BARBARA BAILEY

An Eccentric Marriage
Living with Jim

TAFELBERG

Tafelberg Publishers Limited
40 Heerengracht, Cape Town, 8000
© 2005 author
© photographs Bailey family except where otherwise indicated

Inside cover from left to right: B's grandchildren
Top: commander of what remains of the British Empire with friends – 1997;
Imogen; Flowergirl Saskia
Middle: Ruby; Anna Bailey with Winston; Jasper
Bottom: Frederick; Georgia
Front cover photograph by James Fox
Cover and book design by Nazli Jacobs
Set in Bembo

Printed and bound by Paarl Print, Oosterland Street, Paarl, South Africa
First edition, first printing 2005

ISBN 0 624 04296 0

ACKNOWLEDGEMENTS

About three years after Jim died, my dear friend David Jeppe urged me to go with him to Lionel Abrahams' writing workshop. Every Monday evening for the last 27 years Lionel has held this workshop and has sagely guided many would-be writers, many of whom have gone on to publish. I went as an observer, and at the end of the evening Lionel asked me if I had written anything. I reluctantly read a bit of my diary. I had had no intention of writing seriously or taking part in the workshop. After my reading Lionel twinkled and chuckled in his inimitable way and said, "Go for it! You must publish!"

I am deeply indebted to Lionel for his encouragement, his expert advice and his confidence in me. I feel privileged to have experienced his wisdom and friendship for the last year of his life.

And now his wife Jane Fox with her talent and dedication, carrying on seamlessly with the workshop since he died, has with unstinting and meticulous care become my editor.

I thank Kerry Swift for wading through my typescript and giving me his considered input as my initial editor.

My heartfelt thanks to Nicky Stubbs for her ongoing enthusiastic support and for introducing me to Erika Oosthuysen of Tafelberg to whom I am deeply grateful for making the process of publishing thoroughly enjoyable.

I thank all my beloved friends whether they are mentioned or not, who have weaved the rich tapestry of this 50 years of my life.

Above all I thank my children, Jessica, Beezy, Bundy and Prospero, who have provided me with so much material. When I told Prospero that my memoirs were being published he said, "That's wonderful, Bar! Well done! When can we sue?"

For Jim,
who would have been so proud of me
for getting this published and would have said,
"Well done!" – and wouldn't have read it.

INTRODUCTION

I was in love with Jim Bailey for fifty-one years. I met him when I was nearly twelve and when he was thirty-one. When he died, at the age of eighty, among the many letters of commiseration was one from the South African artist Leigh Voigt who wrote:

> "... I thought: *what on earth is Barbara going to do without Jim!?* ... I remember you told us how you sat in a tree aged 10 and waited for Jim. I can imagine it to be true. Barbara, you have given so much of yourself, especially to Jim whom you loved so, and to all those around you. I send you my sympathy, my love and my deepest friendship. In those hours when everyone else is sleeping and you can't, take up a pen and write – anything, your memoirs, your thoughts ..."

↬

To introduce Jim, I quote the tribute by Kerry Swift, a former *Drum* journalist, given at Jim's memorial service on 7 March at St George's Church, Parktown, Johannesburg.

> "Towards the end of 1975 I received a call from Joel Mervis, who was then editor of the *Sunday Times*. He told me that the publisher Jim Bailey was look-ing for someone to help produce his magazines and asked if I would be in-terested in talking to him. When I did, it was the start of a 25-year friendship that only ended last Thursday when Jim left his well-loved African landscape and moved on to meet old chums elsewhere.
>
> *Drum* changed my life and I believe it changed the lives of everyone who worked there, for Jim was not your normal employer and *Drum* was not your average magazine. It took some time to grasp that he demanded much more of his journalists than other publishers. As an employer he expected more than commitment – he wanted sacrifice. Yet this was no more than he demanded of himself, for he spent the best years of his life and a large portion of his

Jim Bailey

personal fortune developing the foundations of an independent black press not only in South Africa, but throughout anglophone Africa.

And it took time to understand that this was not journalism in the conventional sense. Technical skills were certainly necessary, but they were not a sufficient condition for survival at *Drum*. To join what Jim called the "small circle of friends" and to fully understand what he meant by "life more abundant", one had to learn to see all over again and to understand in a deeper way.

I imagine that all Jim's former working colleagues have their own views of what he was trying to do with his publications. I believe he was not a commercial publisher at all. Essentially Jim was a secular missionary. In publishing *Drum* and other publications across Africa, he set about trying to build something that the politicians were quite incapable of doing. His publications became mass popular educators and trusted advisors in societies where the vast majority of people had no access to an education and fell easy prey to commercial tricksters and political conmen. He saw a common and noble humanity in all people and he used his publications to share this conviction. In this sense, Jim was one of the great democrats of our time.

Perhaps because of his early brush with National Socialism as a Battle of Britain fighter pilot and his subsequent struggles to keep *Drum* alive under hostile conditions, Jim fought off attempts by Grub Street thugs – political and commercial – to exploit the open-hearted decency of the common man. He despised phoney values and suburban vanities. He railed against ideologies that led unwitting people down blind alleys or denied their rights to make their own decisions. He lashed politicians who manipulated or oppressed their citizens, and he used his extensive contacts in Anglo-Africa's social and economic elites to lessen the burdens of the common man. Many of these prime movers were drawn from the small circle of *Drum* friends.

I see Jim as one of the last true heroes. He was certainly the most authentic human being I have ever known. Certainly he was not easy to get close to, and

8

perhaps that is why he was often misunderstood. But for those who persevered, the rewards were great. His humour, his intellectual brilliance, his desires for a better world, his fortitude under pressure, his determination that good should triumph over evil, and his overwhelming love of Africa and its people rubbed off on all his family and friends. It had to, because his enthusiasm for life was overwhelming.

It is often the case that exceptional men are not recognised in their own countries. Jim was awarded a CBE, but he has yet to receive honours in his own land. Yet in the hearts of those who loved him well, he will always be honoured.

To end I wish to quote one of Jim's poems. It was written in memory of a fellow pilot. He and Jim were flying home in their Bristol Beaufighters after a sortie along the Norwegian coast. Halfway back to their base, his wingman's aircraft started failing. Both young pilots knew that death was flying in close formation. Jim kept station as his wingman's plane sank lower towards the North Sea. Quietly, steadily, Jim coaxed him on, talking him home through that cruel night. But slowly, inevitably, the crippled fighter sank into the sea and disappeared.

Jim remembered the episode thus:

A team of swans was flying down the valley,
the hunter fired, one fell with broken wing,
and as she fell she knew that she was dying,
and calling to her friends, aspired to sing.

They, from the frozen winds, replied:
'never shall we forget you, loved playmate,
never in the meadow or on the fjord
forget you, never . . .' their departing wingbeats sighed.

I can do no better than to echo that sentiment in ending:
Nor shall we forget you, Jim
Never in the veld or vlei
Forget you, never . . .

9

B aged 12

Two or three years ago, I showed Murray Crawford a diary I wrote when I was about twelve years old. Murray and I have been friends for nearly sixty years and having read what I wrote, he urged me to write my memoirs. He kept writing to me from Australia where he now lives, to ask if I was working on it. This book is my answer. It is a mixture of genuine diary entries and retrospective stories. I do thank him for nagging me.

12 FEBRUARY 1950. ILLOVO, JOHANNESBURG.
[Verbatim, written three months before I turned 12]

I have fallen in love with the most beautiful person I have ever seen. Just think I've known him for four months and I didn't realise it. The first time I met him he threw a dachshund at me.

Jim Bailey came and I was so pleased to see him. He picked me up and threw me around his head like a lasso and then told me about the RAF. He is a very eloquent young man and I love him as much as Beethoven.

B aged 14 in Jim's pyjamas – Jim in second best

I came into his bed this morning for tea and so did my cats Woffle and Peewee. We discussed the Bushman tribes and Caesar's Gallic Wars and how they trapped stags by cutting almost through a tree, and when the stag leant against it to sleep the tree would topple and they would catch and kill the stag when it fell.

Jim Bailey is very beautiful but he is not a huggy sort of person and I only hug him when he's very sleepy otherwise he hits me. He wrote an essay for me for school and Miss Hodkin gave him 8/20 which proves her stupidity.

B wicket-keeping, Richard batting

1 MARCH 1950

Jim came and we played cricket. Richard[1] hit a ball in my face and my upper lip swelled and went purple. Mummy said thank God my teeth are still in. I cried and Jim looked the other way, which I think was jolly sporting of him. He is deeply understanding as well as beautiful.

---

1 my brother

11

I went and sat in my tree hide-out wearing Jim's cardigan which he left here and thought about him and how lovely for the RAF and Oxford to have him and how I love him. I asked Peter and Roger[2] if he could join our gang and they don't mind as long as he doesn't eat too many biscuits.

B on the left, looking as uncomfortable as she felt at a schoolfriend's party.

I am on the garage roof and they've been shouting for me to come in to supper and I'll not move till the sun has gone behind the pines. The world is very magic and exciting at dusk. I wish Jim were here. He would utter some appropriate quotation from the poets in that hushed exquisite voice of his.

The best thing in the world is Beethoven's 7th symphony and his violin concerto. We were painting the new bathroom and Jim threw a bucket of whitewash over my head and Benny[3] had to cut my hair so Mummy wouldn't see when she came in. She did though. I can jump 3'8" on Matchless, and I can do a back somersault into the water. I have preserved a rarely beautiful bird's egg to show Jim.

DECEMBER 1951 HERMANUS

We are in Hermanus and I found two tortoises and I've called one Jim but I told everyone else it is Tim just to put them on a false trail. I love the sea and the sound it makes and its smell and ice cream and hot chocolate sauce at the shop on the corner.

We all went fishing at the docks and I caught three blaasoppies and one harder, the boys caught lots. An old man like a frog talked to Daddy. He has quite white knees and veins. Sis, he's awful and he kissed me goodbye. I was nearly sick.

I went to the Marine Hotel with Joseph Menell and we took down all the pictures in the passage and shoved them behind the sofas. We found two starfish. One of the

2 neighbours' son
3 Kathleen Talbot-Bentinck, our Irish 'second mother'

tortoises is lost. I am very worried because I think it's Jim. This afternoon I went to the cemetery to see if Jim was there. I cried because of all the tombstones. Say Jim was underneath one of them. I am a Pantheist. Jim is too.

JANUARY 1952 JOHANNESBURG

Jim was wearing a white pullover and he looked saintly. I squeezed his neck and kissed him on the cheek just next to his left eye. He bit my leg and hit me on the bottom and said, "How are we?" Daddy says human bites are very poisonous and dangerous. Maybe I'll have to have my leg amputated when it's gone gangrenous then Jim can carry me and I can have crutches. Lady Stonehaven gave me a red plastic bag which I have eaten. Mummy did a jolly good drawing of Michael Baird. He's a wet but I like him.

Maxine and I rode Timmy and Zeno bareback. We cantered past the swimming pool and slid off the horses into the water. Daddy had a fit because he thought it was dangerous. We also slid off the thatched roof wearing sacks and landed on a mattress. None of our parents think this is a good idea.

The Greek god

But now my poor darling Jim is dying up at Dallowgill[4] with bluegum.[5] Mummy and I are looking after him and mincing the chicken because his mouth is too sore to chew. We played racing demon. He is so wonderful, even with bluegum. I sneak up there every day after school. Nobody knows because Daddy says I can catch it. I hope I do, then I can go up and die with him. He even hits me while he has bluegum. He is perfect in mind and body like a Greek god except for his teeth.

When I die I'm going to be burnt up. Jim is too. I hope we have the same fire. Mummy will be so sad, she thought I would die when I had my double mastoid operation.

4 his sister's house in Illovo
5 Jim had gingivitis. His gums were painted with Gentian Violet

I hunted and loved it. I love the smell of the horses and I love Kotchka[6]. Nadya and I had a sip of everything in the Vladykin's bar and I was sick.

Kotcha Vladykin

On Sunday we had a hunt breakfast outside and Jim couldn't get his jodhpurs on or off. Nadya and I pulled and pulled, finally doing them up with a tie. He looked messy but rather nice I thought. We had a good hunt and I rode Greta who pulled my arms out of my sockets. Typical chestnut. After the hunt I drove the Plymouth round with the Lasches in the trailer and Helly[7] says I drive better than Daddy. Daddy makes me sick he shouts too much and I am going to recede to a desert island one of these days just with Jim and Kotchka. We have just got a new recording of Beethoven's 2nd symphony and I love it best. I love Beethoven as much as Jim when he's not there. It depends.

Jim wrote another essay for me and failed. Miss McKechnie wrote, "Do not try and be clever." Pathetic!

Daddy paid me a tickey not to sing at table. It's all right if we are all singing *Father O'Flynn* or *Patrick McGinty*. But I don't even realise I'm singing and then he tells me to be quiet. He always wants me to wear a dress. I hate hate hate even the word dress. And dressing gown. I would like to run away but I don't know where to go. I want Benny to come.

B and Richard

When I was six Richard and I lit candles at 5 o'clock in the morning and the mosquito net caught alight and then the curtain and we called Daddy and he quickly shut the window so that the flames wouldn't set the thatch alight and he eventually put the fire

---

6 A White Russian who had escaped to South Africa before the Revolution
7 Helmuth Lasch, Olympic sportsman

out. I hid below the tennis court for the whole day and when it grew dark I came back and he was so pleased to see me he wasn't even cross. You never know with Daddy.

I do love Daddy when he tells me about being a doctor. I definitely want to be a doctor like him. He gave me the skeleton and I am learning all the parts of the bones, like epiphysis. Greek because of the ph. I will be a doctor and live in one room with a grand piano and an owl. Anthony is scared to clean my room because of the skull. A dashboard fracture is a posterior dislocation of the femur. It must be horribly sore.

MARCH 1952

I went whizzing down Jellicoe Avenue on my bike to visit Willem Hendrikz. He is so beautiful he looks like Jesus. His hands always look dirty but actually they are clean. It is because he works with metal when he sculpts. He is so kind and gentle. I wish he were my father. We stayed with him at Vygerkraal and he shot a hare and skinned it

Willem Hendrikz

and we had it for supper. The hares eat his vegetables so it's fair. Daddy rode and the gag snapped and the horse bolted and Daddy was very shaken. So was I.

Joanthan Suzman, Richard and B, and Janet Suzman

Jonathan and Janet Suzman came and Janet and I are digging a big hole in our hideout in the hedge. Jonathan is much nicer to me than Richard.

I am sick again and Dr Selby examined me. He is a very orange man and his legs don't belong to his body. Mozie Suzman[8] took me to a concert at the City Hall. Beethoven's 3rd piano concerto is probably my favourite. Edgar Cree conducted. Lettie Vermaak looks as if her hair is painted on it is so smooth. I think she loves

---

8 physician and husband of Helen

15

Edgar Cree. Luckily she leads the violas so she sits right under his nose. Mozie sucked his cigar in the car and filled it with smoke.

Yehudi Menuhin is coming soon. When I first heard him I was 10. I cried and vomited he was so wonderful. I went to the rehearsal with Daddy and when he was playing the fast part of the 3rd movement of the Mendelssohn concerto, he looked down at me crying and said, "Exciting, isn't it!" while he was playing. It was the most exciting moment of my life.

I love music like I love Jim and both make me sick and make me weep. I am slowly becoming convinced that Bach is Everything.

I played the orchestra part written for piano II for Eunice Robinson. Beethoven's 1st and I tried Chopin's 2nd but Chopin is much too difficult for me to sight-read. I feel as if Beethoven is my father. I'm glad he isn't because he had a terrible terrible temper. I just mean his music is my father.

APRIL 1952
Jim left for England. I was sick at the airport and cried in the duckling house for the rest of the day. I wish he didn't make me so unhappy. I wish I wasn't so completely devoid of any will to exist when he isn't here.

AUGUST 1952 SUNNINGHILL PARK FARM
I rode Polyanthus today without a saddle and he got a crazy look in his eye and rushed off at a furious pace, myself clinging to his mane with my head on his neck to avoid branches.

The evening on the farm was beautiful. I felt utterly bodiless. I was filthy and sun browned and scratched, sitting on a trailer full of hay – so happy right inside that I actually enjoyed the itch and scratch of the hay. I was so at peace with the world and had a lovely chat with Daddy in the car on the way home, about operations.

*Toddy Henbury, Jim, B, Monty Denny –
Colesburg in the fifties*

I went to Colesberg with Jim.[9] He promised Benny a trip to Colesberg but he hasn't kept his promise. I made him promise he wouldn't die. He never keeps his promises so it is not very reassuring. He made me drive for hours and I couldn't reach the pedals easily so I had to point my toe to press the accelerator and my leg got cramp. Jim slept and the roads are so straight and long that I found it very tiring. But he was near so I was happy even with cramp. His clothes smell of him and I love it. When he goes away at least I have his jerseys to smell. It lasts about three weeks and then gets so faint I have to imagine it and sniff deeply into the armpits.

It was awful in Colesberg because Jim and Derrick[10] hardly spoke to each other and Jim disappeared as much as possible. Which meant that I mooched around on my own which was better than being with Derrick, who is boring and a bit frightening at the same time. His ankles are like a carthorse. I wish I could love him because he is Jim's brother – but Jim doesn't, so I don't. At

Grootfontein, Colesberg

least Richard and I can laugh together when he isn't being horrible to me.

FEBRUARY 1954 JOHANNESBURG

Chrissie Welles is my best friend. We played duets all morning. The Linz symphony that Mozart wrote in three days! Chrissie's mother Virginia lies in bed with all sorts of creams on her face. When Mummy told her that she is so beautiful it is a

---

9 Jim had inherited farms in the Colesberg area from his father, Sir Abe Bailey, who died in 1940

10 his brother

wonder that every man she meets doesn't marry her, she said, "Oh but Iris, they do!" Jackie is her fourth husband. She told Chrissie that she wished she would play the piano like I do. Stupid woman will make Chrissie hate me. She doesn't hate me.

I love Chrissie's father Jackie and I exercise his polo ponies Wednesdays and Fridays after school. He plays polo for South Africa with Alan and Derek Goodman and Punch Barlow. Derek brought Zsa-Zsa Gabor to our house and Richard was so excited but I didn't think she was worth all the fuss. Lots of scent. I hate hate scent. Moo[11] wears so much I can't breathe. I love her much more when she is not wearing any. I love the smell of Benny. And I love her little whiskers.

Auntie Vera had me for the day and we listened to *Petroushka* by Stravinski and she told me the story and it is heart breaking. I cried and Vera understood. I wish Jim could find me dying or something so that he'd notice me and then realise how much I love him and that I was dying for him. Maybe once I am dead he will realise.

Auntie Vera, my granny and my mother "Moo", in 1914

Auntie Vera and I played the whole of *Ruddigore*. She and I sing lots of the songs with the records. Gilbert and Sullivan is such fun. Jim doesn't like music. This is a tragedy but we both love poetry and he knows lots and lots. When he was asleep I snipped off a curl of his beautiful gold hair. He didn't waken thank God. I will keep it for the rest of my life. It is gold, pure spun gold. He is too beautiful to believe. I wish I was Jim then I could be with him forever wherever he is.

Chrissie Welles is going to school in Switzerland. She is so lucky but she seems a bit sad. Jackie and Virginia are adopting two babies, a boy and a girl. Jackie is flying to London to fetch them. Virginia made Chrissie move out of her room into a much smaller room so that the babies can take over hers. Chrissie is pretending to be excited about the babies but she obviously says exactly what Virginia wants her to say. I am really sorry for her because she is not Jackie's child and she worships

11 my mother

her father who is so famous and he has no time for her. Orson Welles was only 19 when Chrissie was born and he wanted a boy so she was christened Christopher. They should have had me – I'm as close as they'd get.

I wish Daddy didn't get so bad-tempered. We went to a restaurant for a treat and he shouted about the food and we all wanted to vanish or die. He was so embarrassing and I cannot think why he does it. It made me ill with misery. Moo and Richard hated it too. I also had to wear a dress which was enough punishment.

I wish I could share music with Jim, but we do love playing smiff-miff together. Grass, bushes, flowers, earth, pines, etc. and then we decide on our favourite smell. Mine is rained-on earth after drought. I remember when I was seven and I had my mastoidectomy and I came back from months in the Lady Deadly[12] and there were violets in freshly wet earth under my window. I will never forget what it meant to me, ever.

I love Yeats and Matthew Arnold, and Jim. And Spenser's *Epithalamion* – I have learnt the first verse for Jim.

Maxine Lautre and I were riding Timmy and Zeno and they bolted home and we sped past our mothers who were horrified – flat out into the stable where I only just ducked the doorway. Shaking like a leaf I dismounted catching my knee on a bucket and split it open to the bone. I could actually see the whiteness of the patella. Maxine's father, a surgeon, was going to stitch me but I said no thank you, I want Daddy to stitch it. So Moo drove me home and Daddy put four stitches in and I was so pleased because Mr and Mrs Case were there and I was very brave and didn't murmur and they were impressed.

---

12 Lady Dudley Nursing Home

In the early 1950s Jim bought a farm near what is now known as Lanseria, some 25 miles north west of Johannesburg. He called it Monaghan after the county in Ireland where his mother's family, the Rossmores and Westenras lived. He stayed in an old cottage across the Jukskei River which runs through the middle of the property. He had no domestic skills. He slept on a bed with no sheets, he considered them to be superfluous. He grew onions in the garden and his meals consisted of bacon and eggs, with or without onions. A maid cooked his meals for him. My mother called his house 'Naught for Your Comfort'.

At this time Jim bought a magazine called *African Drum* from the Springbok fast bowler, war hero and journalist, Robert Crisp. To edit it, he brought out Anthony Sampson, who was at Christ Church, Oxford with him. Between them, with a small and talented black staff, they set about turning *Drum* into a vibrant magazine serving the rapidly developing communities around South Africa's cities, especially Johannesburg. Jim was totally committed to this venture because he knew there was nothing like it in the country. He modelled *Drum* on *Picture Post* and threw himself into the work, spending much time, energy and a considerable amount of money, to provide a vehicle for the black, Coloured and Indian writers and photographers that he met as he travelled around South Africa, and later across the sub-Saharan continent.

During my early teens, I went to some of the parties for *Drum* staffers and their friends. As it was during the 1950s, at the height of apartheid, the parties were held at 'Coney Island', a little stone hut on the river near the furthest northern boundary of Monaghan Farm. The road to it was so bad that it was unlikely that the Special Branch would follow us (the Special Branch took a close interest in what Jim was doing and in the goings-on at *Drum*). They also had journalist informants placed in opposition publications such as the *Rand Daily Mail,* the *Sunday Times* and the *Sunday Express,* in which Jim was the major shareholder. Jim's response was that he always knew who they were and it was better to leave them be on the principle that it is better the devil you know than the devil you don't. But it created subtle pressure and meant that he had to be cautious in all his relationships, at times even with his own staff.

I knew Jim thought these gatherings were great fun, so I pretended even to myself, that I thought so too. But with hindsight I was confused, bored and terribly tired. On one occasion a guest arrived at the party unconscious with liquor, and was carried in. Jim thought this hilarious. He plied his guests with alcohol to "relax them and free them of inhibitions." For me as a teenager the parties grew more and more unappealing as the people became more and more inebriated.

Can Themba, Henry Nxumalo, Casey Motsisi and Lewis Nkosi sometimes came for meals. They drank heavily which I always found tedious. What saved me from boredom was the dancing. I adore dancing, and dancing with black men during my teenage years spoiled me for evermore for dancing with white men.

I occasionally went to shebeens with Jim and again dancing was wonderful, but I didn't drink and the

nights grew long – too long. There was also the fear that the police would raid the shebeen. Selling liquor was illegal and mixing with other races was illegal. One had to be prepared to dash out of a back door or jump out of a window and hide or make a getaway. For these reasons he rarely took me along. It was too dangerous.

The two people I loved seeing from *Drum* were Todd Matshikiza and Nat Nakasa. Todd was small in stature, had an infectious broad grin and had just begun work on his famous musical, *King Kong*. *King Kong* went to Broadway, and was the making of the singer Miriam Makeba, who decided to remain in self-imposed exile rather than return to apartheid

Jim and B at a shebeen, 1958

South Africa. Todd wrote as originally and superbly as he composed music. Jim called his idiomatic prose-style 'Matshikeze'.

Todd came to the farm often, and we played piano duets together and had much in common. He was joyous, lovable and a wonderfully talented man. Nat Nakasa was gentle, and delightful company. I remember helping him learn to swim in our pool. When he eventually went to New York to live in the "free" world, he was so homesick and lonely, he committed suicide by jumping out of the window of a skyscraper.

After these *Drum* bashes, Jim drove many of the guests back to where they lived in various townships. It was sometimes 5am when he went to bed. If he was staying with us at my parents' house, I would worry about him having an accident, or being arrested for being in the townships. They were valid worries.

I wrote all the times I kissed him (he never kissed me) on the wall behind my bed in pencil in Greek lettering. I was 16 when I wrote the last entry and the total was six. What a curious adolescent I was. I dressed like a hobo to be like Jim. I thought he was poor because of his clothes and his car and the way he lived.

I copied his writing so accurately that on occasions he and I have not been sure which of us has written it. He often held a cup of tea by holding the actual cup, not the handle. So do I.

My obsession with him was curious. I didn't want to marry him as much as I wanted to be him. I remember wanting my head to be inside his head and my arms and body to be within his so that I became part of him. Thus I wouldn't exist without him.

Throughout my teens I spent hours on our garage roof waiting for him. As he never indicated in any way when or even whether he would come, it was unfulfilling to say the least. He spent some of his time in Johannesburg at the *Drum* office, and often visited his Colesberg farms where he was breeding racehorses and Merino sheep.

As *Drum* grew and he opened offices in Fleet Street and in various parts of Africa, he travelled extensively and I regularly cajoled my long-suffering mother to drive me to Palmietfontein Airport to meet him after a trip. Quite often he didn't arrive when expected. I would wait until the last passenger was seen coming off the aircraft – and then weep, and sometimes vomit with disappointment. I do not know how my mother could have stood me.

I was so obsessed and so single-minded it must have been dreadfully difficult for both my parents. My mother quite often gave me my supper to take up onto the garage roof when I was so sure he might arrive that I wouldn't come down to eat.

Jim rarely played cricket more than once a year. He would stroll onto the field looking like Rupert Brooke, take three or four wickets, score the most runs, and then stroll off for another year. I would watch his every move and if he fielded near the boundary, I would take him a cold beer. I loved the smell of the room where they donned their pads, the sound of the studded boots on the cement floor, the smell of the freshly oiled bats, the red stains on their white flannels. Jim's cricket flannels dated from 1938, the year of my birth, when he was up at Oxford. His shirt had the laundry marks of his house at Winchester where he was schooled. I still have it, shirttails well below my knees, the cream flannel rough on the skin. He didn't play seriously at Winchester or Oxford because cricket would have taken up far too much time for his liking. On his school report of 1934 when he was 14 his housemaster wrote that his cricket was "hampered by his lack of restraint."

Old Wykhamist Malcolm Burr wrote and had published a delightful collection of portraits of Old Wykhamists among whom were Anthony Trollope, Thomas Arnold, AP Herbert, Cecil King, Arnold Toynbee, GH Hardy – and Jim Bailey! I had the pleasure of meeting the Burrs when they contacted me to talk about Jim's Winchester days.

Jim's older brother Derrick captained Gloucestershire at cricket. I was so proud of this fact. He was fed up with Jim for spending all his free time either with a trout-rod or a shotgun, but Derrick was to discover that Jim's leisure pursuits, particularly his hunting skills, were to save his life many times when he and so many young men like him took on Goering's Messerschmitts over the leaden skies of London during the Battle of Britain.

In 1934 when Jim and Derrick were invited to Lord Walsingham's famous shoot at Merton in Norfolk, there were 15 experienced shots spending the weekend, and the 14-year-old Jim shot over half the bag.

When I was 14 I clearly recollect him shooting a duck which very nearly dropped onto my head. I saw it falling out of the sky and then heard the bang. I still find the pause between sight and sound enthralling. Over all the years I knew him, Jim always had a Labrador and each one has behaved impeccably. I read a perfect description of a Labrador by Elizabeth Jane Howard. It ran, "*she was a noble and resigned creature, hell-bent on loyalty.*"

I acted as Jim's second gundog and carried his birds. I hated it if they weren't completely dead and was too shy and nervous to ask him to finish them off. If anyone else were near me I would give him the injured bird to kill rather than let Jim know I hadn't the courage to do it myself.

About that time he asked me to walk the boundary of Monaghan Farm and chase guinea-fowl into the guns, and to try and prevent them flying into Rod Douglas's neighbouring farm. I walked too fast and thought I might have gone too far, so I crouched behind some bushes and watched ants for a while. The birds were flying over me, shots were being fired, guinea-fowl and francolin were plummeting down. Showers of pellets fell round me. I was too embarrassed to come out of

Jim in aunt Doods's hat

my hiding place so I stayed put and got a pellet in my leg. It stung like fire and oddly enough hardly bled. When I rejoined them they had all wondered where I was. I was too frightened to tell Jim in case he was cross. If I had been shot to pulp, my only worry would be of Jim's disapproval.

I loved the shooting season; filling Jim's cartridge belt, assembling his gun, finding the whistle to wear round his neck to keep the line in order and so forth. He had a tweed jacket with poacher's pockets that he had worn since he was 16 years old. He wore it until he was 74 and then found he couldn't do up any of the buttons. So I wore it, and carried his birds in the pockets. The sleeves have been darned over and over again and it is interwoven with seeds and burs, and never dry-cleaned as it would disintegrate. I still have it.

He wore an extraordinary garment on his head to keep the hair out of his eyes. His aunt Doods had knitted it for him when he was in the RAF. I cannot imagine what she had in mind when she made it. It amused and puzzled his friends for many years.

In 1955 when I was seventeen I had typhoid and was ill for three months. I ended up with a thrombosis in my leg and thus, although able to write matric, was not allowed to move around. So I wrote the exams at home. As I had done no school-work for three months since I became ill, I was unprepared and treated the whole process as if it were a game. A very tiring game, but at least, I thought, it would soon be over.

An old lady, Mrs Cheesman, came every day to invigilate. My parents, Benny and Jim were my only visitors. I was supposed to be in the Fever Hospital, isolated. It was due to my father being a doctor that I was permitted to stay at home. My parents and Benny wore white uniforms when they came into my room, and I had separate eating utensils and the bathroom my brother normally shared with me became a sterilised wash place for me alone, and everything I touched. Jim was the exception. He came in and smoked cigars and I remember my temperature going up, and feeling terribly shaky, but that was fine by me! I think my parents gave up trying to discipline him.

I was about 17 the first time I spent a night at Monaghan with Jim. My parents thought I was staying with a girl friend in Sandhurst. I slept on the bed with him. There was only one single bed. He slept soundly with all the blankets on him – a bed fascist. I was very cold on the bare mattress and was too shy of him to pull the blankets onto me in case I woke him. He didn't hold me or make any kind of advances. It was hell, and I thought I was in heaven just to be near him.

I passed my matric exams and went to the University of Cape Town to the Michaelis School of Art for three years to do a Fine Arts degree. I wasted long hours trying to find out when Jim was coming to Cape Town which he did at least four times a year for family meetings and to visit the Cape Town offices of *Drum*. I occasionally saw him, but went bananas if I heard he had been to Cape Town and I had missed him.

It was obligatory to go to the Freshers' Ball which was certainly not my cup of tea. I was told I should bring a partner. I invited Jim, who fetched me, but we didn't even go into Jameson Hall. He drove me straight off to Simonstown. I was dressed for the ball, uncomfortable and self-conscious. It was dark when we reached the Simonstown harbour and we 'borrowed' a rowing boat that was tied to the pier and rowed in the inky water which was illuminated with lights off parked yachts, and from the shore. A perfect way to spend the evening but it was chilly so Jim took me to a cafe in Simonstown and sat me on the glass top of the heated container for hotdogs.

These were politically horrific years. I frequently demonstrated with fellow-students at the University of Cape Town, some of whom were eventually imprisoned. Some fled the country.

Having Jim as part of my life kept me closely in touch with goings-on of which otherwise I would have had no idea. UCT students were very involved and aware, but Jim was in a unique position in both the black and white publishing worlds.

I lived in residence and spent many weekends with Deb and Denis Cowen. Denis was Professor of Law at UCT and Deb I had known since she worked on *Drum*

25

when I was 15. Their home was a haven for me and I adored their first baby Diana, nicknamed Woozle. I babysat her so often that I grew to love her deeply. It is thanks to Woozle that I was in any way prepared for my own first baby, Jessica, when she was born. My letters home were filled with Woozle – and, of course, Jim. Items cost 'Jim/6 or 5/Jimpence'. I wrote his name sporadically throughout my letters without meaning or context, ' I-2-3 Jim, 1-Jim 3-hop, 1-2 Jim hop', in between saying how much I enjoyed learning Chaucer and the history of the English language.

I did life-drawing every morning at the Michaelis and all the models somehow resembled Jim, and when I learnt about printing linocuts I wrote Jim's name in Greek as a pattern for a scarf.

When I was home on vacation, I went with him to visit friends in Sophiatown before its residents were forcibly removed. I taught the piano there for a brief while.

1956 FRASERBURG ROAD[13]

This is absolutely unbelievable. I am in Fraserburg Road which is beyond description awful. I am hitching a lift from UCT to Johannesburg with John D, a fellow student who is dull, humourless, and who plays dreadful music on the wireless all the time. We have broken down several times in his Ford Prefect and now we are well and truly stuck. The garage proprietor has come out of a tree and makes a snail look like Roger Bannister. It is horribly hot and sticky. I have a headache and there are wasps and flies in plenty in this room. The cold water is hot and there is a maid here with a wart on her neck the size of a cherry. I have an upset stomach and my feet are dirty and the water is still too hot to use.

John's Ford Prefect breaking down.

John is in the next room. We are awaiting a local farm manager, Mr Duminy. Please God may he come today and fix the car. I would play the piano here except the notes stick. How I long for amusing company. Jim would do, of course.

---

13 subsequently renamed Leeu-Gamka

My dislike of Fraserburg Road holds no bounds. It is abominable. There is no grass whatsoever and a very hot wind is blowing smelling of trains and lavatories. How I wish I were home – or anywhere else . . .

There is a mangy goat eating some very dingy lettuces that grow beneath my window, and John spilt some coffee on my table. It is now a flat, sweet-smelling varnished patch covered with flies. My hair is filthy. How I long for a cold bath and how I want someone with whom to laugh it off – it being Fraserburg Road. To cheer myself I have gone through some of the score of the *St Matthew Passion*. I'm so glad I packed it for Paddy Duncan. I tried to sing but my throat is full of Fraserburg Road.

On an odious little dresser stands an even more odious chipped enamel washbasin with red flowers painted thereon. Next to it is a limejuice bottle filled with water and some dusty pink towels. The pink is not dusty, the towels are. It amazes me that the walls are not brown. They are fairly clean and cream-coloured.

The telephone has just rung – maybe it is Mr Duminy. When I have finished writing in the book I shall make my Will. John came in and told me that he slept well, the lucky beast. I suppose if the goat and the hotel owners can live here, so can I. Warm flat beer is truly awful.

The evening meal was memorable for the remark made by the waiter about the pudding. When he brought it to the table I asked what it was. He said it was steamed pudding, but: "it is a bit shabby, Ma'am."

I slept here. Just think of it – lying naked on grey sheets and a hot lumpy pillow. I did sleep, though. The car parts arrived by train early this morning and a wasp came in at 5am. I dodged it sleepily round the room for a while and then went back to bed and resigned myself to being stung. I cannot go to the lavatory because it smells so bad I shall be sick. I peed outside.

The three charming things about Fraserburg Road are two secretary birds and a huge baritone St Bernard. The hotel is full of Coloured infants whose faces are covered in flies and their mothers don't seem to mind.

I have been playing my recorder at the reservoir which is filled with dirty water. Somehow Bach doesn't feel at home here.

At the station this morning some men on the Jo'burg train leant out of the window and asked me, the local yokel, what station it was. When I told them in my squeaky little English voice their jaws dropped.

The breakfast! My gastric and duodenal walls had better be lined with zinc. Thick dry heavy porridge, lukewarm; then overcooked eggs lying in a stagnant lake of oil of dog with rubbery meat-straps. A huge Afrikaans woman with a moustache was mumbling at the next table. I looked at her inquiringly and she said: "I despise tea-leaves in my coffee."

Why couldn't all this have happened in Colesberg where Jim may be 45 miles away at Grootfontein?[14] My stye is growing larger, an infant is screaming incessantly – the flies have probably eaten away the skin on its face.

Later – We left in the newly-mended car and broke down 25 miles outside Colesberg! I hitched into the town while John was towed to a garage. I phoned Grootfontein from the Central Hotel, praying fervently. The chance of his being there was remote. He answered the phone. He will be here in an hour to fetch me. I do hope he's nice to me most of the time. Just think! From Fraserburg Road to Jim and Naval Prince![15]

When I was still at UCT, I had an emergency appendectomy. This had its hilarious aspect. Firstly, the surgeon only gave me one stitch in the weeny incision he had made – to show off to my father. This was early days for keyhole surgery. My friend and fellow student Christopher Gill came to visit me the evening before my operation. I lay on my back on a trolley that spanned the bed for taking trays of meals and Christopher pushed me down the corridors of the hospital at high speed. We had a whale of a time.

Christopher Gill pushing me flat out down the corridors on the meal trolley

14 one of Jim's farms near Colesberg
15 stud stallion

My doctor and the surgeon arrived and gave us a wigging, and we all had a jolly evening chatting and laughing. At the time I was in my second year at the university and one of the English set books was Christopher Marlowe's *Doctor Faustus*. When the doctors had left the ward, one of the old biddies next to me, seeing the title of my book and having witnessed the bonhomie of my doctors, leaned over and said, "You are a one with the doctors, aren't you!"

The other patients in my ward were mostly octogenarians and when Christopher arrived, he looked round at them and bent down to whisper to me, "Do you believe in mercy-killing?"

I was flown home – a huge treat because I always went back and forth to university by train, which I enjoyed greatly – but I had never flown. I still had my single stitch in my abdomen so I didn't walk comfortably. My parents were about to have a dinner party and Jim was with us and my mother asked him to wear a suit for the party. He didn't have one, so she told him to go and buy one.

He took me, and we went to the Belfast in Rosebank. Because I wasn't allowed to walk he carried me sitting astride his shoulders, holding my legs hanging down in front. He went to the suit department counter – I navigated – and he said, "Um, I want to buy a suit." There was an open box with a new suit on the counter. He said, "That's fine." The salesman suggested he try it on and fussed around, but Jim insisted it was fine, paid for it, took it and rolled out of the shop, wearing me on his shoulders.

That evening, he came down in his new suit. The pockets were tacked up with orange cotton, the label hung on his bottom, the trousers came down to his mid-calf, and he couldn't button the jacket. It was at least three sizes too small.

Despite being as hygienically unaware as he was, Jim spent long hours of his life in the bath. As a child he didn't seem to have been taught how to wash. His idea of washing his hands, for instance, was to run the tap feebly and hold the tips of his fingers under the dribble of water – no soap – then wipe them on a towel.

He was genuinely unaware of dirt on himself or his clothes. He bathed every single morning in order to shave, but made no attempt to wash in any way. He did use soap to wash his hair which he often forgot to rinse. He cut his hair himself, very badly, and when he started to go grey, he bought dye and tried to dye it himself. We called it his mango-orange rinse. He had no idea how extraordinary he looked, but he so hated aging.

We mostly bathed together. It was a relaxed happy communicative time for us. I have marks on my shoulders made by the taps – of course I had the tap end. He would occasionally twiddle the hot tap with his toes to add hot water, which dripped on to my neck and scalded it with fair regularity. Jim stayed in for such ages that quite often when friends came they would sit on the closed lavatory seat to converse with him. He would continue adding hot water by toe-twiddling.

Benny, my Irish 'second mother', had been with my family since before Richard and I were born. She stayed with us for the rest of her life. When I had my own children, Benny lived with us on the farm. One morning when Jim was in the bath, Benny knocked on the door and said, "Close your eyes, Jim, I'm coming in." Jim, being Irish too, closed his eyes.

Benny would sometimes come at him with a facecloth and wipe around the convolutions of his ears, muttering, "Just look at the dirt of you!" What amazed me is that he let her. We loved her dearly, and she loved us unconditionally and was a great source of warmth and security and a lot of laughter.

Benny

Jim never put any garment in the wash-basket and we had to sneak in and grab his soiled clothes while he was in the bath. He was angry if he caught us at it.

Jim was renowned for his dress-sense. The only complete suit he possessed was his wetsuit for spearfishing. He had jackets of some suits and trousers of others, but as most of us seem to land up with single socks, he couldn't keep a full suit of clothes for any length of time.

For meetings in the city, be it London or Johannesburg, he would always wear a tie. With it he might wear a striped beach shirt or a checked farm shirt. Most of his clothes had permanent ink stains where he had had leaking pens in his pockets. He even had an ink-blue groin which I noticed from time to time

Jim in his only suit

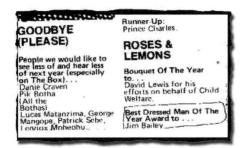

GOODBYE
(PLEASE)

People we would like to
see less of and hear less
of next year (especially
on The Box)...
Danie Craven
Pik Botha
(All the
Bothas)
Lucas Matanzima, George
Mangope, Patrick Sebe,
Lennox Mohvohu..

Runner-Up:
Prince Charles.

ROSES &
LEMONS

Bouquet Of The Year
to...
David Lewis for his
efforts on behalf of Child
Welfare.

Best Dressed Man Of The
Year Award to...
Jim Bailey

From *Style* Magazine January 1982

when we bathed. At first we thought it was a bruise, but together we diagnosed it to be ink. With his 'office' outfit, he would wear clod-hopping boots or veldskoene more often than not, with a fair amount of cow dung stuck to them.

Jim spent long hours driving back and forth from Johannesburg to Colesberg to inspect his farms there. The distances between farms and dorps in the Karoo are great, and very often there were gates to be opened and closed on the seemingly endless dirt roads. It was necessary to close them for the livestock that grazed there.

On one of his trips he gave a lift to a young man carrying a large suitcase. They drove many miles and reached a gate. The young man climbed out to open it. Jim drove through the gateway, and carried straight on to the next town about 40 miles further on. He only noticed the hitch-hiker's suitcase on the back seat and realised that he had left him behind when he stopped for petrol.

Another time I was with him when he gave a lift to a hitchhiker, and Jim amused himself by arguing that the earth was flat. The poor chap was young, uneducated and took Jim absolutely seriously. I grew more and more embarrassed for the hiker. Jim thought it was very funny. The bewildered young man was greatly relieved to bid us farewell when we reached the next town. Me too.

Living on Monaghan Farm at Lanseria, Jim drove daily to the *Drum* office which was in Eloff Street Extension – on the southern side of Johannesburg. Schoolchildren often thumbed lifts to the end of our dirt road. They all knew Jim and waved him down with gusto when they saw him coming. Once, he opened the back door for six of them to clamber in. I phoned him at the office that afternoon and he said the children had spent all day at *Drum* because he'd forgotten to drop them at the end of our dirt road. I asked him didn't they say anything? He said they seemed to make a lot of noise at first but he told them to pipe down. I can hear his very familiar phrase, "Can we have some peace?" Happily he brought them home that evening. I was worried – and I am sure they were – that he would forget about them.

"My hinterland is there."

My first paid job in 1958 was to do a drawing of Jim for an article on him by Anthony Clarke in a publication called *Contact* which Anthony helped start with Patrick Duncan and George Clay, and which was soon banned on account of its liberal policy. Anthony Clarke worked on *Drum* for a while before opening what is considered to be the best second-hand bookshop in the country, Clarke's, in Long Street, Cape Town.

While I was at UCT he became one of my dearest friends and a great influence on my world of reading, particularly poetry. He loved music and played various instruments badly, and we had many sessions of side-splitting music-making. I spent my happiest hours in his house in Hof Street, which was filled with books, records and his encyclopaedic knowledge. He wouldn't allow me to buy books in his shop. He would only give them to me. In addition to being awarded the Military Cross for bravery during the war, he was later given the Freedom of the Town of San Sepulcro for saving what Aldous Huxley called "the best picture in the world", *The Resurrection of Christ* by Piero della Francesca. Anthony was in the artillery, and HV Morton told the story of how he refused to shell the town of San Sepulcro, knowing that if he obeyed orders he would be destroying one of the world's greatest paintings. He could have been court-martialled.

Anthony's attitude towards his cancer was phenomenal. When asked how he felt, it was always, "I'm fine." He never learned to drive a car and not long before he died, I invited him to come and stay on the farm for a while. He hardly ever went away from Cape Town, so it was a great honour that he agreed to fly up, and I fetched him from the airport. He wouldn't let anyone carry his case and was excited to be shown to his guest-room. It was so rare that he was a guest in someone else's home. Jim loved having him in his library and they shared so much and had great admiration for each other. During his stay we had a fire on the farm and all the children, plus myself and Jim, went as usual to help beat it with wet sacks. Anthony, weak with cancer, absolutely insisted on being part of the fire-fighting team. His could barely lift his arms yet he was cheerful and his courage was a lesson for us all. He was gentle, unassuming and rather shy, and as brave as anyone I have known.

32

In July 1958, Lindy Serrurier and I drove up from UCT, where we were at Fuller Hall together, to Johannesburg in a Volkswagen that broke down about 40 miles outside Middelburg in the Karoo. We walked to the nearest farmhouse where the farmer, Mr van der Merwe, telephoned the garage in Middelburg. He had checked our car and diagnosed its problem. We needed a mechanic to tow us there.

The van der Merwes were very kind and gave us enormous helpings of Karoo mutton, with potato, rice, samp, beans, pumpkin. This was midday in a temperature of about 30 degrees. Mrs van der Merwe took us into her bedroom and showed us her jewellery. They were going to a farmer's meeting; Mr vd M dressed up in suit and tie, and Mrs vd M wore a costume with quite a lot of her jewels on her ample bosom and off they went in their huge Cadillac.

Lindy and I waited for the mechanic who arrived soon afterwards. He had a cleft palate. We were both 19 and were in paroxysms of mirth all the way to Middelburg. I had my eyes glued to my binoculars for the wondrous birds of prey that wheel over the Karoo landscape. It was a hazardous journey and Lindy had to yell at me regularly because I was at the wheel while we were towed. We stayed at the Middelburg Hotel and laughed until we eventually fell asleep. There was a photograph of a wedding couple in an oval convex frame on our wall. The bride was coloured in with vivid red lipstick and a green wedding gown.

Our car was fixed next morning. We loved every moment of our journey.

Francis Wilson was in my English class at UCT. He was going out with Lindy and I told them if they married, I loved them both so much that if anything happened to me and I had children, they must please take them and bring them up. Besides loving him dearly, I always wanted to sit next to him during our lectures because he had a thermos of hot tomato soup which he often shared with me. He was the son of Professor Monica Wilson, an anthropologist at UCT, who became a good friend to Jim and me. Francis was to become Professor of Economics there.

Some years later Lindy and Francis did get married, and they came to live in the cottage on the farm while Francis was on sabbatical. It was wonderful for me to have their company because Jim was away so often. Lindy and I spent time on the horses together. She was working for Jim at *Drum* at the time. Francis designed and constructed the most extraordinary filter for our swimming pool. He is definitely influenced by Heath Robinson, and it worked! When Jim was home we often played very noisy games of racing demon on the floor. This became a sort of ritual whenever we saw each other for many years to come.

In 1958 during the Christmas vacation, I became ill at Monaghan and had a high fever. Jim kindly brought me a meal on a tray in bed. On the tray without a cloth, were onions he had just picked in the garden, complete with skin, roots and soil. No plate, no knife. With the onions was a bottle of brandy – no glass.

He decided he had better drive me home. I was shivering, it was pouring with rain and the river was only just fordable. But in the dip of the dirt road the water looked too deep to cross. Jim stopped the car and asked me to test the depth. Being the besotted twit I was, I got out of the car in the rain and waded into the pool. I was only up to my knees in water so we drove through. That was one of the times I was relieved to go back to my loving, caring parents.

When Jim was 40 he decided he should marry and have children. He asked the farm-manager's wife in Colesberg how much it would cost him to keep a wife!

He married a pretty blonde schizophrenic whose parents explained her behaviour by saying she had an artistic temperament. She had frequently been in closed wards in an asylum and they never breathed a word about it. After being re-admitted many times, she said that pregnancy would cure her. Jim was very ignorant of this disorder and believed her. Tragically, their child was to be committed to a mental hospital at the age of 19 with the same illness.

I was in my third year at UCT when I heard that Jim had married. I put myself to sleep with trichloro-ethelyne – obviously and fortunately not enough. I also considered driving off a cliff into the sea. I then went to Oxford, became friendly with Jeremy Taylor, and married him the day he finished his last exam for his degree in Modern Languages. Jeremy's French was so good that he was chosen to translate simultaneously for Mendès-France when he came and spoke at the Oxford Union. He is a superb mimic and a natural self-taught musician.

In Oxford a few days before our wedding I was at a chemist buying some medicine. It was after 6pm and while I waited for my prescription to be prepared, a lady came in wanting lipstick. The chemist refused to sell her any as it was after hours for the sale of cosmetics. She was very put out and begged him to relent. He refused. My mother, having heard I was to marry, had gone clean off her rocker and had sent me some lipstick. I have never worn make-up, ever. So I told the distraught lady that if she followed me home when I had bought my medicine, I would give her some lipstick with the greatest of pleasure. It was exactly the colour she wanted – shocking pink.

I climbed on the back of Jeremy's two-stroke put-put and we wobbled along, being followed by a chauffeur-driven Rolls Royce, in the back of which was the very elegant lady. When she followed me into our digs in Wellington Square, a couple of Hungarian mathematicians who lived upstairs came down into the entrance, their eyes wide with pleasure.

"Congratulations, Dame Margot!" they said.

It was Dame Margot Fonteyn, who was being awarded an Honorary Doctorate at Oxford the following day. I had no idea that it was she. She was thrilled with the lipstick to match the shocking pink lapels of her academic gown.

Next morning Jeremy and I joined the throngs watching the procession of those receiving honorary degrees. Amongst the old bent and wizened academics in their various robes was beautiful and graceful Dame Margot. I received a two-page letter of thanks from her, to which she added some Zulu bead necklaces for our forthcoming wedding. She had no idea I was from South Africa so it was a most extraordinary coincidence that she chose this present.

Jeremy and I married in Binsey Parish Church in Port Meadow outside Oxford. I chose this church because it was tiny and ancient, and because the priest looked exactly like Mrs Tiggywinkle. I walked up the aisle with my teddy bear instead of a bouquet. Austin Farrer, the Dean of Trinity College Oxford, where Jeremy was a scholar, took our wedding service.

We sang our way round Ireland with Jeremy's guitar, and then I brought him to South Africa when he had graduated. He had never been here before.

Our first jobs were as teachers at St Martin's School, whose founder and headmaster, Michael Stern, was a great anchor in our lives. Jeremy taught French and Latin; I taught art and took the chapel choir. I also taught maths to all the Standard 6's. If I had been asked to teach any higher classes, I would have been unable to. That Michael Stern talked me into teaching maths at all shows his single-mindedness. I enjoyed it immensely.

Jeremy directed a charming production of *Twelfth Night* at St Martin's. The cast was chosen from boys throughout the school. I produced the music for the play, played the harpsichord and had a small group of instrumentalists, one of whom was Oliver de Groot, who became one of the best clarinettists in the country. He was 13 at this time. On flute was Sterling Wilson, who also had one of the most beautiful singing voices I have heard in a boy. He is the son of Lettie Vermaak who was a leading viola player in South Africa.

Twelfth Night. *Front row: Jeremy Taylor, B, Jerome Muegens, Peter Klatzow.*
Second front right: Sterling Wilson

Sterling was also in my maths class and was unbelievably lazy. At 14, he was very tall for his age and lay sprawled over his desk, closed his eyes, and got 26% for a test. I told him that if he occasionally opened his eyes and looked at the board he might get higher marks. He unfolded himself like scaffolding, very slowly, stood up, and languidly announced, "Oh Miss. I'm so tired."

He was taken out of St Martin's and sent to school after school where he did very badly. I met him again a few years ago and reminded him of this story. He said he is still tired. He is now in his 50s, has made a fortune and lives like a prince. So much for school results.

On 16 November 1960, Jessica was born. She arrived three weeks early, before the end of the school term. The staff and boys at St Martin's made a big fuss of her and I loved taking her to school and showing her off.

When Jeremy left St Martin's he fell in love properly for the first time, with a beautiful dancer who was part of the cast with him in a musical show, *Wait a Minim.* Andrew and Paul Tracey and Jeremy were the key musicians in the show, which was a great hit here, and then it travelled and succeeded in London and on Broadway.

With hindsight I knew I had been living a lie – I was so deeply Jim's. I was 21 and Jeremy was 22. I had no idea who I was or what I was doing.

In 1962, when Jessica was 20 months old, Beezy was born. I was playing the harpsichord for a rehearsal of *The Beggar's Opera,* and I excused myself when the labour pains were about five minutes apart. Beezy was born around 6pm and I phoned our conductor to tell my fellow musicians I had had a son. They found another harpsichordist for the evening performance.

Our dear Russian friend Kotchka Vladykin came to visit me in the nursing home. He looked at Beezy and said, "Varvara dallink, he is very sweet leetle boy, but you must agree that he is no Rudolph Valentino."

When Beezy was eight months old, he became seriously ill with gastro-enteritis. He was hospitalised and when I saw him in such distress I found it unbearable. When he saw me it upset him terribly, so my very dear friend Stanno Opperman offered to visit him each day for me, until he was well enough to come home. When Beezy

Benny with B's children, Jessica and Beezy, in 1963

arrived he was hoarse and had almost lost his voice completely from screaming. He was only in for three days but it seemed like months. He was bruised on his wrists and ankles and neck where they had tried to find a vein for a drip.

Two years later when I pulled a violin case from under the bed, he fainted. To Beezy it must have looked like a doctor's bag. For some years, he had episodes when he would stop breathing and turn blue. He had every sort of test for petit mal but thankfully he grew out of these 'fits' when he was about four.

Jessica aged two at St George's Church where she sang solo

Jessica at the age of two was an odd little one. She had a curious habit of licking her finger and stroking her eye-lids with the wetted finger. She learnt long complicated songs with all the words long before she knew what they meant.

At the age of two and a bit she sang the unaccompanied solo of 'Once in Royal David's City' at St George's Church, Parktown. She had a phenomenal ear. I took her to rehearsals of the orchestra from time to time. She pointed to the cellos and said, "I want to play that." She waited until she was seven to begin learning with Betty Pack.

Meanwhile in 1963 Jim's wife ran off after a man in Canada. Huge relief and quickest divorce possible. I begged Jim to marry me. He said that marriage was destructive.

He was living at Monaghan with his three-year-old son Jonathan, and stayed with me and my two little ones at times during the week in my digs in an old house in Eton Road in Parktown, Johannesburg. I was teaching art at St Katherine's, a small private prep school for girls, to make ends meet. I even sold my Pariani saddle, to help with the finances. My parents had been begging me to move in with them, but I wanted, desperately, to be independent.

Jim wrote his book *Eskimo Nel,* in longhand.[16] I then copied it out in its entirety in my own hand because Jim's writing was so illegible. For his subsequent books I learnt to type. I typed for him, kept his home and started helping with the farming during the week – and went on begging him to marry me. He once wrote to me, "People do not marry their playmates."

Then, just before a *Drum* trip to Salisbury in 1964, he said, "Bribe a magistrate with a bottle of whisky or two to marry us in a garden somewhere on Friday afternoon."

---

16 later re-published by Bloomsbury as 'The Sky Suspended'

To do this he left before the end of a SAAN [South African Associated Newspapers] board meeting. I was told by one of the other SAAN directors that as he was leaving the boardroom he had said, "I am about to make the second biggest mistake of my life. I am getting married."

It was a white wedding: Jim wore white shorts because he was playing squash afterwards. I brought a curtain ring because I knew he wouldn't bring one. He never did give me a ring. The wedding took 10 minutes and then he left to play squash. That night he went to Salisbury without me. It remained a joke throughout our lives together. He went on the honeymoon without me.

My mother was very worried about my marrying him. She said, "Darling, Jim is a wonderful man but he will make the most dreadful husband."

Over our near 40 years together our game was that I often asked him to marry me. He said he would consider it. He loved the idea of being free and pretending that we weren't married and that he had no responsibilities.

For the first 25 years of our marriage he was away between five and seven months of every year. So I learnt to farm at Monaghan, to be mother and father and disciplinarian to the children. Jim was away on an average of between two and six weeks at a time. The longest absence was over 10 weeks. That was terrible for me. I hated his going away, particularly as I had no idea how long it might last.

He never phoned from anywhere in independent Africa because it was too dangerous. He was aware that BOSS was watching him. Our phones were tapped. Occasionally he phoned from London and said he'd be heading south soon. Oh what did that mean? I had very little idea of the danger he was in at this time. He didn't discuss it with me. I suppose he knew I would react by wanting us to leave the country so that he would be safe.

On one occasion in October 1964, Mr and Mrs 'Digniformer' (as we called people who were conventional in the extreme) were coming to lunch. Jim asked me to make sure there was a good lunch, and what is more he asked me to wear a skirt. This was a very tall order, but I did as I was bidden, greeted them on their arrival and led them onto the verandah to offer them a drink. Mrs D wore a pale blue costume, large costume jewellery, stockings and court shoes, hair in a tight perm, careful make-up. Mr D was dressed in a dark suit, boring tie and highly polished shoes.

The verandah looks down onto the swimming pool and while I poured their drinks, dressed in my skirt and blouse, I looked down and saw Jim on his hands and knees, his head down over the filter, his back view facing us. He was stark naked. I swept our guests into the living room. They were a little puzzled to be taken indoors so suddenly, and then Jim rolled in having put a small towel over his shoulder. It didn't even reach his navel. He greeted them warmly, shaking hands with them both – he had beautiful manners always – and then he went on to the bedroom to dress for lunch.

When he was about a year old and only just walking, Beezy disappeared from the farm kitchen. He wasn't in the garden or anywhere in the house. My heart froze. We ran down the road towards the river, which is about a quarter of a mile away, and there he was, clutching his blanket called Gentle Ninganing, his tin double-decker bus and his cuddly animal called Jesus. He was perfectly content and not a bit worried about being so far from the house.

In November of 1964 I took the children to the Oyster Box, an hotel on the Natal coast, to join my parents who were staying there. Jim was away for a month so it was a welcome treat. We went by train overnight, and arrived for lunch, after which I put them on their beds to rest for an hour before going to the beach. When I went in to fetch them, there was no sign of the two-year-old Beezy. A major hunt was organised and I felt more and more desperate as the minutes ticked by. All over the hotel we searched; the waiters were alerted and the whole staff was eventually commandeered. There are miles of beach below the hotel and I felt ill with anxiety.

Eventually I ran down to the ocean and with my binoculars searched the beach as far as the eye could see. There was a group of four fishermen with their rods over their shoulders, walking along the edge of the water about half a mile down the beach, and only just visible was a tiny speck following behind them. We hared down towards them. It was Beezy, perfectly happy, trotting along after the fishermen, who seemed relieved to have him retrieved.

Beezy was a very original child. He was also naughty. When he was an infant, I regularly put my finger in his mouth and scooped out whatever he had in it. A scoop once revealed six buttons.

He sang all the time he played. He played long imaginative games by himself and either sang or kept up a running commentary, so that when he was silent it usually meant he was doing something that he shouldn't. Once, when I had dressed them all for a Christmas party at the Inanda Club, Beezy in a little pale green silk suit that my mother had bought in London, white socks and shoes, hair washed and brushed, I put him in his room and shut the door while I dressed the younger ones. He was quiet, and when I went in to fetch him he had opened a bottle of black ink over his head.

Jim never raised his voice to the children. When they were naughty he laughed. But he liked quiet and all through their childhood, I kept them quiet for him. This was no easy task. As we saw his car drive in, when we were all sitting at the big kitchen table doing homework or eating or whatever, the decibels would decrease dramatically. When we drove the 900 miles to Plettenberg Bay, they had to whisper in the back of the car. I ended up being like a mother superior of a Trappist monastery. A very fierce one too. They often disappeared until Jim had gone to his library. But when the mood took him there was much laughter and wrestling and games with him. The children were all sensitive to his needs and acted accordingly.

He once asked me, "How many children have we over the age of seven?"

They loved him and he taught them to fish and shoot and was a valuable and hugely supportive friend to all of them when they grew up. He always encouraged them to do what their hearts desired. He let them be who they were, and when they were old enough, they understood how precious and rare a gift this was in any parent. He legally adopted Jessica and Beezy when they were five and three. He was so fond of children that he would gladly have adopted more.

Samuel Modiba lived at Monaghan all his life. He was a boy of about 12 when Jim purchased the land, and we first saw Samuel when he was ploughing the red earth behind a pair of even redder oxen. He and I ran a Hereford Stud for 27 years together. We drove the cattle in on horseback. How I loved cantering after wayward calves, shout-

Samuel Modiba with B on Kleintjie

ing at stubborn cows, becoming more and more familiar with the veld grasses and flowers, and avoiding holes made by all sorts of creatures. It was a blissful part of my life.

One of Samuel's eyes looked out to the left. He was wiry and bent his head forwards when he wanted to impart information. He spoke no English, I spoke no Tswana and we communicated in indifferent Afrikaans.

During spring, the calving season, while Jim and I breakfasted on the verandah, Samuel would stalk up the lawn to us, and hold up one, two or three fingers, depending on how many calves had been born during the night. After breakfast I would collect the marking equipment for the new arrivals. Each calf had a number tattooed in its ear. The Hereford Breeders Society had a letter of the alphabet representing each year, so according to the letter in its ear, we would know when an animal had been born.

Samuel would pen the mother and then rugby-tackle the newborn calf. We would weigh it, and then he'd sit astride it while I tattooed it and gave it an intravenous injection against heartwater, a tick-borne disease which is one of the main causes of death in cattle in this area. We used Zebo oven polish to rub into the tattoo and the heel of my hand was ingrained with black for most of every spring.

These limpid-eyed babies, red with white curls on their foreheads, smelt delicious and their anxious disapproving mothers would be mooing and stamping the dust while we processed them. When it was over, the calf would trot off to its mother, none the worse for wear, and they were reunited, the calf butting the udder for a good drink after all its manhandling.

During these Hereford-breeding years, Jim and I had the pleasure of choosing names for over 100 calves annually. If we woke in the night and uttered Tamberlaine or Tchekov, it required no explanation. That 'T' year he wanted to call a calf Tampax but we thought the Breeders Society might have objected. It was endless fun and I was desolate when the herd was sold.

Every winter on our farm, a group of male youths go off for a month's initiation. The weather is often below freezing at night, and they go naked, bathe in the river each morning, and are circumcised, the wound being dressed with leaves with healing properties. A fire is kept alight for the duration of the month and a tough one it is. Over the years desperate mothers have come to me secretly to beg for antiseptic cream, and occasionally I had to use antibiotics. While out riding my horse I have sometimes caught a glimpse of a white-painted face of one of the initiates which hastily disappears when it sees me.

Recently I asked our gardener, Sam's brother Joel Modiba, what they learn and do during their initiation. He said they become men. He said no-one will ever tell what they do. They are sworn to secrecy. It is now 2004 and the winter 'school' continues to take place on this farm. I still do not know exactly where it is.

On the 9th November 1965 we were fishing down at the river. Jim harpooned a 5ft barbel then lost his spear in a smaller one. Meanwhile I was starting labour pains on the bank. Jim kept saying, "Give me a few more minutes." The pains were growing more frequent and when we finally left the river, we had no time to gather any belongings at the house. I arrived at the Florence Nightingale Nursing Home to give birth, equipped with a fishing bag and a copy of Augustus John's autobiography, *Chiaroscuro*. I went to the reception desk and said I was going to have a baby. They asked my name, and after searching their book, they told me I was due in three weeks time. I said I knew that but that I was going to have it now. They argued. Luckily my doctor arrived and whisked me smartly off to the labour ward.

I had phoned my father when I started labour. As he had recently had his second coronary thrombosis, he said he had better not come to be with me, and wished me well. So it was a wonderful surprise to see him walking into theatre in time for the birth. The umbilical cord was wound round baby Alaric's neck and he needed extra oxygen. Shortly afterwards I looked round to see Papa sitting on a chair against the wall, with his newborn grandson on his lap, sharing the oxygen mask, sniff for sniff.

Having dropped me at the nursing home, Jim drove all the way back to the farm and fetched his pyjamas for me, and nothing else. No toothbrush, no comb, nothing but huge men's pyjamas.

It was pouring with rain when he returned. He lay on the bed with me to rejoice in the birth of Alaric. He was sopping wet, having walked through the rain from many blocks away where he had parked his car. The nurses eventually shooed him out, visiting hour long past, and said it was the first time they had had to change all the bedding for a husband.

Father Aelred Stubbs CR, whom I had met while teaching at St Martin's, christened Alaric, and Francis and Lindy Wilson were the godparents. Aelred has become a wonderful friend and often comes to the farm.

APRIL 1965 ENGLAND

Shirley van Velden took me to her parents' house near Cookham. We met the Master of the Queen's Swans, who dresses in a smart red uniform with buttons and braid, and looks after all the swans on the Thames. We went walking by a stream and I needed to pee urgently, so I squatted down behind a tree. I hadn't learnt about nettles and possibly broke a record jumping up from a sitting position. Dear Shirley picked some dock leaves to ease the sting, and I wore them in my knickers for the next few hours.

The following March (1966) Jim had been in West Africa visiting the *Drum* offices (he eventually had 22 offices in Nigeria alone) and I joined him when he reached London. I had been haemorrhaging slightly since Alaric's birth in November and Jim reluctantly agreed to accompany me to see a doctor. The doctor wanted to perform a D&C straight away. I told him I wished to fly back to South Africa and have it done there. He telephoned my father, a doctor, who booked me into the nursing home direct from the airport when I arrived so my children wouldn't see me until after the operation.

The London doctor injected me with something that he said would make me warm and drowsy, and said I was to stay in bed until I flew the following evening. Jim and I left the doctor's rooms off the King's Road, and I assumed we would take a cab back to the Lansdowne Club in Curzon Street where we were staying. I assumed wrong. It was a lovely evening and Jim wanted to walk. We walked for a while and then I suggested a cab. Jim kept walking. I was not in a good way and eventually asked him for some change for a cab.

Jim came in hours later. I was too young and I suppose frightened of him to insist on a taxi immediately.

For the first decade or two of our marriage Jim hated me playing the piano. He always said, "Can we have some peace?" So as he walked into the living room I used to stop playing. As I grew up – that is when I was about 50 – I played on and he accepted it. Why oh why did it take so long?

44

But when Jessica practised her cello, I told him never never to stop her practising. He heeded me. I do not regard his attitude to my piano-playing and my reaction to it as a sacrifice. That was how it was. I wished to please him.

Eventually he mellowed, but it took about 25 years.

In May 1967 we went together to Athens. Jim's knowledge seemed limitless and he enjoyed imparting it. He spent most of the time in the Athens museum. He was writing a book on the Bronze Age that Hodder & Stoughton were publishing. He needed illustrations for the book, which meant I was to draw vases and various artefacts in the Athens Museum.

I find museums exhausting and Jim sweetly led me in the crook of his arm while I closed my eyes, until we reached the relevant artefact. I would get on with the drawing he needed and when he came and fetched me, he was grateful and appreciative, and led me out again. When I had drawn what he needed, we went to the Acropolis together. It was as if we were visiting his gods, which I suppose we were. He told me about entasis – the almost imperceptible swelling of the columns.

One night we supped at a taverna under grape vines. At a long table was a lively party. There was a very attractive man who was holding forth and captivating his audience with such charm and power that he captivated us as well. We couldn't hear what he was saying and we fabricated his character. We decided he was called Gustav and that he spoke 10 languages fluently – and I was falling in love with him rapidly. The Greek dancing started and a sunburnt lady took me off into the circle, while Jim was left at the table. After prancing around the restaurant with hands held high I looked across the room and there was Jim in the chain of dancers, holding Gustav's hand, almost helpless with mirth.

Our last day in Athens was hot and I suggested going up the coast. So we rolled our bathing suits in towels and took a bus, which was mostly filled with old women in black. There were only a few seats on the bus and a big empty space at the back where we sat on our towels on the floor. Soon we saw a beach and turquoise sea so we hopped off. Jim had never done anything like this – i.e. catch a bus.

He longed to snorkel and there was a man doing just that. We put on our swimming costumes and when the snorkeler came out of the sea, I chatted him up while Jim lay nearby on the sand and slept. The man lent me his goggles and snorkel, which I handed over to Jim and in he went.

Later we all drank retsina together. Then the wind came up so we put on our jumpers and watched some teenage boys playing volleyball on the beach. Jim went to sleep again and I couldn't resist joining the volleyball game. After about half an hour I suggested we all swim – by sign language. I spoke no Greek. They had no English.

I was wearing my bikini under my clothes. I started to undress and they did likewise. When they saw I was not a boy, they were very shocked. Evidently in Greece, girls do not play volleyball on the beach with boys. They must have thought I was a really effeminate boy and a very, very poor volleyball player. As I was 29 and a mother of three children, I was tickled pink.

The last time I was mistaken for a boy I was 32 and the mother of four children. I was asked to sing in the St Mary's Cathedral choir because the Archbishop of Canterbury was taking the service and they imported some extra voices for the occasion. I wore a cassock and sang with the choristers. As we filed out after the service, I heard one old biddy saying to another, "Of course it's a boy, look at 'is boots!"

Jessica and Bundy, 1967

Three generations – Papa, B and Jessica, 1968

At Easter 1968 I bought three white chocolate rabbits for Jonathan, Jessica and Beezy. Alaric was rather too young for chocolate. I put them on the mantelpiece in the living room so they would be a surprise for them on Easter morning. Jim came in late the night before, long after I was in bed. At dawn, when I led our three excited offspring in to find their Easter bunnies, there were two bunnies and some scrunched silver paper and cellophane. Oh Jim!

46

At this time Beezy wrote letters to God which I was to post through Jessica's godfather, a priest. Beezy thought this would be the quickest way of reaching their destination.

Beezy, 1967

> "Dear God,
> You are such a dear you give us the veld and sky and the farm and everything. If I was God I would be a dear to you, but too late, you're one to me."

School was very hard for Beezy. He was dyslexic and little was known about it then.

Having his wild imagination and having to tow the line was not easy for him. Even in Kindergarten his first report read, "... He prefers to sing when the rest of the class is playing with plasticine, and to draw when they have outdoor activities. William (he was christened William James Sebastian) does not obey orders. He appears not to hear and we suggest that you have his hearing tested."

Poor little Beezy was always in trouble, at school and at home. I remember chasing all of them round and round the kitchen table with the wooden spoon. If I caught them, they got it on the backs of their legs. Beezy was the main victim.

6 JULY 1968
Essay written at school by Jonathan, aged nine.

"My Mother"
My mother is very fascinating. She is like a man because she has never in her life worn a dress in my sight. She drives tractors and cars a lot. She loves fishing when ever my father goes fishing she does. She is very nice and kind because she gives me a whole easter egg full of chocolates long after easter day. She is a good type-writer and has to help my father a lot.

Jonathan excelled at school work and at games. He learnt easily. His schizophrenia was evident but only became unmanageable when he was in his late teens. I once asked a psychiatrist to hypnotise me into loving him with all my heart. The psychiatrist said that if he could do that he could change the world.

In September we drove to Dullstroom in the Eastern Transvaal to fly-fish with Jonathan Gluckman and his wife Lois. We fetched them in our car and they met Jim for the first time. Jim and Lois sat in the back, Jonathan and I in front, and we all chatted congenially for the three-hour drive to Belfast. There we stopped for petrol.

Jim and I went to the café to check *Drum* sales, while Lois went to a vegetable shop. When we came out, Lois was waiting on the pavement and she asked Jim, "Did you get what you wanted?" Jim looked at her, puzzled, and politely asked, "Who are you?"

SEPTEMBER 1968 MONAGHAN FARM
The Muscovy ducks have 10 little ducklings who march solemnly behind their mother across the wonder-lawn in the courtyard outside my bedroom. Mehercules the hedgehog lives there too.

While bringing the Herefords in on horseback with Samuel I spotted a baby hedgehog that I wanted to take home for the children. Samuel gallantly dismounted and made a little cradle out of his filthy handkerchief in which he carried it back to the house.

Mehercules' diet consists almost entirely of snakes. He is tiny yet he devoured a whole night adder about 2ft long, all in one night.

Samuel's cradle for carrying his hedgehog while on horseback

On 22 May 1969, Prospero James Thomas was born. I had toxaemia and wanted to give birth at home I felt so rotten. Then I remembered the cord around Alaric's neck, so off I went to the Florence Nightingale. Happily, Meggy (Meredith Hill) had come to help with the children while I was in the nursing home. Meggy was travelling around the world after working on Vogue Magazine in New York. I met her through friends at St Martin's Church in Dunkeld. She was free to come to the farm for a while. She meant to stay for three weeks, and made it very clear that the one thing she couldn't tolerate was illness of any sort. Within days, all the children had chicken pox one after the other. Then they all had mumps, Beezy had encephalitis following the mumps, and a few weeks later, I had mumps and encephalitis. Two months later I had pneumonia. This was all within nine months of Prospero's birth. Meggy wound up staying for those illness-stricken nine months. Poor Meggy, lucky me.

She described to me the supper she shared with Jim the night that Prospero was born. It was their first meeting and Jim didn't say one word. Meggy kept on trying to make conversation but failed to get any response whatsoever.

Prospero was born smiling. When most children are woken from a sleep they groan or grunt. Prospero grinned before he opened his eyes. He was charming and easy and attractive throughout his childhood. He got away with murder because of his charm. He still does.

When they wanted something, the other children usually used Prospero as their spokesman to tackle me or Jim. He usually succeeded. I was also too worn out to argue by that stage of my life. It was easier to let him have his way, rather than be nagged.

Alaric alias Bundy was accident prone all his life. He swallowed a drawing-pin when he was about three and I nearly had a fit and rung my father who told me to relax, and that it would come out the other end and do no damage. Papa was right.

Jonathan aged 11 threw Bundy aged four into the swimming pool and he sank like a stream-lined brick. I rushed to the pool from the verandah and jumped in and hauled him out. When asked why he did it, Jonathan said: "He falsely accused me."

When all the children were stealing biscuits out of our neighbour's larder, they all ran home and the only one caught was Alaric who was about five. He didn't run as fast as the others and the neighbour gave him a hiding which was so awful – I wished she had given me one instead.

He was a very good little boy and loved his school work and had more prizes than any other child in his class all his years at the Ridge. Every term we had a ritual of Jim reading their reports with them, one by one. On these occasions Bundy positively purred.

He was very literal. When asked what he was reading, he would tell you and add that he was on page 243. He was totally dependable and one could rely on him to do what he was told. He was a nut-brown boy and one could lean on him. The headmaster of the Ridge always relied on Bundy to ring the bell for break. It was Bundy who knew all the numbers of our cars, telephones etc. He was very necessary in this otherwise scatter-brained family. He was also the only one who slept deeply. We could use him as a hot-water bottle while he slept, move him from one bed to another without waking him. The others used to play a wireless loudly in his ear and he wouldn't move an eye-lid.

Throughout their childhood Jess often shared a bed with him, warmed her icy feet on him and adored him.

19 SEPTEMBER 1969
Selwyn, a tiny baby jackal, has become a pet in our house. Strabismus, our Siamese cat, hisses at him and he takes not the blindest bit of notice. Selwyn will eat anything. Yesterday I saw something dangling out of his backside and slowly pulled an entire shoelace out of him.

Selwyn devours anything.

When Selwyn grew up he ate chunks out of a mattress, and I eventually had to give him away to a lover of jackals.

23 NOVEMBER 1969
Bill Wilson and Jim had a business lunch. Bill is Deputy Chairman of Anglo American and he and Jim were taken to a smart restaurant in a chauffeur-driven Mercedes. After their very congenial lunch, they climbed into the back of the grand Mercedes and carried on their conversation for about half an hour until someone came and told them they were in the wrong car.

DECEMBER 1969

There are four huge pipes under our causeway which often get blocked up by branches and debris washed down in the floods.

The river was a few inches over the causeway when the family who live in the farm cottage went for a walk. They have young children and they took Bundy (Alaric), now four, and waded over the causeway where the water was so low as to only cover their feet. They crossed slowly, picking watercress, watching yellow-bill duck and Egyptian geese and spotting the sporadic rise of barbel.

When they had nearly reached the other side, they realised Bundy had disappeared. The wet surface is slippery and Bundy had fallen upstream into the river, been washed through the only pipe of the four that wasn't blocked and had reappeared downstream. It happened so quickly and he was hauled out none the worse. I can barely muster the courage to write about it.

The river can rise 20 feet in summer. It happens very suddenly when there has been a huge cloudburst in Johannesburg. Almost exactly seven hours later, a wall of water, terrifyingly powerful, rushes down and then there is no sign that our causeway exists.

Once, when Jim still lived in 'Naught for Your Comfort', his house across the river, he parked his car on the road about 10 feet up from the river because the rain was such that he thought he might be marooned if he drove across. In the morning, the roof of the car was bobbing up and down, just visible in the middle of the now-mad river which flowed strongly enough to sweep the car into its torrent. The road alongside was totally submerged.

In this state, the Jukskei has taken the lives of the aged, the drunk and some little children on this farm. It has sometimes taken up to a week to find the bodies which have been swept downstream for a mile or more.

JANUARY 1970 MONAGHAN

Jim phoned me from the *Drum* office. He had a SAAN board meeting and could I bring his shoes and socks. I phoned and asked my brother Richard to lend him some – Richard is only 15 minutes away from *Drum*. He would save me having to drive for close on an hour.

Jim's daily routine is to check on the farming until mid-morning, when he goes to *Drum*. On this occasion, he had driven to the river which was too high to traverse, parked our side of it, and waded across. Having inspected the farm, he waded back again to his car and drove to town leaving his footwear behind.

21 MARCH 1970
Celebrated Bach's birthday with all the James family, as they are fellow Bach-lovers. This year we had Deborah, Simon and Melissa James on piano, flute and viola, and Jess and self on cello and piano. John Silver came and played guitar. We all sang choruses from St Matthew's Passion and the Christmas Oratorio.

I made a cake with BACH iced on it. Bundy, aged four, wouldn't come in for tea and I found him under the trees in the drive. He told me he was waiting for Bach to arrive. He'd seen the cake and didn't want to start without him.

When I see Bach's name printed on the cover of music I want to show my respect by kissing the cover, or bowing my head. This is a genuine response that has been deep inside me since I was a child.

I was confirmed in Oxford when I was 20, and I told Austin Farrer, who prepared me, that my difficulty was that I couldn't see much difference between God and Bach. Austin's reaction was unforgettable. He said, "Exactly. That is how you worship. You understand worship through music, and so much of the greatest music has been written for that purpose. Likewise the painting, sculpture and architecture over so many centuries."

For me it is like a believer taking Communion. When I play Bach well, self disappears and Bach plays me.

I go to church for the music, and am often inattentive during the sermons, but once I heard a priest saying, "... and in the words of that great and mighty giant, Johann Sebastian Bach, *All music is for the greater glory of God*." Every cell, every atom of my mind and body beamed.

I cannot remember who it was who said, "Beethoven is the music of Man, Mozart is the music of Angels, Bach is the music of God."

When I was in my late teens, my parents took me to a recital by Roselyn Tureck, the famous pianist, whose interpretation of the works of Bach was unique, convincing and stylised. There is a story that the great and wondrous harpsichordist Wanda Landowska and Tureck were invited to a party in New York and the host tried to keep them apart. Landowska however spotted Tureck across the room, and went over and greeted her warmly. Tureck, amazed, said: "It is wonderful to meet you – but I am truly surprised that you are so friendly!" Landowska responded: "Why not? After all, you play Bach in your way, and I in his."

barthroated Apalis

APRIL 1970

This morning I nearly stood on a 5ft boomslang in the Karee courtyard – it slithered up the Karee and disappeared.

In the afternoon Letta, our cleaning lady, wounded a rinkhals with a broom, outside my room. That is frightening. I don't need a wounded rinkhals on the loose.

I saw a bar-throated apalis in the celtis in the kitchen courtyard.

22 MAY 1970

Petrus Mashlangu drove a boomslang out of the honeysuckle by burning Horseshoe tobacco. It worked perfectly, causing the snake to slide out and away, slightly stunned by the pungency.

I was bitten by a spider and reacted badly enough to need cortisone.

Around this time we noticed that our Frisian cow had been producing less and less milk yet her udder filled unfailingly for the evening milking. We grew suspicious that someone on the farm was milking her before dawn on a regular basis.

We put a spy onto the case and one morning, a 6ft leguaan was witnessed suckling her. This had been going on for weeks. Fanie, our farm manager shot it dead with a .22.

Jim then insisted that we should eat the leguaan. We figured that the only person we knew who would know how to cook it was Kurt Jobst. When I phoned to ask him, he didn't bat an eyelid or laugh.

"Put it in a cauldron of boiling water, sit on the lid while the leguaan thrashes itself about thus ridding itself of its poisons," he said. When I told him it was six foot long and dead, Kurt said, "Chrrrist!"

Previously, Jim had been on Durban beach wearing his red sweater and someone had mistaken him for a lifesaver. This filled him with such vanity as to believe lifesavers such as he could eat leguaans – no trouble at all . . .

Kurt Jobst died in a car accident in May the following year. He was one of the most gifted metal smiths and designers of his time. He had a pronounced limp due to polio as a child, and he was a tireless womaniser. A terrible driver even when he was sober – it was a wonder he lasted as long as he did. I was asked to play the organ at his funeral. I said I would cry and thus wouldn't be able to see the music, but he really loved Bach so I braved it.

I went to the crematorium the day before the service to try the organ, and was met by a deaf dwarf pushing a wheelbarrow. He was the only person there. I showed him my music and he pointed to a side door that was open into the crematorium. The tiled part at the back was visible through another open door, and there were trolleys with covered bodies lying on them. Apparently they all burn together because of the cost of white heat. The organ was a harmonium that had to be pedalled constantly to produce sound.

At the ceremony the following day, which was cold, a wind blew from the heater near me, causing the pages of my Bach to keep waving about and turning. As I couldn't take my hands off the keys, I blew furiously at the fluttering leaves to enable me to see what I was playing. How I kept going I do not know. It was a nightmare, but Kurt would have revelled in the story.

8 SEPTEMBER 1970

We came home to find the farm on fire and about 100 hectares gone. Beezy and Jess fought gallantly with the farm staff, using wetted sacks tied onto sticks. Black faces, black clothes, black bathwater, black on the carpets, bedding, curtains etc., and the smell of burnt veld for many days.

This happens almost every winter. Driving home we see flames and pray they are not on our property. Great walls of fire come from the north-west and are fanned by the prevailing wind, and our firebreaks however wide we make them, are meaningless if the wind is high.

19 SEPTEMBER 1970
First four artichokes ready for eating, and orange and lemon blossom filling our nostrils from the paradise outside our bedrooms. The Arabic for 'walled garden' is 'paradise', and paradise it is. I have planted gardenia, brunsfelsia, citrus, and jasmine there – I am sometimes woken by the scent wafting in.

20 SEPTEMBER 1970
Mocking chat male outside bedroom – so dapper. First time on this farm.

Killed a small snake in the swimming pool first shot. Then next day a rinkhals outside the bedroom – three shots, three holes in rinkhals. Then a horrible big rat in my room – first shot. All with a pellet gun. Dead-eye Dick, that's me.

4 NOVEMBER 1970
I shot a 5ft Egyptian cobra with the pellet gun. It was coiled up on a clutch of hen's eggs. It had swallowed two so that it looked like this. It was so fat and full that I pumped its head with pellets before it had woken enough to rear up and look threatening. I had an enthralled and admiring audience consisting of all my children, the gardener, the nanny and three of the farm workers. They gave me courage and I felt I was saving them all from a terrible monster.

November 4th 1970 . Having swallowed eggs .

Prospero [aged 18 months] comes to Jessica's cello lessons and has his sleep in her cello case while she plays. I take his little eiderdown and tuck him in. During her trio lessons with Gerard Korsten and Elna Stein, the two other mothers sit and knit, their fingers 'weaving in skilled unmindfulness'. My handwork while listening to these three ten-year-olds playing Schubert or Beethoven, is to remove black-jacks from Jim's socks and jumpers. Betty Pack's ashtrays gradually fill with bits of wool interwoven with blackjacks and burs.

Betty Pack, the doyen of chamber music in South Africa, was a key part of our lives for a decade. Almost every good string player learned the cello with Betty, the violin with Alan Solomon, and all of them played in her orchestra. String playing in this country is much the poorer since she died and since Alan emigrated to the United States after his beloved violin was stolen from his home. Amazingly, it was recovered eventually from a pawnshop.

December 1970
I was lying in bed with Jim at the crack of dawn when there was just enough light to see what I thought was a very thin black snake on the carpet. I woke Jim and said that it must either be a shoelace or a snake. He said it must be a snake because there are never any shoelaces in the house, and he went back to sleep. It was a snake.

December 1970
Heard desperate cries coming from behind the library. It was a hare with its ear impaled on a thorn branch, being attacked by an eagle owl. Part of its back had been eaten away. Jim finished it off by breaking its neck. Such stuff as nightmares are made of. Thank God he was home.

Jim left a note in the kitchen, "Gone to Nairobi and London."

20 June 1971
Beat about 200 guinea-fowl into the guns. Wonderful fun – saw it all happening down near the river.

Cantering along fast, watching birds dropping out of the sky and then seconds later, hearing the shot. Always fascinating, the different speeds of sight and sound.

Bundy and David his cousin, aged five and six, were lost for a short time in the very long grass. Found weeping, poor babes.

1971
I interviewed Prospero on an audio tape.
    "How old are you?" I asked.
    "I'm four," came the reply.
    "No you're not, you are two."
    "I'm four. I can swim."[17]

When Prospero was two he cut his forehead open and had to be stitched. I held his hand during the process. He didn't cry at all and afterwards he said, "Sank you doctor." This gives some indication of what he endured when his four elder siblings played 'doctors' with him.

One evening Jessica, aged 11, was driven home to the farm after a concert where she had been playing trios. Jim and I had gone to bed and were asleep when I heard the car drive in. We sleep two courtyards away from the main house where all the children have their bedrooms, so I phoned Jess on the intercom and told her to bring baby Prospero, aged two, to my room for the night so that he would not wake her early in the morning and she could sleep late.

She was wearing her long white concert dress. Prospero was asleep and she carried him in her arms, slipped in her new white shoes and dropped him. His scalp was split open on the tile skirting. She arrived in my bedroom almost as white as her dress, carrying Prospero. There was blood all over her dress and shoes and the carpet. I had been deeply asleep and it was close to midnight. I leapt out of bed, fetched towels and started to clean around the wound. Prospero took it quite calmly and didn't make much fuss. At this point Jim wandered in with a book open in his hands and said, "Would you like a piece of Herodotus?" He had noticed nothing untoward.

---

17 He swam for the first time when he was six

I told him to take Jessica in under the blankets and hold her close and hug her. She was in bad shock and needed care far more than Prospero did. I was busy cutting his hair, washing the wound and finding antiseptics. I asked Jim to fetch a hot sweet drink for Jess. Off he rolled to the kitchen and was away for nearly half an hour, returning with a plastic mug of tepid milk that leaked. He said he had put the milk on the stove but wasn't too sure how to switch it on.

His roly-poly walk was so much part of Jim. Many of his friends and employees imitated it. He told me when he landed his Hurricane at an airfield during the war, he saw a pilot 'rolling' away down the path. The walk was very familiar. It was his brother Derrick.

Above: Jim and James Fox 'doing Jim'
Above left: Jim greeting Nicky Oppenheimer at
Bridget's 60th birthday
Left: Joel Madiba 'doing Jim' with Grace
Lekutle and Maria Skosana

21 JULY 1971

Raymond Dart and Jim walked across the farm discussing ancient history with such fervour and concentration that when they came to a fence they stopped and carried on talking. I physically turned them round to face the other way, and like clockwork toys, they proceeded without pausing in their conversation.

11 APRIL 1972

Prospero, nearly three, saw a cobra under the piano and had the good sense to run and call me. Later, while I was playing the piano and all the children were busy in the living room with me, a cobra slid in through the front door, down the three steps, across the room with us all watching, and out the French doors. It had taken a short cut instead of going round the house.

Bundy as squadron leader, 1972

At this time Mark Douglas-Home, at the age of 19, was the editor of *Wits Student*, the weekly University magazine. He published on its front page a photo of a toddler looking down a lavatory. A caption bubble emerged from the toddler's mouth containing the words, "Excuse me, are you the Prime Minister?"[18] The offending edition of *Wits Student* was banned. Mark was followed to the Ogilvie-Thompson's house where he was babysitting their children while they were abroad. The telephone rang there at 2am and Mark was told 'they' were coming to get him. The following day he came to us and stayed in hiding at the farm. After a few days he was given 24 hours to leave the country. His uncle, Alec Douglas-Home was British Foreign Secretary at the time which adds a certain piquancy to the saga.

After he had been in South Africa in 1972, Mark went to Oxford. While he was a student there he formed a select little group who made it their mission to take gnomes from one garden and place them in another garden. They were successful until Mark was caught mid-gnome.

Mark is at present the editor of the Glasgow Herald. Jim once gave him some advice which he always regarded as the best he'd ever had in journalism. It was simply: "be irreverent."

---

18 Dr B J Vorster at this time

16 May 1972 Scotland

Spent a delightful weekend with Edward and Nancy Douglas-Home[19] near Gala-shiels. Jim caught a 10lb salmon in the Tweed. Edward and I sat on the bank and watched him. At one stage, Edward in his understated gentle manner said, "Watch Jim fall into the Tweed". Which he did, up to the neck.

Edward knows every stone in the river and Jim was trying to negotiate the river-bed with a salmon on the end of his line. Edward didn't warn him to take care, he just sat and chuckled. Mark helped Jim up onto the bank and carried his fish for him.

Edward and I finished The Times crossword – he is addicted as are all the Douglas-Homes.

26 May 1972 London

Spent my birthday morning listening to Yehudi Menuhin and Maurice Gendron rehearsing in the Royal Festival Hall. Listening and looking at Yehudi is my idea of heaven. Gendron teaches at the Menuhin School. He is a beautiful cellist.

In June 1972 we went to Rooipoort, near Kimberley, to the wonderfully pictur-esque shooting box built for Cecil Rhodes that he never saw because he died in 1902. I think it had only just been completed. This was where we were invited every year by Julian and Tessa Ogilvie-Thompson to shoot guinea-fowl, Namaqua sand-grouse and springbok. Other people shoot larger buck and I don't want to think about it.

The original horse-drawn buckboards were restored and used. Being at Rooi-poort was like winding the clocks back a century; doors with inlaid stained glass, china door-knobs, the original china washing-bowls and chamber-pots in the bed-rooms; high iron beds, huge baths with clawed feet, enormous fireplaces with the original tiles, the woodwork and metalwork all beautifully preserved.

On the train en route to Rooipoort, Clewer, our black Labrador gundog, slept

---

19 Mark's parents

under the bunk, carefully hidden by rucksacks. When the steward came to make up the beds, Clewer's tail thumped a greeting. I quickly did a little tap dance to match the tail wagging which mystified the steward. He thought I was dotty. But it worked.

Clewer is a matronly and stately Labrador. When we told Beezy that she was invited to the Rooipoort shoot, he said, "Oh Bar, can you imagine all the hat boxes!" For this occasion she was named Aunt Augusta.

Which reminds me that when Gorna Albu took her little dog on a train, the steward told her no dogs were allowed in the compartment. Gorna, holding her little dog on her lap said, "It's not a dog! It's a monkey!" and grinned so charmingly, in her inimitable twinkling way, that he left in silence, open-mouthed.

Aunt Augusta's model for the duck board. June 28th 1973

Gorna

Gorna once arrived for lunch with us at the farm wearing white gloves that were still stitched together. She said it made up for her lack of shoes. Gorna hated wearing shoes and would go everywhere barefoot if at all possible.

1973 MONAGHAN

I shall not plant Namaqua daisies again next spring. They come up beautifully healthy and just as they are about to flower into carpets of yellow and orange and white, the hares tuck in. When I caught one red-handed, it loped off in a relaxed manner pretending it hadn't seen me. This happens every year, so I give up.

20 JUNE 1973

Prospero has mumps. I thought he was merely putting on weight for the last three days.

He and I made little brooms out of pine-needles wrapped around sticks, and we sold them to the ducks who parade past the bedroom.

Whenever I listen to the concertos or symphonies that we had on 78s as children, I still know exactly where the record ends and the next one plops down onto the turntable.

All the Beethovens we had were with Furtwangler conducting the Berlin Philharmonic – and Schnabel playing the piano concertos. Heifetz or Menuhin played most of the violin recordings.

Cortot, Casals, Thibaud, Milstein, Simon Goldberg, Lili Kraus, Edwin Fischer and so many more we had, and I still prefer most of these recordings to the modern perfectionists.

15 JULY 1973
Letter from Jim from Nairobi:

Sweetheart,

I got through immigration at Jan Smuts and dropped my boarding card. This I did not expect and as I stooped to collect it, the sound beloved of Captain Hook, shattered the silence of the building – my pants had again split. An inane smile passed across my face as I thought of all that had passed between us. (I had stitched his split pants several times)

Hoping my alabaster skin was not in evidence, keeping my legs together, I made my way across the bare hall endeavouring to fathom how extensive was the split without actually feeling for it, which would have given the game away.

Walking across a public hall without knowing if your balls are hanging out is not nice.

I shall soon be reduced to either wearing heavy armour or a kilt:

All love,

Captain Hook

In September and October 1973, I took Beezy and Jessica aged 11 and 12 to London and Oxford.

Beezy has been a highly original and fancy dresser since he was about six. He always wore a hat: a tam o'shanter, deerstalker, Nigerian hats that Jim had brought him, an opera hat that could concertina flat, Raymond Dart's top hat, a real sailor hat with HMS Something on it – can't remember – among countless others. He wore flared jeans and a denim jacket fairly permanently during this trip. James Fox bought him Beatles badges to sew onto the jacket, and a saucy denim hat.

We stayed at the Lansdowne Club which has squash courts and a big swimming pool, and is otherwise an old-fashioned stuffy club for landed gentry and dowagers spending the night in London on visits from their country houses. The children thought the club was hilarious and wondered how one could tell if some of the codgers reading the papers in the grand pink and gold sitting-room, were alive or not. They decided the way to tell was that if one nudged them from the side, they'd keel over if they were dead.

Jess and Beezy were well behaved while we were there, but one evening when we left them and went out to dinner, I phoned the club to ask them if all was well. The man at the reception desk put me through to our room to speak to them and there was no reply. I was worried and asked the receptionist to try the television room. He said, "Mrs Bailey, if your children were in this club, I would know it."

We rushed back. Jessica was there but no Beezy. I froze. Lost in London aged 11. Centre of London, early evening. Our children, brought up on a farm with no experience of traffic. Oh God!

Jess confessed they had been to Piccadilly and that Beezy was trying to get a job in a souvenir shop. Taking directions from Jess, Jim and I hastened towards Piccadilly and there was Beezy in his funky jacket and hat, very happy in a huge shop full of all the tourist junk dear to his heart. The owner told us Beezy was too young to be employed but he was a very bright lad and would be welcome when he was older.

Jess and I went to all Paul Tortelier's masterclasses televised by the BBC. Six hours a day for three days. Riveting.

Then I went to hear Arthur Grumiaux rehearsing the Bruch concerto in the Royal Festival Hall. As I was the only person in the auditorium, Grumiaux asked

me to test the balance, which meant that I had
to move to various parts of the auditorium to
see if the orchestra was balanced for the soloist.
He had no idea who I was and assumed I was
part of the larger orchestra, I suppose. I
absolutely loved it.

When I told Sir Colin Davis, who was conducting, that I believed the officials in the Royal
Festival Hall probably thought I cleaned the
lavatories there, he said I wouldn't be able to
do that at Covent Garden because *he* cleans
the lavatories there. He has been resident conductor at Covent Garden for quite some years.

Arthur Rubenstein aged 86, rehearsed
the Greig and Mozart K466 piano concerto with Andre Previn and the London
Symphony Orchestra. Jessica and I went to the Artist's Entrance of the RFH and
the man on duty was new and would not allow us into the rehearsal.

I told him Mr Previn had invited us personally. He said he would telephone Mr
Previn in his dressing-room and asked my name. I held Jessica's hand so tightly that
my nails dug into her palm, and prayed. There was no reply, he said, "Mr Previn is
already on the rostrum." Thanking God, in we went – swiftly.

The Greig was memorable, the Mozart not: for me Rubenstein is not a Mozart
player. After these major concertos, the 86-year-old sat and played Chopin waltzes
and Mazurkas for his own amusement. What a treat and how awful it would have
been to miss it! I am so glad I didn't take no for an answer. Like my darling Papa.
Thank you Papa.

We also saw the aged Leopold Stokowski rehearse his own versions of Bach organ music. So wonderful.

In July, back at Monaghan, Jess returned from an orchestral camp in Durban. She
had had gastro-enteritis there and passed out playing Bach during the competition
in which she was taking part. A month later she had encephalitis. Mercifully, Papa
was at home, and Jess moved in to the Main Branch which is what we all called
my parents' house, to be nursed by her doting grandparents. John Clarke, the art-

master at Woodmead, where Jess was schooled, had encephalitis too. Jess was then 13. Twelve years later she married John and they have lived happily ever after.

23 NOVEMBER 1974 MONAGHAN
Jess (just fourteen) played the Elgar cello concerto with the Johannesburg Symphony Orchestra. Neil Chapman conducted. Great triumph, Jim and I and Papa and Granny were all there – four curtain calls and standing ovation from the orchestra!

Jim has been away more than seven months of this year. Oh how I wish he could change his life to be here at home more often.

As Jim's *Drum* office was in London's Fleet Street, the Temple Church was three minutes walk away. Jim and I used to go to choir practices there on Friday afternoons. During their break, the choristers played football outside the vestry among the ancient tombs, making a terrible din yelling to each other. Barristers leaned out of their Middle Temple windows to tell them to shut up.

I am passionate about church music and it is the only kind of music that Jim found familiar. He grew up in a music-free family and went to school at Winchester where there were two services a day and three on Sundays. It put him off church for life, but I did lure him back to introduce him to the beauty of the great choirs in England.

He also loved playing games on the lawn with the choristers.

He was having a board meeting one Friday afternoon, and I took eight of the choirboys up into the *Drum* office to fetch him for football. His secretary said we were not to disturb him. I reckoned the meeting had gone on long enough, opened his door and led my small boys in where they performed a can-can while chanting, "We've come to take you to tea! Whoops!" The board members seemed to evaporate and Jim roared with laughter and obediently followed them out for tea and football.

Playing with children was his way of knowing it is never too late to have a happy childhood.

We have been managing and helping finance a school on the farm for close on

30 years and every weekend there were football games on our lawn with Jim looking like Gulliver among the Lilliputians. As Jim grew older, the children had to be younger – he hadn't the strength to play with 12-year-olds. So, in his 70s, the Grade 1's and 2's came to play with him. He loved it and so did they.

For the last decades of his life, Jim turned nine every birthday and we celebrated by inviting the 9-year-olds of St Mary's Waverley to come to the farm. Our friend Claire Rossouw was the principal of the school. When Claire left, Alison Hallett who followed in her place continued the visits. The Standard Ones came every year on the 23rd October and were wonderfully supportive, bringing toys and jumble for our little farm school. Each year Jim had sheaves of illustrated birthday and thank-you cards from all the girls, which he treasured.

Between 30 and 40 girls would arrive with a few teachers and the mothers who drove them. I have such tender memories of watching Jim being led along by a swarm of little girls, all competing to hold his hand to walk to the river and to cross the swinging foot-bridge, and on to our school where they played games, sang and shared picnics.

Then the tractor would be ready and they would all climb onto the trailer to be carted up to the house singing, the two schools swapping songs, the wondrous sound carrying across the valley.

Then came dancing and ball games on the lawn. The winners were rewarded by being allowed to throw Jim into the swimming pool. There were shrieks and squeals while they dived off his shoulders and bombed him until it was time to leave.

He only declined taking to the water for the first time when he was 78 and a sick man.

During the 1978 birthday party, our nine-year-old Prospero drove the Land Cruiser bearing tired teachers and one little girl with her leg in plaster. The Land Cruiser appeared to be driverless because Prospero was barely visible as he peered at the road ahead between the steering wheel and the dashboard. Most of the thank-you letters read that this was the highlight of their visit.

One of the games played was 'Brother, brother, are you there?' Two children lay facing each other blindfolded, armed with rolled-up magazines, their free arms linked. Jim never changed his mode of speech to accommodate the black children whose English was minimal. He would say, "Keep your weapon poised to enable you to strike your opponent. Guess his whereabouts when he answers to 'Brother,

brother, are you there?' Silence is essential to avoid the attacker knowing where to land his blow." Fortunately, he gave a demonstration.

Every year he would thank me over and over again, for the happiest of days.

Once I flew to London to join Jim and was seated on the plane next to a young man who was autographing for a seemingly endless queue of passengers. He and I had the four middle seats of the row to ourselves. When the queuers had finally re-seated themselves, I apologised for my ignorance, having no clue to his identity, and bashfully asked him why he was so famous.

He said, "I'm embarrassed to tell you that I play squash." It was Jonah Barrington, who had been the world squash champion for several years. He was now in his late 20s.

We had our meal together and chatted happily. He told me he was in love with someone a bit older, and wondered what to do about it. He was natural and easy company. I told him we stayed at the Lansdowne Club in London where there is a swimming pool and squash courts where Jim loves to exercise after a day in the office. Jonah told me he was taught squash at the Lansdowne Club by the great Egyptian player, Jahangir Kahn.

It then dawned on my wicked mind to play an irresistible prank on Jim. I was always trying to find squash partners for him in London, so I suggested to Jonah that he should play Jim, lose the first couple of games, and then . . .

He was perfectly willing to do this and we plotted, planned and went to sleep sharing the four seats, lying full length head to foot, Jonah's feet resting on the back of my head.

As I drifted off I thought of the appropriate handful of friends who would enjoy being spectators at this match. Sadly, it never took place. Jonah was not in the country when Jim was free, but Jim has squirmed with glee at my story ever since.

Jim was deeply sensitive to my feelings in some circumstances. We saw the film *Death in Venice* and I was so overcome with Mahler and the beauty and tragedy of it all that when we came out, I couldn't speak. We walked straight into a woman who hailed us very loudly and asked after the family and talked on and on. Jim took my head and sort of burrowed it face-first into the thick jumper he was wearing and led me away from her. He then kept silent and held his arm around me.

On the other hand, when I was lying next to him listening to the recording of the child Yehudi Menuhin playing the Elgar violin concerto with Elgar conducting, I was so moved by the music that I wept. It was in the early days of our marriage and Jim was irritated beyond speech. He stomped out of the room.

He was so jealous of my love for music. I wish now that I had had the strength to talk to him about his reaction. And mine.

Waffle-eating competitions were held during every holiday in Plettenberg Bay. Jim would round up his friends between the ages of six and 12 and take them down to Sasha's restaurant by the sea. I would order the waffles in advance to give the restaurateur proper warning, so that when the party was seated, the waffles would arrive all at once.

"On your marks, get set, GO!" – and a dozen or so competitors, hands strictly held behind their backs, would frantically munch their way through their waffles. Their faces were covered in cream or ice cream and maple syrup. Their shrieks were muted by their full mouths.

I tied Jim's tresses in a ponytail to keep them out of the food. He always took part, was always the only adult, and usually came last. The winner was rewarded with a second waffle.

These competitions went on for more than 20 years. Children unknown to us would sidle up to us on the beach asking if they could take part in the waffle-eating competition. Ex-competitors who were over-age came as spectators and referees. No hands! Older ones were promptly disqualified if they cheated.

Sasha's, alas, is no more. But I am still greeted on the beach by strangers, now in their 20s and even 30s, who tell me they took part in the waffle-eating competitions.

MARCH 1975 MONAGHAN
We gave a recital at the Lindbergs' soirée. Jess played Bach's 3rd unaccompanied cello suite – complete. Then she and I did Fauré's Elegy. Then a Beethoven Trio with Gerard Korsten on violin and Ilana Stein on piano. It all went well.

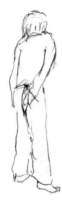

MAY 1975
Jim glorioso! He came into my bedroom and in a petulant little voice asked why no mending was done in the house. He demonstrated by showing me how his pyjama trousers were split from guggle to snitch at the back. I told him to take them off and turn them around. It was his fly. Jim nearly fell over laughing – and didn't change them around.

In June of that year Jim decided to test the worthiness of the gynaecologist who was to perform a hysterectomy on me by playing squash with him. He seemed satisfied.

He came to the nursing home to be with me while I lay waiting to be wheeled up to theatre. I was delightfully doped with the pre-medication. Jim stood at the foot of my bed reading *The Scholar Gypsy* of Matthew Arnold. The nurses put me on the trolley to take me to theatre and Jim followed, reading loudly in the corridor, in the lift, and was about to enter theatre with me. It is a long poem and they stopped the trolley for the last verse and then explained to Jim that he was not to follow me into theatre. I found it very touching.

It was mid-winter and we had been invited to the annual weekend shoot at Rooipoort with our old friends, Julian and Tessa. As this operation was fairly sudden, and as I couldn't join them, they sent a huge and magnificent vase of flowers to the nursing home. Darling Jim arrived bearing a grubby plastic cup in which he had put a baby lettuce that he had picked in our vegetable garden. Its limp leaves clung to the sides of the cup looking flat, dried out and forlorn. I wasn't sure if it was to be eaten or it was meant to be decorative. Either way I loved it and showed it to everyone.

June 1975

Since I've been lying on my bed at the farm recovering, Bimble cat has caught no less than six mice in my bedroom. He is now called Air-Vice Marshall Rentokil Streebs-Greebling – all those stripes on his arms prove his rank. His scent is a mixture of mouse blood, trodden grass and chamois leather, and I love him spending all day sleeping off his nocturnal murders on my bed.

25 September 1975

Prospero saw his first crimson-breasted shrike and said, "we must write it on a piece of paper because it is so important."

We have a 14-year-old French girl living with us for a month to learn to speak English. Prospero, aged six, has taught her to say "shit" and "bugger up mate!"

Christmas 1975

Jim, Robert and Papa – three very odd Kings of Orient were for our Nativity Play.

Our family had some kind of show every Christmas Eve. Jim or I wrote a play and various friends who were staying at the time took part. One year Andrew Tracey came in playing the bagpipes in his kilt, and then had all the children performing a song from 'Wait a Minim' about a mediaeval maiden locked in her chastity belt. Jess, who was about 10, sang the part of the maiden, Jonathan was her husband who had gone off to sea and taken the key to her chastity belt, Beezy was the locksmith. Andrew played the guitar and was the narrator.

In the first play the children did I can only remember that Jonathan was the 'man of the house' bringing in the Christmas goose for their dinner. The goose was real and there were feathers all over the living-room because Jessica who was about five couldn't take hold of it properly so there was a lot of squawking from the goose and from ladies in the audience who took fright. Jim caught hold of it and took it out.

Jess and Beezy were forever dressing up and doing their own acts with no prompting from me. I have wonderful tapes of Beezy interviewing himself on radio in various voices, and Jessica being a wicked mimic taking off people we knew.

70

They dressed Bundy in a white tutu when he was about three or four and taught him a bit of ballet.

I think the last play they did had Beezy, Bundy and Prospero performing Noel Coward's *Three Juvenile Delinquents*. They did enjoy dressing up for this. Jim was so proud of them all when they performed.

Eventually they grew older and refused to perform and found me a pain in the neck when I wanted them to do so. They had become teenagers and the plays came to an end.

Simon Preston, organist and choirmaster at Westminster Abbey, arrived to stay. White-bodied from the snows of England and never having been to South Africa, he lay in the sun, burnt his bottom bright red and subsequently ran a fever.

Roodewal Laerskool was a three-teacher Afrikaans school on the border of Mooiplaats. A charming red-roofed building with sash windows around a courtyard, with a bell in a pillared structure in the centre. There were 45 pupils, aged between six and 12. Jessica spent six months there when she was 11, before going to Woodmead. I asked Mr Goodchild, the headmaster, what colour shoes she should wear – brown or black. He answered: "No, Mrs Bailey, they don't wear shoes until about April." Jessica loved being there, and helped teach English. Bundy aged five spent his first year there and became fluent in Afrikaans. This stood him in good stead for the rest of his schooling, and he ended up writing Afrikaans A-levels at Eton, which he could do with ease. He was one of two pupils at Eton writing Afrikaans – they found a teacher in London.

In January 1976 we sent Prospero to Roodewal School for two days. Jim and I lay in tears on the bed both mornings, and that was the end of his schooling. I taught him at home for two years. He went to the 'Shhh School for Boy'. This is what I inscribed on his exercise books as it was illegal to keep a child out of school without going through the proper channels. Too boring to do that.

Roodewal School is no more. It was closed when the African National Congress came to power. The local Afrikaans community would have rather razed it to the ground than have black children there. I tried very hard to make it into a music and ballet school for all the locals of any colour. No go.

Once while I had Jonathan, Beezy and Bundy as weekly boarders at the Ridge,

71

the end of the long winter holiday drew nigh, and I packed all their trunks and drove them to the Ridge on a Tuesday afternoon. Term always started on Tuesday afternoon for boarders. I was a week late. The three Bailey boys had an extra week's holiday because I just had a feeling about when they should go, I hadn't looked at the school diary. The headmaster had thought we had gone abroad and didn't bother to telephone.

Bundy craved convention and chose to go to Bishop's, instead of Woodmead where the others went, after he left The Ridge. He loved being in Founder's House and was proud of doing well at his school work. The others didn't seem to take much notice of school.

My attitude to school certainly influenced them. Jess hardly went to school on Fridays because she had her cello lesson and trio on Friday afternoons and school was often too much. Steyn Krige, headmaster of Woodmead, was wonderfully understanding and supportive and I never had to lie to him. He said that Jessica's work was strong in most subjects and it wouldn't matter at all if she missed most Fridays.

Prospero grew tall very fast and it wore him out, so Mondays he often stayed home because he was exhausted.

MARCH 1976 MONAGHAN
Some chain-smoking, hard-drinking journalists came to lunch with Jim. I didn't want to see them so I climbed on the roof and stayed there for about three hours. The children brought me my lunch and some cushions and my current book. Jim didn't mind, so all was well.

Jim and I went to London in October 1976, and stayed with Thomas and Valerie Pakenham. Jim had toothache and when we breakfasted together, he asked Thomas the name of his dentist. At the time Thomas was writing his book on the Boer War and in his obsessive way, spoke of little else. While talking without cease, he dialled, and then spoke into the telephone.

"Oh, hello, is Dr Murphy there? Oh dear, I am so sorry. When did he die? Four and a half years ago – oh I'm so sorry. Has someone taken over his practice? Could you please spell that name? Z-y-n-z-a-k. Unusual name . . ."

He made an appointment for 11am that morning. He tried to pronounce the name again – "Zynzak."

Jim said, "I don't trust the relaxed end of the alphabet."

Val stormed in and said, "Thomas, why don't you go to your mother's dentist? Why do you go to a National Health dentist! You're a millionaire! Ring your mother and ask her the name of her dentist!"

There was not another word on the subject of toothache. Thomas went to the dentist. Jim went to his office in Fleet Street.

That evening when we were all re-assembled at dinner, Thomas said that the dentist had been perfectly charming and wanted to refill all his teeth.

26 MARCH 1976 MONAGHAN

Trout fly (silver doctor) embedded in the tip of my index finger – beyond the barb. Peter de la Harpe pushed it through and broke the barb off with pliers. I took a mouthful of Jim's jersey and held onto him tight – and was silent. It was the first time Peter showed respect for me. We liked each other from then on. What one has to endure to seal some friendships!

Years later, after telephoning me several times and threatening that he would inject himself with a fatal dose of pethidine in the arm, he committed suicide by blowing his brains out with a shot-gun. The poor man had had several operations on his spine, and was possibly depressive. His wife Tessa went into the bathroom and found his body.

11 MAY 1976 LONDON

Staying with Shirley van Velden in "the pink nest". What a friend! There's Prospero aged 6, myself, and for over a week of the time Jim - all staying in a tiny room with a single bed and a camp bed for Prospero. There's about a foot's width of space to stand.

The purpose of the trip was for Prospero to meet his godfathers, Alan Howe and Gilbert Smith.

Alan Howe was the gamekeeper at Bletchingdon in Oxfordshire where Jim grew

B and Alan Howe

up as a boy. Alan taught Jim to shoot and fish and was probably the main adult influence in his life, Jim being the child of absentee parents. His mother was flying across the world and his father was mostly in South Africa and about 60 when Jim was born. At the time of our visit, Alan was in his late 80s and was thrilled to meet his godson.

Gilbert Smith and his wife Daphne were wonderfully kind to us and had us to stay at Long Crendon.

Luckily for Shirley we were away quite a bit. But I cannot believe how she stood having all of us in her flat, in spite of Prospero going to school at Hill House during the day.

Bletchingdon Park Estate, where Jim grew up

MAY 1976 LONDON

Colin Davis rehearsed the London Symphony Orchestra in the Royal Festival Hall – Beethoven's *Eroica*. He is so excellent and so funny. I will try and make all my trips coincide with Colin Davis conducting in London.

Jim and I took Shirley with us to Petham near Canterbury. We had been invited by Major and Mrs Thompson to see where Jim had force-landed his Defiant in their hedge when he was shot down by a German Messerschmitt 109 in 1940. He had unwittingly flown under some high-tension cables when he landed. His gunner, who had jumped out of the turret of the crashed aircraft, pointed them out to him. Jim had been concentrating on steering the plane between the poles planted all over the fields to forestall German gliders, and had no idea about the high-tension cables.

The Thompsons were charming and took us to meet Charlie Mills, aged 93. He was the vicar of Petham who had helped Jim out of his wrecked plane and given him whisky. It was only the second time Jim had drunk whisky in his life. Charlie was a little man with braces and very few teeth. The Thompsons had kept a small piece of Jim's Defiant and of the ME109 that Jim had shot at and Charlie was very excited about meeting Jim.

When Jim had crashed into the hedge, the pilot of the ME109 had parachuted in the nick of time, his aircraft plunging into the earth three fields away. He was captured and locked up in a horsebox. Jim, in his book on his war experiences, pointed out the advantage of fighting over one's own country. Jim was treated as a hero. The German was to spend the rest of the war in a prison camp.

Before they took him off, Jim asked to meet and speak to the German pilot, who was pale and shaken and complaining of a sore back. So Jim organised a mattress for him to lie on. In Jim's school German, they discussed their respective aircrafts … The German said that, in general, he judged Spitfires to be better than Messerschmitts, Hurricanes not so good, and Defiants no bloody good at all.

Our visit to Petham happened because Major Thompson had read Jim's book, *The Sky Suspended,* which describes the Petham adventure in one of the chapters. They had found our address through the publishers.

16 June 1976
Students in Soweto demonstrated against having Afrikaans imposed as a medium of instruction at school. It was a peaceful protest until police started shooting at them and killed one, and wounded scores more. Jim says if this does not cause civil war here, it will be a miracle.

9 October 1976
Jess excelled herself at a masterclass with Pierre Fournier. He made her play every movement of Bach's 1st unaccompanied cello suite. All the other partakers in the

class were asked to play only one movement – and he didn't let some of them even finish that. Then Jess played Schubert's *Arpeggione* sonata. He has invited her to learn with him in Geneva!

December 1976 Plettenberg Bay

Bundy sang the 'Once in Royal' solo at midnight mass at the Plett. Catholic Church. Peter Behr and Bundy pretended to be confirmed Catholics and took Communion so that they could have a sip of wine.

Poseidon (Jim likes to be called that) speared a leervis and two Cape salmon off the Beacon Island rocks. His new habit – I have to wake him at 5am every morning. Sometimes he goes spearfishing, sometimes he goes back to sleep. I cannot fall asleep again. Not a good arrangement as far as I am concerned.

A happy New Year's bash at Nicky and Glennie Behr. Much dancing and boozing. Ian McAdam, who was knighted for his surgery, stitched Russell Steven's bottom which he had cut sitting on a glass. No local anaesthetic was used – or indeed was necessary – as both of them had drunk enough not to feel a thing. Ian laughed so much while he was stitching that in the sober light of New Year's Day, Glennie, a practical GP, had to restitch the wound.

I swam right around the wreck, a ship that was wrecked off Robberg beach about 40 years ago. Philip Johnson who swam with me, poked his speargun into the palm of my hand. It bled and was quite deep. Old Ena Behr treated it with cotton wool soaked in Friar's Balsam. It stung like hell and she said I was allowed to scream for exactly half a minute and then it would be fine. It worked a treat.

Poseidon and I were saying how sad it was that we hadn't seen a Knysna loerie this holiday when a few seconds later one flew across the road, apple-green flashing its scarlet under-wing.

Jess arrived on New Year's Eve having toured Israel with the orchestra. Betty Pack said she was moved to tears when she watched Jessica planting a tree near Jerusalem. Jessica said she had been asleep on the floor of the bus when the members of the orchestra were tree planting!

They played 22 concerts in 20 days and Jess was almost permanently exhausted. She also got lice in her hair from the house in which she was billeted in Tel Aviv. To make up for it all, she heard Rostropovich play Dvorak's cello concerto. After the concert he received all his fans with Jess tucked under his arm.

She begins matric this year, just turned 16.

FEBRUARY 1977

Superb weekend trout fishing with Jonathan and Lois at Dullstroom. I caught four trout over one-and-a-half pounds.

Lovely warm rain and Squeezie[20] and I spent Sunday morning together in the happiest way possible. We fished the new water from the weir – Tom's stretch – and onward until the pool below the cottage. The tumbleweed was in full bloom, pale classical pink and crimson Watsonia along the water's edge.

Squeezie and I are a formidable team: his skill and experience with a fly, my agility for climbing down banks or along overhanging branches to net his catch makes a great partnership. Prospero came too. Unfortunately he has recently learnt to whistle which he seems to do most of his waking hours. It is a breathy slobbery tuneless whistle, and when we heard it getting close, whilst we were fishing intently, our hearts sank somewhat.

The apple tree outside the cottage was heavy laden and we picked them wet with rain and very crunchy.

8 FEBRUARY 1977

Prospero had a tonsillectomy today and reacted badly to the anaesthetic. He and I spent the night at the Katzenellenbogens so that he would be near a doctor if

20 Jim

needs be. When I woke in the morning Prospero's bed was empty, so I went to Jessica and Josie's bedroom and knocked on the door. I was invited in and there was our Peanut snuggled down in between them in their bed. Dear kind Jessica and Josie.

MARCH 1977 MONAGHAN

During the last month I have killed three Egyptian cobras. In the courtyard outside my bedroom Bimble was having his siesta near the font. When he woke he walked over to the Brunsfelsia where he became fascinated by a 5ft cobra. I grabbed the said striped animal by his tail and whisked him into the bedroom. Then I shot the snake with the pellet gun.

The next one was eating the dog's food outside the kitchen. I shot it.

The most dramatic was a 4ft cobra that slid behind the bookshelf in the bathroom while I was on the loo. My parents were visiting, Papa having recently had a coronary. Mother, a Londoner through and through, is convinced I live with snakes hanging from the trees like bunting and is petrified.

Dealing with the dog-food thief

I was therefore worried about both my parents' reactions. Papa had seen the cobra from the bedroom and was quite gleeful about dealing with it, and together we wondered how to approach it.

I phoned Jim at the office for advice on how to get it to come out from behind the bookshelf without endangering ourselves. He was in the middle of a meeting and had his office 'be-brief' voice on and told us to pour boiling water onto it – which we did. Papa did the pouring while I waited with loaded pellet gun at the ready.

The boiling water certainly made it move. I shot as soon as I saw its head. We both wore diving goggles. Cobras spit accurately into your eyes at a distance of four feet and then it spreads. Papa clobbered it with a polo stick.

Eventually we went in to lunch and I asked Piet our farm manager, to get the corpse out from behind the bookshelf. I'd had enough.

The corpse hissed horribly. Cobras put on an act whereby they lie belly-up as if dead, then when you are most vulnerable, they twist round and strike. Piet killed it good and proper.

There is a polo stick in every room in our house for dealing with snakes. It allows one to keep one's distance. Jim played polo for an English team touring Nigeria; Papa played polo for the Eastern Transvaal. So we have a sufficient supply of polo sticks.

26TH APRIL 1977
Trip to London with Jessica and Alaric. Betty Pack gave Jess her last lesson and sent her off to audition with Joan Dickson at the Royal College of Music, which she did successfully. Fournier wrote and confirmed his offer of lessons at his home in Geneva for three months before she starts at College.

Jess had a lesson with Jackie du Pré. It was so upsetting seeing Jackie so ill and deformed by MS. Jess found it too much to bear. When I sat at Daniel Barenboim's piano in their flat, I felt as though it might do a Sparky's Magic Piano act for me. Would that it did!

Yehudi Menuhin invited Jess to come and play to him at his house in Highgate. Yehudi had known my father well ever since he played the lead violin in the Guy's Hospital orchestra. She asked what she should play. He asked her to play a Bach slow movement. He listened with his eyes closed in a trance-like state and then said, "You are very, very musical, which is not surprising coming from a family like yours." Purr purr. It was about 11 am and Yehudi was in slippers. His heavy-duty British nanny came and told him to come and dress himself to go to Norfolk. He is not of this world and has to have a team of efficient nannies and drivers to see him through the day.

Heard Hephzibah Menuhin rehearsing Bartok with Yehudi conducting. Superlative pianist. I chatted with Yehudi who loves Hephzibah so much and is so proud of her with good reason. He then played Bach's E major concerto. After the first movement he asked Diana, his wife, who was sitting half way up the stalls, what she thought of it. She shouted back, "It was awful, darling." He then calmly repeated it and continued the rehearsal.

We heard Pincus Zuckerman play Mozart – a unique experience. This, and hearing Christ Church Cathedral choir singing *Beati Quorum Via* of Stanford, under Simon Preston, organist and choir master of Christ Church, have been the great musical highlights of this trip for me.

Saw our beloved Gaffer Blackwell. He told us that Appleton church rang muffled bells for three hours when his wife Christine died.

Jim ordered countless books from Blackwell's in Oxford. He had met Gaffer, the owner, while he was up at Oxford, when Gaffer was very helpful and good to him.
During my life with Jim I wrote many many letters ordering his books from Blackwell's, addressing them directly to Gaffer, not realising that they would be handed on to the various departments in Blackwells. I addressed him as my beloved Gaffer, etc. etc. Here are copies of some of his answers.

"Oh Priceless Pearl,
I write in dismay to tell you something unique in my experience happened with regard to your cable.
The German publisher has instructions to send the Eusebius by air at our expense. It is the least we can do in view of this extraordinary happening. May it reach Lord Jim soon and safely.
Yours for ever and ever,
Gaffer."

"My dear Rapturous One,
I salute you happily, for I have found ... two copies of Josephson's EDISON,
now out of print. These were picked up in the second-hand market, and they
come to you with all my best wishes, only equalled by my best wishes to Jim.
So hurrah on all sides!"

"Oh Glowing Light of Dawn!
I have been radiated by your letter.
We have sent off at once the Gilgamesh Epic. Etc., etc ..."

"Oh Fairest, outweighing many lakhs of rubies!
Thank you for your gracious note and fragrant enclosure ...
I still hope that one Sunday morning I shall learn that you and Jim and one
or two of the delightful children are coming down the drive."

"Oh Scrumptiousest ... Is there any hope of a visit this year? Christine and
I, who share a birthday, are about to score between us 172 years, being of the
same age, and even ancient monuments are apt to collapse ..."

THE GAFFER ... "The world's greatest bookseller, and a great citizen of Oxford."

Sir Gaffer Blackwell, as he appeared in the London Times

On one particular visit to Oxford I went in to Blackwell's and on the offchance of his being there, I asked the person at the reception desk if Sir Gaffer was in. He asked my name, used the telephone, smiled, and said go straight up to his office on the first floor.

I knocked on his door, and hearing his voice, entered. There were about five men in the office. They were all seated and were obviously deeply involved in a meeting. Gaffer stood up – he was very tall and thin – and held his arms out for me. I went towards him and he enfolded me. Nothing was said. The men slowly disappeared out of the door, and when they had all left the room and closed the door, Gaffer said, "That's better."

MAY 1977

Lovely weekend at Firle, Sussex, with Dinah and Christopher Bridge. Heavenly, sunlit English countryside. James Fox, Dinah's son, and Jessica having a high old time. We all walked over the fields to Charleston where the painter Duncan Grant still lives. Quite a few of the Bloomsbury paintings are there but not great ones, I felt. The house was dark and Duncan Grant ancient. I wish I had read what I have now, about the Bloomsbury Group – before I went to Charleston. It was a waste.

I rode a very wobbly bicycle on Newhaven pier.

SEPTEMBER 1977 MONAGHAN

In a restaurant a man greeted Jim, and Jim asked me who it was. "Our dentist," said I. So Jim rose and went over to the dentist and cordially chatted with him. A few weeks later we were in a restaurant and this time Jim went straight up without hesitation and greeted the dentist in a friendly fashion. It wasn't our dentist.

26 SEPTEMBER 1977

Having kept bees for years and been stung regularly, I have suddenly became allergic. From one sting I had acute bronchial spasm. My eyes disappeared, so swollen was my face. Huge weals of urticaria covered my scalp and entire body. I was faint and nauseous. Jim lay on the bed next to me after I had had adrenalin, cortisone and antihistamine. My breathing was like a leaky bellows pumping mud, and he said, "Would you like a chocolate log?"

The next time I was stung, when I lay gasping and swollen after treatment, Jim asked if I would like him to read to me. I nodded. He read from the book that was next to his bed, *The Gospel According to St John,* in Ancient Greek.

SEPTEMBER 1977

On our way to a bird-watching weekend on the Natal coast, Tessa O-T and I are staying the night at the Ghost Mountain Inn. During dinner last night a tight-lipped young woman let out a blood-curdling shriek which silenced the dining-room.

A cat had rubbed against her legs. The cat was taken out by a waiter, the door shut, and chatting and eating resumed.

At the end of the meal the woman walked out past our table, and inconsiderately and unthinkingly, I miaowed, *pianissimo*. She spun round on her heel and said: "What did you say?"

"I said: 'Meeow.'"

Eyes beady, lips even thinner, she spat: "Well, it's in very bad taste."

It certainly was and I regret having meowed, however quietly.

Tessa O-T

1 OCTOBER 1977 MONAGHAN
A young man came to be interviewed by Jim for the job of farm manager. He was slightly late and apologised profusely explaining, "Sorry we're late but my brother has just been munched by a hippo."

11 OCTOBER 1977
Jess played her matric music exam and I accompanied her. It is a 45-minute exam and she was last candidate of the day. When the examiners had heard her play her first piece, they settled down to enjoy themselves and asked us to play the whole Brahms E minor sonata, instead of only the required first movement. Their remarks on her report were encouraging indeed.

During the holidays, the boys spent a lot of their time on the roof to avoid being tasked by Jim. He couldn't abide seeing them lying by the pool or relaxing in any way. He would immediately think up some task of Herculean proportion. For instance, "Could you please water all the citrus." Or their most unfavourite, "Would you please go and take the stones out of the van Otten land." The van Otten land is about 30 hectares square and full of stones even after 40 years of continually removing them – and evermore shall be so.

He was always polite, and usually unreasonable. I used to hide if I wanted to read or just swan around. I would often climb onto the roof. Long years later our beloved friend Nicky Stubbs gave me a t-shirt with a picture of Jesus on it, with the caption 'JESUS IS COMING, look busy'. I still have it.

One day, Jim was lying in the bath demanding something unreasonable of the children while Jess and I were in the bathroom. Jessica went up to him and said, "Jim, don't you start your rot!" and walked out of the room. Jim immediately melted, and said, laughing, that Jess reminded him of his mother. Jess was never frightened of Jim and he had great respect for her. As soon as he knew that anyone was nervous of him, he was autocratic.

Prospero

In April 1978, age nine, Prospero won the Victor Ludorum at The Ridge prep school (he won it every subsequent year also, until he turned 13 and went on to Woodmead). He won the 75 metres, the 150 metres, broke the 100-metre record and the long-jump record. As he was the fourth and last son we would have at The Ridge, I was asked to give away the prizes. So I presented him with the Rhodes cup, the Victor Ludorum cup, and kept congratulating my constantly victorious grinning child. What was more, we won the mothers-and-sons race, and I was embarrassed to have to present myself with a box of chocolates.

He brought a Ridge friend home for the weekend. We fished, we climbed on the roof, we rode, and at the end of the weekend, the little guest said, "Gee, Bailey, I wish *my* mum was a boy!"

1 JULY 1978

Jess was asked to play in Pierre Fournier's masterclass at the Grahamstown Festival. When she came onto the stage to play, so did the TV lights and the microphones. She was the star.

84

Shoot on the farm. The guns were Jim, Peter Moses, Christopher O-T, Reiny Cassirer, John Lippiat, Tony Lea, and Alexander Caccia. Piet, our farm manager, asked if he could bring a friend who was a gunsmith and could service Jim's guns very well. At first Jim refused, because he never has strangers wielding a gun at our shoots, but after Piet had asked again and again, he relented.

At 10.30 am Jim came walking towards the house bleeding profusely from his face and neck. I was horribly alarmed because I couldn't see where the injuries were until I had cleaned him up a bit. Alexander Caccia had actually seen the gunsmith turn round and aim straight at Jim while they were walking after guinea-fowl. The gunsmith and his very unpleasant dog left before we had realised it.

All we could find out was that his name was Ian. He disappeared. Piet said he didn't know how to contact him and didn't know his surname. He was never to be seen again.

I went with Jim to have a pellet taken out from between his eyes, and one out of his ear lobe. It took ages for the doctor to find the pellets, which he did under an x-ray screen so we could watch the instruments getting nearer to the pellets. I sat on the floor next to the operating bed and held Jim's hand. These two places – the same ear and between the eyes – were where Jim was wounded when he was shot down during the war. Extraordinary coincidence.

Being the proprietor of *Drum* is more dangerous than we know. I know our telephone is tapped and that I have to lie about our residential address when I am anywhere but South Africa. But I didn't know they want Jim out of the way. Our right-wing neighbour told me recently that the Special Branch used to come regularly to ask him if 'Bailey' was home.

6 AUGUST 1978 MONAGHAN
Squeeze is in London. The BBC asked him to talk on the Ancient Atlantic Route and Thor Heyerdahl on the Pacific. Just Squeezie and Thor! He is so chuffed.

Prospero was using Jessica's hula-hoop. She said he could have it for keeps if he let her spit on his face. He readily agreed on the deal. Our wunderkind cellist, aged 17. Prospero is nine.

28 AUGUST 1978

Planted aubergine, onions, courgettes, carrots, red peppers, squash and pumpkin.

We have breeding stock of approximately 150 pairs of guinea-fowl on each farm, as well as francolin, and a few pairs of swempie and redwing partridge. There are 19 warthog on Mooiplaats.[21]

Only Wally survives out of my six ostriches. He panicked during a shoot and caught his leg in the fence from which he allowed himself to be extricated with as much resignation and stoicism as an aged Labrador.

14 SEPTEMBER 1978 LONDON

Went to London leaving Squeezie with a bad cold. The orange blossom and syringa were in full bloom and for all these reasons it was very difficult to leave.

Winchester Cathedral for Evensong – William Rufus lies buried there. Choir superb. Then Salisbury Cathedral where Sir David Willcocks happened to be rehearsing the London Bach Choir singing Bach motets, followed by Evensong with the Salisbury choristers dressed in emerald green. Not a great choir, Salisbury Cathedral.

Sir Georg Solti with the Chicago Symphony Orchestra did Brahms *3* and Mahler 1. Ooooh! Wondrous! Also a rehearsal of the Philharmonia with Ricardo Muti conducting in the Royal Festival Hall. When the soloist came on, everyone was asked to leave the auditorium. There were only about four people there, myself being one of them. The reason was that the piano soloist was Emil Gilels, who is Russian. The powers that be were particularly careful to ensure that Russian musicians

---

21 a farm which Jim bought near Monaghan

were guarded when they toured Europe. Rudolf Nureyev's leap to his freedom to the Western world set it off. At Orly airport in Paris, Nureyev leapt over a crowd of people by climbing on the counter of the customs desk and literally doing what only Nureyev could do. A superhuman leap! Once he was out, he was free and Russia had lost him. My father was there, at Orly at the time, and witnessed this historic happening.

Back to the Festival Hall, when asked to leave the auditorium, I left the stalls and crept into a box and lay prone until the lights were lowered and Gilels started playing the Schumann Piano Concerto. I wept. What a musician!

At Christ Church, Oxford they sung a Palestrina Mass, and it was ravishing. Simon Preston conducted. I wish the organ had finished being repaired, such a cathedral with a piano is very unsatisfactory – like eating caviar off a paper plate.

Jess and I heard Tortelier play Schumann at a rehearsal. He is so vain! He throws his profile at the audience and shows off very well. His profile is lovely so it 's fair enough.

Picking vegetables with Robert and Jo Loder in Wiltshire, walking through the fields near their house, we heard an old man say: "It's no good gettin' old wivout gettin' artful."

At Brinsop with the Tom Baileys, Jim and I slept in one narrow single bed and hearing moorhens instead of traffic, enjoyed it so much we didn't rise till 10 am. The gamekeeper at Brinsop, Evan Rogers, is 82 and whispered to us all about the partridge and pheasant. Jim shot three pheasant and it rained. I hid in a ditch and familiarised myself with the grass and stalks and flowers round me, all dripping wet. It was the happiest moment of my trip, knowing Jim was squatting nearby with a 12-bore. Then about 50 duck took off from the pond. We walked back sopping wet, picking blackberries.

On the train from Hereford to London we sat opposite an oldish man with no hair whatsoever on his face, arms or legs. He wore black shiny leather shorts and he was reading a book entitled, *Shropshire Witchcraft, Folklore and Ghosts*. I ached for any of my children to be there to share this with me.

Jess is getting on well learning with Joan Dickson and hopefully the Royal College will do her well. Leaving her in London was very painful. She is staying with the Pakenhams, which isn't too far from College.

5 FEBRUARY 1979 JOHANNESBURG
Had an operation to remove my gall bladder. Horrible, with tubes up my nose, drips in my arm and so very ill.

Exactly four weeks later: back on the operating table being opened up to remove pus. Yuck!

Jim away for a month and I am spending that time with my parents who are nursing me devotedly.

22 FEBRUARY 1979
From a letter from me to Jim:

> " . . . Kenneth Clarke writes of Lady Colefax's handwriting: 'she wrote frequently to the London Library for books, and Mr Cox, that unforgettable character who for 50 years sat at the issuing desk, used to keep her letters stuck with drawing pins to the shelf behind him, and glanced back at them from time to time hoping that light would dawn'. Does this remind you of someone?

> My Love of Loves, I broke a wishbone and wished that I could be your leatherbound 1654 copy of the Essays of Francis Bacon, in your hands, to receive your love of books and those words you love so."

16 March 1979: Fishing with Peter and Joan Moses near Dullstroom

Beezy, Prospero, Jim and I saw a moon rainbow – my first. So romantic. Then spring hares like kangaroos. Beezy calls them cabbage-mice. We stayed in a log cabin. It was happy and relaxed and Jim was completely content.

There was a fearsome storm when were out rowing on the lake. I was rowing, Jim fishing, the waves choppy, a howling gale, and we were swept into the far side of the lake. I shivered myself blue and Jim fetched the car, and the sun came out.

These fishing weekends make our life so good and I feel closer to Jim than at any other time.

24 March 1979 Monaghan

Pilly[22] came home from the Royal College having lost 20 lbs. She undressed and I got a terrible shock to see how thin she was. I had no idea how much she hated being in England and away from home. She must put down her cello and have a gentle time here. I want a daughter, not a cellist. Poor poor Pill to have been so unhappy and I truly didn't know.

She wants to do bookbinding with Papa. I am so very worried and sad about her. There has been too much pressure on her being such a gifted cellist. Oh dear, oh dear, and I am partly responsible.

April 1979

At Sports Day, Prospero broke the 150-metre record. He broke the long-jump record. He tied with his own 100-metre record from the previous year and won the under-10 Championship cup. Jim has come last in every short-distance race he has run in his life.

He enters the father's race at The Ridge readily every year and always comes last by quite far. This time, however, one of the fathers fell over and hurt his ankle and Jim stopped to thank him. It was the first time Jim had come second last. He was very chuffed. Great guffaws.

---

22 Jessica

26 May 1979

I had the happiest birthday of my 41 years. In the morning I caught three trout, Beezy drove me to Mooiplaats and back to do so. In the afternoon I shot three pigeons with six cartridges. The day was cloudless and beautiful and then in the evening we held a sudden birthday dance. Alexander and Arabella Caccia, Sarah Brown, Dot, Anthony and all of us Baileys danced to the Beatles. Jessica arrived late with Faucet (Dr Robert Millar) who had taken her to the races. Prospero and Sarah Brown are both  just 10 years old and they danced so sweetly it was unforgettable. Prospero in a top hat. Sarah, pretty Victorian Sarah, in a straw boater with cherries on it. Sarah is the granddaughter of Dulcie Howes, the great doyenne of ballet in this country. Genes will out.

December 1979 Plettenberg Bay

Bundy is getting pretty hot-stuff on water-skis. Took Diana Murray to Plett. with us and she is a delight - she and I laugh so much we can't stand up. Louis did some under-water photography.

Wondrous spearfishing below the castle with Murray Crawford. Jim came nose to nose with a 9-foot shark but it went away quickly enough. I would have had a heart attack if I met a shark.

Friend Henjo was playing patience, and when I asked him if he ever cheated, he said in his heavy Polish accent, "No, I never cheat, but sometimes I push it a bit."

On the way home in Port Elizabeth, I played duets with Virginia Fortesque – Faure, Ravel, Schubert. I enjoyed it enormously. She is very good company.

17 April 1980

Jess had an exhibition of painted ostrich eggs at Linda Goodman's gallery and sold them all.

6 JUNE 1980 MONAGHAN

The bank manager of the Trust Bank, with seeming total irresponsibility, is offering to lend us a huge sum of money – indeed is enthusiastic to do so. He came out after lunch at short notice with a set of beautiful bird prints to present to me, but ill-advisedly went down to the river with his son with a .22 rifle. There he encountered Beezy and Peter Johnson. PJ told him he was a Nature Conservation Officer and as the bank manager had no licence for his .22 – and anyway a .22 is an illegal weapon – PJ would arrest him for trespassing, among other things.

Peter Johnson and Jim discussing tactics

A frail peace was subsequently made between the two – but the bank-manager was mightily impressed.

21 JUNE 1980

Jim and Beezy invited by Julian O-T to shoot at Welgelegen, next to Sasol's artificial rubber factory. After the Sasol sabotage, the company had quickly run up a guard platform. The youngster on duty on the platform, seeing a posse of men advancing towards him armed with double-barrelled shotguns, Weimeranians, Labradors, and Wisselers, radioed his HQ that an attack was imminent. At once a platoon of soldiers armed with automatic rifles advanced on Julian's hunting party.

Julian put down his gun, took off his camouflaged top and advanced to meet them, figuratively waving a white flag. A parley was held and eventually two very nice lieutenants admitted that the owner of the farm might be permitted to shoot his own guinea-fowl. So the shoot was resumed.

9–30 JULY 1980: A VERY EVENTFUL TRIP TO ENGLAND

George Thalban-Ball, organist and choirmaster of the Temple Church in London, seems to put black boot polish on his head to keep his very thin hair black, but his scalp is also polished entirely black. He is 83 and still going strong. George is one of the great figures of church music of the century, both as organist, choirmaster and composer.

One Friday, when Jim and I arrived outside the vestry we saw a little boy in the rubbish bin. He was crying. We fished him out and asked what was wrong. He said the other boys had called him a Nazi spy – his surname is German. 1980 it is now and he was victimised, as in the *Lord of the Flies*. We took him back to the Lansdowne Club for a swim and an early supper to cheer him up. We telephoned his father, who had a heavy German accent, and we explained what had happened. He wasn't too surprised.

Ernest Lough, the famous boy soprano that was, is now about 60 and still sings in the Temple choir. I think he said he has sung there for 50 years. He and a tenor and I sung *Rejoice in the Lord Always* and *I will lift up mine eyes* by Walford Davies. It was a great treat for me. Walford Davies was the organist and choirmaster of the Temple Church before Thalban-Ball. Between the two of them they covered almost a century.

At the 40th anniversary of the Battle of Britain the airmen who had served during the B of B were invited to the Guildhall for a grand banquet. All the fighter pilots were lined up to meet the Queen Mother. When she shook hands with Jim she only came up to his waist so tiny was she and she said, "I remember your mother and father well, and how good of you to fly all the way from South Africa to be

Grootfontein

with us tonight". How on earth she could know who was who and remember what to say? Very impressive.

Soon after the war, the king and queen spent the night at Grootfontein, the stud farm near Colesberg, when they toured South Africa. Sir Abe and Lady Bailey had a room built on specially to accommodate the Royal Family. On the roof of this room was a water tank, which fell through into the room the day before the Royal visit. So after all that trouble, they spent their night in a spare bedroom.

At the Battle of Britain banquet I stood immediately behind Jim when the Queen Mum did her round. I was about 20 years younger than almost everyone. Jim borrowed his brother-in-law's dress suit, and wore it with a checked shirt. He enjoyed introducing me to his friends, and was very moved to meet them again, but there were too many that had been killed during the war for it to be an entirely pleasant reunion.

He wrote a beautiful piece about it for the London *Sunday Times*. I had thought of all these men, whose names I had known since my teens, as glamorous young fighter pilots who flew with Jim when they were all in their early twenties. Of course they were now grey or bald old codgers and it all seemed unreal.

30 AUGUST 1980 MONAGHAN
My camellia is flowering! I have planted all my summer vegetables. There is blossom on the peaches, pears, apricots and plums, and the buddleia is in full blow. The spring is exciting and precious because it is so short a season, and the birds have gone mad.

cabbage-whites and lucerne
butterflies amongst the primulas
1980

SEPTEMBER 1980
Hundreds of primulas have seeded themselves in the mossy brick verandah again. They are the colour of a bishop's vest. The butterflies love them, cabbage-whites, yellow lucerne butterflies with a hint of lime at the edge of their wings, and tiny lavender-coloured ones. The warmth of the sun is still welcome, before the relentless heat of summer. I am sitting on the lawn eating my lunch, enjoying it all.

The white butterfly migration is on and has been for days. They fly more or less from west to east – I don't know why or whither, but I know they fly on and on until they die. Curious, beautiful and a bit tragic. "If we ask ourselves the reason for our never-ceasing motion, we reply without compunction that we haven't any notion."

19 SEPTEMBER 1980
Gilbert Smith, Prospero and I went to Londolozi. I went off on foot, as is my wont in search of unusual birds, and was escorted by a game ranger who seemed bored. I

came to a dry river-bed with thick bush on both sides and saw a red-helmet shrike. It was a first so I focussed carefully and then realised there was a leopard standing looking at me, about eight feet away. I was paralysed. The leopard was a fully-grown male, dark, exquisite, staring and stock-still.

The ranger was directly behind me and had his gun held behind his head with both hands. He didn't move. After a very very long time – like about three minutes – the leopard turned and sloped off down the river-bed. My heart was beating so fast I could hardly breathe.

I asked the ranger if that had happened to him before. He said no. I said was it not the most extraordinary experience? He said yah. I later learnt that he had been studying mice on Marion Island for the last 18 months. Maybe this made him lose his ability to respond to thrills.

When the leopard had gone, we went to see the spot where it had been. There was a flattened circle of grass where it had been sleeping. I lowered my cheek down onto the place. It was still warm. What a privilege. It had been like having seen a god.

Back at camp I was told how lucky I was. Trapped between the bush both sides of the riverbed, the leopard had two options. One was to leap onto me from a stand-still, front claws to scalp me, back claws to eviscerate me. The other was to do an about-turn.

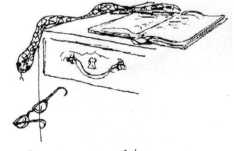

30 September 1980 Monaghan
A memorable day
The Earth Mother visited Jim's desk in the library in the form of a 5ft boom-slang that knocked his reading glasses off the desk. Luckily Jim witnessed it otherwise he would have blamed Bimble. By the time he had fetched a polo stick the Earth Mother had disappeared.

boomslang witnessed by
Jim knocking his glasses off
the desk. September 30th 1980.

A few hours later while I was sitting under the pines behind my bedroom with Bundy and Meggy, my friend and neighbour, a small plane flew so low over the house that I told Bundy to phone Lanseria Airport and complain. He did so, only to be told that the plane had crash-landed into our ploughed field just beyond the house.

I drove there immediately, shaking with nerves and dreading what I might find. Come on Barbara, you're a doctor's daughter! Be not afraid, you must do all you can to help.

The plane was upside-down and squashed. Four unscathed men were walking around it. One was a black man who had been taken up for the first time. He said he has decided that flying is literally for the birds.

12 OCTOBER 1980
It had rained and Angela Lloyd and I had a perfect day fishing. It rained, it blew, it shone, the water was rough, it was smooth, we fished from the boat, we smelt buddleia, and everything sparkled. Memorable.

1 NOVEMBER 1980
As I was opening Jessica's bathroom cupboard for some hand cream, a night adder dropped out onto the tiles. I fetched Squeezie to kill it. He was naked, ready to climb into his bath and said, "No, not just now I think". So I said, "It gives me the heebs. You're here. You come and kill it. It's in Jess's room". He said, "I'm not dressed for it". Then he put on his woollen hat, his new red sweater and nothing else at all, grabbed a polo stick and walked over to the children's bathroom and killed it.

Our mornings are happified by Napkin, Prospero's tiny white rabbit who enters as soon as we open the bedroom door. Napkin takes his eating very seriously and Jim says if he develops a good sense of taste he could get a job as a cook at Maxim's in Paris. Bimble and he get on fine, but Bimble wishes he'd play more imaginatively.

1 DECEMBER 1980

Told Squeezie that I saw Bea Smithers who is now married to Birch Bernstein. So he said, "Oh yes, I nearly greeted Birch Bernstein the other day; but I couldn't remember his name – and it wasn't him."

12 JANUARY 1981

Beezy went off to the Air Force. Bundy and I both wept to see him go. The three months basic training sounds truly hideous. Beezy is admirable, giving superb imitations of the various types at Valhalla. He is in a soggy tent with some extraordinary company. He is actually managing to like it and is enjoying reading Colette as an antidote. When we visit him, he is greedily hungry for Bach. He sits in the car and listens for the duration of our stay.

Beezy was originally posted to the Infantry in Middelburg. I wrote and told the powers that be that his grandmother, Lady Mary Bailey, was a world-famous aviatrix, his father a Battle of Britain fighter pilot in the RAF and that as a matter of course, Beezy must serve in the Air Force. That was immediately agreed upon.

As a next step I asked for him to be based at Lanseria where there is an Air Force base, just five minutes away from the farm. The reason I gave is that I lived alone most of the time because my husband's work took him away. And living alone on the farm was not desirable. That was agreed.

Next I said that Beezy was an artist and would be useful working in the Air Force Museum and organising exhibitions and air shows. That was also agreed.

So we bought him a little put-put and he went off at 5 to 8 in the mornings, came home most days for lunch and arrived back just after 5 pm, bored stiff but happy, having plenty of time to read books on the history of art.

1 FEBRUARY 1981

Jess had a phone call from someone called Bruce Attwood who went to her exhibition at Linda Goodman Gallery. He said Jessica had obviously never seen a hot air balloon because her paintings of them were inaccurate. He asked if she would like to see one. He said he would come to the farm and fetch her at 4.45. Naturally we assumed it would be in the afternoon. However, he arrived before the sun was thinking of rising.

Bruce and Jess took off from our front garden at dawn in a rainbow-coloured balloon. I stood in my pyjamas and waved to her as the basket quietly wafted over the chicken house, over the trees, over the road and away. So romantic and beautiful it was. They came back at about 11 am and we all breakfasted in the garden.

23 FEBRUARY 1981
Letter from Gaffer Blackwell, aged 92:

> "Superlative Barbara
> I offer 100 000 thanks for the Valentine, which, like the heroine in the melodrama, I am sewing into my stays."

Jim came home from a short absence in a new car. He had parked at Jan Smuts Airport for three days. Prospero, Alaric and I were in the drive when he arrived and Alaric congratulated him on the new car. Jim said it was nothing of the sort.

It was indeed a white Toyota, like his, but that is where the similarity ended. His had four gears, this one had five. His was red inside, this one was blue. His had done about 80 000 km, this one had done 400 km.

I said he must phone the airport and report it. Jim said no, it is a splendid car and it will do fine. He would like a bath and there was no hurry.

I dial the airport police and pass him the phone. Jim says, "Um, I want to report a car. My children tell me it is not mine."

The police ask whose it was. "Don't know," says Jim.

Police ask the registration. "Don't know – hold on," and he asks Alaric.

Jim then explains that his key fitted this car and he drove home . . .

Police ask the registration of his own car. "Dunno. Hold on," says Jim and asks Alaric.

Police ask his telephone number. "Hold on a minute." Asks Alaric.

Police suggest that as it is late, Jim should return the car to the airport next morning. He was told to inform the police where he parked it and find his own car.

Next day Jim drove off to swap cars at Jan Smuts. I telephoned him in the afternoon to ask if all had gone well. He said he had a job of work to do and he hadn't had time to go to the airport.

He did take it back on the way home.

Bundy was a very reliable little boy. One evening Jim arrived home late. A friend had driven him from town all the way to the farm because Jim had parked his car to go and meet this friend, and then couldn't find it.

When he came in we phoned the police to try and locate the car. This was before car theft was rife. Neither of us knew the car's registration number and the only person who would definitely know was our 10-year-old Alaric. It was well after lights out at the Ridge School where he was a weekly boarder. The matron had to wake him to fetch him to the phone. He told us the registration number and the police found the car within the hour.

MAY 1981 MONAGHAN

I enjoy hot air ballooning more than I can say. We go nearly every weekend. Three tons of air, 85 000 square feet of silk balloon and floating like a dream. Today we flew over Jack Scott's farm, kudu, baboons, giraffe, duiker – all reacting in various ways. Carl Jeppe came ballooning and took photographs, loving the whole experience, and we lay in a heap on the balloon in the basket trailer on the way home in a state of delicious physical exhaustion.

Beezy and I flew with Bruce over a mealie field and as we drifted low, a courageous black cat hissed at us. We floated slowly, slowly over our own trees, touching, peeping, so intimate. Then along the river, almost skimming the water. It was 5am and I imitated a cock-a-doodle-doo. A man came out of a cottage in his pyjamas and was so excited to see us he asked us in for tea. We drifted on, explaining we couldn't stop, and we waved to each other until we floated out of sight.

This evening a storm was brewing, thrilling evening light in the sky, and then an emergency landing, just missing a bedlam of telephone wires. We banged down onto our side and crashed on stones and it was quite rough. Then it poured with rain. I LOVE ballooning.

After today's trip we landed in a 30 mph ground wind and really got pounded. Every time we touched down, the balloon filled with air again and we were lifted up, only to get thwacked down again and again. The wireless dug into my thigh and caused bad bruising. This trip I didn't enjoy.

This morning we landed at Mooiplaats and Beezy and Bruce and his kids went down the mine in one of the dolomite sinkholes and were charged by a porcupine as big as a PIG! Then Bruce caught a little bat and we studied its face, which is exactly like Dracula.

15 JUNE 1981

Jim ran in and fetched me at 11 am and we both saw them – a pair of fish eagles wheeling high above the house, calling. Godsent. This is the fifth time I have seen them here. I still find it hard to believe.

9 JULY 1981

Our cat, Bimble was found tampering with a 4ft boomslang in the karee courtyard by Bundy who yelled hysterically. I was laid up with tickbite fever, so Beezy potted it with the 20 bore because I was unable to contact Mike Perie, the snake collector, to come and collect it.

I am glad we have reached the stage of trying to save snakes rather than killing them. They were too threatening for me when the children were tiny.

10 SEPTEMBER 1981

Francis Grier (organ scholar at Christ Church, Oxford, composer and pianist) and Colin Carr (cellist from the Menuhin School, now performs world-wide) came and spent the only free day of their tour with us on the farm. Some years before I had been in the organ loft at Christ Church during a service when Francis was playing.

I had arranged a balloon ride for them and then to take them to catch a trout and see the blesbuck and other animals – in other words, give them a real treat of a day in the South African countryside.

That day it snowed in Johannesburg for the first time in about 80 years. It was freezing and wet. So I had a wonderful day making music with them, but it wasn't quite the plan. Francis accompanied Jess and it was heaven.

7 OCTOBER 1981
Three baby robins have hatched in the courtyard under the light fitting. Mrs Robin is almost too tame and I fear for the fledglings when Lord Bimble learns of their existence.

My bedroom guest for the summer
October 1981

During the rainy season every year there is a slightly hair-raising moment when we put our shoes on in the mornings. Have you ever put your foot into a shoe in the toe of which is a frog? This happens regularly and it is our habit to shake our shoes out thoroughly before putting them on our feet. Even if you are wearing socks, it is terrible to feel a frog there. Last year a frog took up residence in one of my trainers and I just left him in peace and didn't wear them for the whole summer. I grew fond of him and missed him when he left after about four months.

NOVEMBER 1981
My mother had an extraordinarily large repertoire of the songs of George Gershwin, Cole Porter, Noel Coward, Irving Berlin etc. She was born and brought up in London and as a child, she and her sister attended rehearsals where George Gershwin played the piano for Fred and Adele Astaire's dance numbers. Their uncle Julian Jones directed the shows at the Hippodrome and sometimes took his nieces to rehearsals.

I took Bruce Attwood and Mary Murray to Sun City where Frank Sinatra was performing. Mary and I often sing Golden Oldies. Mary knows lots of Gershwin and Cole Porter etc. and we were thrilled to be able to go and hear Sinatra together. The enormous audience at Sun City were seated in a U shape around the stage, and we had seats on the side of the stage where we had a good view of the first row of the audience in the central section.

While Sinatra sang, Mary suddenly leant over and whispered to me, "Barbara, look at that man in the front row!"

There was a man in the centre of the row, on his knees, with a beatific expression on his face, his hands slightly apart in a worshipping position.

It was my brother Richard.

11 DECEMBER 1981

We had a grand supper under the stars in the bush camp. Henrietta and Alexandra Hawson came. Henri is eight and she took Bruce by the hand and looked up into his face, throwing her head back and putting her arms around him she said, "Bruce, who's your lawyer?"

Henri has a list of rules pinned to her bedroom door. They are made to be obeyed by her elder sister, Alex.

1. Wipe your feet.
2. Be kind.
3. Do not mess about.
4. Do not say rude words.
5. Do not fiddle.
6. Close the door when you go out but not at night.
7. Do not play the piano if you have not asked me.
8. Do not stand on the beds.
9. Do not sing unless you ask me.

26 FEBRUARY 1982 MONAGHAN

I went to the movies with Angela and when I got home Papa gave me the message that Jim had gone to England. Jim had told me nothing about it.

Huge Ewen Fergusson lay in our Mayan hammock and did it serious damage. (He's the British Ambassador, and Imogen calls him the Bombassador). I subsequently fell through it on my coccyx onto the brick verandah. I cried in Beezy's arms for a long time. He was so kind and sympathetic. Very comforting.

19-26 April 1982 Mauritius

Jim and I were going for a week and 12-year-old Prospero said, "And me!" – which could be his middle name.

Spent most of our days snorkelling over the coral. Jim discovered a fish trap about 200 metres from the shore. In it were two biggish fish, so he swam back to fetch Prospero and off they went in a kayak to collect them. It was clever of him to find the trap again. He stole the first fish out of the trap and its spine pierced his hand and caused him acute pain. Being Jim, he not only persisted in catching it and putting it in the kayak, but almost howling with pain, went under water again to catch the second. Prospero had to row him all the way back to the beach, his hand being unusable.

We went to a Mauritian doctor who wanted to cut open the wound to let the poison out and was preparing to do so and then stitch it. He said the cordonnier has poisonous spines and Jim would be in pain for a long time. I said NO to the cutting and stitching, and the doctor was disappointed to have nothing to do. He looked very bored when I first saw him at the door of his surgery.

We asked the fisherman who rents out the boats what to do about it. He told us, when stung by a cordonnier spine, pee on it immediately and the pain will cease. Jim did, and it did.

Lovely Gauguin people, graceful, gentle. Their boats and sails are wonderfully picturesque. The sails are of dark beige canvas, home-stitched. Sunsets magnificent silver and gold like I have not seen anywhere else.

I went to the Pampelmousse Gardens in Port Louis. Saw the Ficus Religioso – extraordinary tree, like an Edmund Dulac. It is so called because according to legend it was in the Garden of Eden. And the giant water lilies whose leaves must be nearly five feet across. I was so sad that Jim wouldn't come with me. He preferred to "do a bit of reading."

18 JULY 1982 MONAGHAN
We lit the fire in our bedroom and Squeezie came to bed in his corduroys and jersey. We had steak, mushrooms, tomatoes, sausages – a royal meal as far as we are concerned. We lay and grinned like a pair of Cheshire cats so content were we.

24 JULY 1982
Thirteen guns – 106 white-faced duck, 60 guinea-fowl, 10 francolin.

For me this was the best shoot by far. Did the first walk – about 200 guinea-fowl flew to the wrong side of the river as we lined up!

I beat on Kleintjie my horse, and spotted a poacher. I crept up on him while he was setting snares for leguaans but was nervous to do anything about him while I was alone, so I rode away quietly.

With Jess's help, Ingrid von Hone did the lunch superbly. That was the biggest bonus for me – they enabled me to spend the whole day out with the guns.

After lunch we were waiting for the duck-flight and I saw the poacher again. I ran and fetched our friend Martin and his retriever Brufen, and we had an enthralling hour on the river. First Martin shot to miss the poacher, who got the message. Then Martin and I waded along the edge of the river, he taking all the wire snares the poacher had set and flinging them deep into the middle of the river.

Then he shot a duck, fell over and was totally submerged, grappling for his gun. Then he ran after a duck he'd shot, put his foot in yet another snare, fell hard onto his kisser and really hurt his knee on a rock.

He came back dripping from top to toe, limping, and said he'd never had a better time in his life.

The sun, the river, the bare trees, the winter veld, silly little clouds, and then hundreds and hundreds of white-faced whistling duck wheeling over – it was very heaven.

Jess had prepared the mulled wine and all the food. The fires were lit. She was splendid. We gave Martin a change of clothes. The Fergussons and Angela stayed on and Beezy played his wind-up gramophone. We danced, and it was a merry evening indeed.

After everyone had left, and the whole family having just gone to bed, both farms caught fire and Jim, Beezy and Prospero fought fires until the small hours. What a day!

Bimble, when fat, which he is, and in the tugboat position with his paws folded beneath his chest, is a Transatlantic Hovergoose.

what the baboons have left of our mealie crop

Baboons have eaten our mealie crop at Mooiplaats and have left cobs all over the farm. I am frightened of baboons.

It is good to be alive to breathe air that is clear and cold at night and sweet with rain. Picking my first broad beans. They all fell over in a sort of swoon a month ago and seem to be bearing only now, in their horizontal position.

About this time I went to Nairobi with Jim and we stayed at the Norfolk Hotel which was owned by our dear friend Jack Block. Jack was a nut-brown small firework of a man with a devilish sense of humour. He and I teased each other unmercifully every time we met. We had an ongoing competition 'mobbing' each other.

On this particular trip I telephoned his wife Doria and asked her to give me the name of any friend of theirs in London. I told her what I was up to and she happily complied. I then asked her to put Jack onto the line. In a hopefully disguised voice I told him that I brought loving messages from our common friend, and that I was in Nairobi for a few days and would love to meet him. He was as charming as ever and asked my name and where I was staying. I gave him a name and said that I was staying at the Norfolk. Jack said he had to be at the Norfolk for a meeting at 9.30 am and suggested we breakfast together beforehand. Excellent plan said I.

The dining room at the Norfolk is divided from the entrance foyer by a row of potted palms. Jim and I sat at breakfast watching Jack pace up and down looking at his watch and growing increasingly impatient. Eventually Jim attracted his attention and Jack was surprised and delighted to see us. We hugged each other and Jim urged him to join us for coffee. Jack said, "I'd love to – but some silly bitch said she'd meet me here at 8.30 and it is now after 9.00 and there seems to be no sign of her." We talked him in to sitting with us where he could watch the foyer. He was very distracted and I eventually let on. I led by one game to nil.

Jack then organised for us to meet the Leslie-Melvilles who bred Rothschild giraffes, which have quite different markings from the ones we know. We were to go to their estate outside Nairobi in time to feed the baby giraffe with bottles of milk, after which Jack and Doria would join us there for dinner. We had a view of Mount Kilimanjaro on one side, and Mount Kenya on the other, both snow-capped, and these curiously beautiful giraffes strolling around the lawn. Jim and I climbed scaffolding to be able to reach the baby giraffe to feed it, and with us were three American field students who were staying with the Leslie-Melvilles to study the giraffes.

While we sat having a drink and waiting for Jack and Doria, I told the L-Ms all about the morning 'mobbing.' Their response fired me up and I asked Mrs L-M if she happened to possess a wig. She did, and she enthusiastically took me upstairs where she dressed me in fishnet stockings, mini-skirt, patent leather high heels, lamé top, masses of make-up and dark glasses. I stuffed cotton-wool in my cheeks, which changed the shape of my face alarmingly, and planned to ask for a double vodka whereupon Mr L-M would give me water with ice and a slice of lemon. Jack Block knows I don't drink alcohol.

The problem was Jim, who couldn't possibly keep a straight face, so he agreed to leave the room before giving anything away.

Jack arrived and was introduced to not three but four American zoologists, and when he asked where I was, Jim told him I was still feeding the baby giraffe. I took my seat next to Jack and asked him if he were married. He explained that his wife Doria was unable to join us that evening. I said, sotto voce, "That's great!" and sidled nearer to him. I then asked him if he would take me on a safari. He muttered that would be lovely but mumble mumble. I said, "You know you really are cute!" and climbed onto his lap and shouted across to Mr Leslie-Melville to pour me a double vodka.

Jack was blushing and squirming with embarrassment and trying to be polite the while. He said his keys were digging into his leg and tried to prise me off his lap without giving too much offence. This is when Jim went beetroot and left the room to explode out of earshot.

This charade continued for about 15 minutes and eventually I sighed, "Oh my golly it's so hot!" and tugged my blonde wig off and spat the cotton wool out of my mouth.

Jack was so overcome with surprise that he yelled and slapped his thighs and became almost apopleptic and joined Jim in the hall, both of them making a terrific din.

Game, set and match. Mrs Leslie-Melville made me a gift of the wig and the rest of the outfit.

Within a year of the Jack Block scene, I went to Jan Smuts Airport to meet Jim after a long trip, and rigged myself up in the airport toilets as a blonde tart. As I saw Jim pushing his luggage trolley along I tapped him on the shoulder and said in a Cockney accent, "Are you Mr Balfour from London?" He ducked sideways and said, "No," apologetically. I teetered after him and said, "Do you know a Mr Balfour off BA 056 by any chance?" He said, "No - I wish I did." I was at a loss so I went on following him, and the group of women who had watched me change in the toilets stood wide-eyed, holding their hands over their mouths. I swung my hips at Jim and he tried to avoid me until I yanked the wig off and removed my dark glasses. He yelped and nearly fell over with mirth. He made such a noise when he really got going that there ended up quite a scene. People crowded round wondering what it was all about.

He giggled about it all the way home in the car. We had been married for at least 20 years – and he had seen me in this outrageous get-up in Kenya and had been in on the 'mobbing', and he still didn't twig. What I called Jim's Après Laugh could be maddening. He would suddenly start laughing with no explanation. When questioned, it was usually about something that had happened days before. Eventually I gave up wanting to be in on it.

I went in my blonde tart outfit to Clarke's Bookshop in Long Street, Cape Town. Anthony was at his desk behind the counter and I told him - in a whiny voice - that I was getting married soon and that my fiancé was decorating his study in blues and greens and we wanted some books for decoration. I pointed to a row of large green ones - volumes of Gibbon's *Decline and Fall of the Roman Empire* - and then a collection of blue volumes the other side of the room. Anthony, crouched down behind the counter, his lips tight, his face crimson, his eyes filled with tears, was trying to explain what they were. I didn't listen at all but added they're just the right colour for my fiancé's study. He spluttered out that these books were expensive and rare. He was trying so hard to control himself and be polite - and at the same time to alert his assistant to come and enjoy the scene. I was really getting into the swing and wanted to be shown more green books and told him about the curtains we had chosen.

Eventually off came the disguise. Anthony was writhing, and continued to enjoy the blonde fiancée visit for months on end.

Every member of my family has used the wig. It has done a lot of mileage over the last couple of decades and we still have it.

18 September 1982
Heard first nightjar of the season.

Imogen Cooper spent the day and played Schubert wonderfully. We played the F minor Fantasia duet. What bliss for me.

19 September 1982
Our Chamber Choir performed a concert in the Market Theatre with Donald Swann. He had composed songs about the Hobbit, which he played and sang, interlaced with our singing. A beautiful evening. He is a marvellous musician apart from being an angel not of this earth.

107

Donald and I came back to the farm exhausted after the concert and letharged in the kitchen on the sofa with hot drinks, watching totally mindless Afrikaans soap-opera on television with the sound switched off. It seemed perfectly apt for our mental state.

28 SEPTEMBER 1982

I was playing Schubert duets with Donald Swann and Jim came up to the piano to say goodbye to us. I was leaving for England in the afternoon.

When Jim had left, Donald's eyes filled with tears. I said, "Don't cry, Jim is only going to the office. I am the one that is leaving."

He said, "But Jim has gone. He has gone into the world, and I love him."

18 OCTOBER 1982 OXFORD

I went to see Gaffer Blackwell in Blackwells. He is 93 plus. He says he doubts I will see him next year. He explained he was a spirit, a ghost. Yet he goes to meetings at Beaver House.

Tom quad in full sunlight, the Broad after rain, sunlit, Trinity gardens, the Grinling Gibbons altar in the chapel. Then down the Turl to Duckers. Oxford is at its most sublime.

Deb with whom I always stay in Oxford, has been married to Tony Honoré for about a year or so and he is systematically getting rid of a lot of her stuff, and a lot of stuff she has. He likes plain white walls – and Deb's way of life was very different.

He has dealt with Deb's huge sofa in a very original way. It was in a state of advanced disrepair, and seemingly too big to get down the stairs. How it was brought into the flat is a mystery. So he chopped it up and removed it piece by piece and then burnt the bits. *Sic transit gloria* Deb's awful old sofa.

Christ Church Cathedral Choir superb under Francis Grier. Simon Preston is a hard act to follow.

Simon now has Westminster Abbey Choir singing more and more beautifully. He and I played the Bach C major double harpsichord concerto on organ and piano, which was great fun. He's performing it on harpsichords with George Malcolm in November.

B and Simon

Taking Gail Schrire to the Abbey was amusing. After Evensong we were walking in the cloisters on our way to visit Simon in his beautiful digs which go with the job of organist and choirmaster, when several black-clad clergymen passed us bearing a coffin. Gail's eyes were like saucers. When we told Simon he giggled and said, oh yes corpses get taken to lie in some private chapel. He then took us to hear the little choristers of the Abbey playing at their orchestra practice. Little boys on huge instruments like tuba and trombone and cello etc, playing very well considering their ages and sizes. Simon calls them The Neasden Simfonia. It being after 7 pm, some of them were in their pyjamas and dressing gowns.

JANUARY 1983 MONAGHAN
Bimble died while we were in Plett. I loved him more than any cat I have had. I cried for days until Jess took me up to Peter Berning our doctor. While I sat on the lawn outside his rooms weeping away, Jess went in and said for God's sake do something about my mother. He gave me muti and it worked.

Jim and Morné du Plessis opened the batting for our motley cricket team against Keith McAdam's Invaders. If the ball goes into the duck pond it is six and out. Morné's economy of movement is a delight to behold – it is such a privilege to witness great professional ability, in whatever field. Morné eventually hit a catch on purpose out of politeness. Not so with our Jimothy. He remained batting until the end of the innings.

Bundy is loving Eton and has written regular good letters home. I am so proud of him, and I hope he is making the most of this extraordinary opportunity.

He has no belief and is therefore excused chapel. For those that are not Christian or are non-believers, there are various speakers that come to Eton to talk to those boys while the others are in chapel. Bundy wrote and said, "guess who came to talk to us on Monday? Solzhenitzin!"

Eton is a privilege beyond one's imagination. If a boy has a particular talent or interest, almost anyone in the world can be conjured up to come and give a class.

4 FEBRUARY 1983

Raymond Dart is 90 today. We were invited to a banquet at Wits to celebrate along with the Vice-Chancellor, Professor Bozzoli, and the Hammond-Tookes. Dart didn't cry which was surprising. He cries readily.

Jim, Philip Tobias, B, Raymond and Marjorie Dart

When we got back to the farm, Prospero, who is in his first term at Woodmead, said I have to come and listen to a wonderful man who is taking assembly at school this week.

Prospero was spot on. We met Bishop Launcelot Fleming and his wife Jane.

We invited them to Monaghan, and when we were all sitting on the lawn having tea, Launcelot christened our new kitten. He asked Prospero to fetch water, and Prospero, whom Launcelot calls Ganymede, asked, "Won't tea do?" He considered it for a while, and then said, "Why not!"

Monkeyboy in his christening robe

As Launcelot is bishop of Norwich, was bishop of Plymouth and looked after the Royal Family at St George's Chapel in Windsor, he is properly qualified to christen Monkeyboy Launcelot Bailey. A very flexible broad-minded bishop! He and Jane have become very loving and wonderful friends.

Jess is playing in the National Orchestra for the symphony season. She is the youngest member of the orchestra by quite a bit.

25 FEBRUARY 1983
Jess played quartets, quintets and sonatas with Ernst Kovacic, Lettie Vermaak and Virginia Fortesque. She was sight-reading and having great fun. Jess played like a dream, at home with all these professionals, especially in the Schumann quintet and the Mendelssohn trios.

On 26 March 1983 we all went on a skiing Trip to Kitzbuhel. It was Jim's idea to ski there because he had been there in 1938. At that time he went there to improve his German, taking his trout rod with him. He was surprised to find it snow-bound. And even more surprised that there was a Luftwaffe training camp in Kitzbuhel. He spent evenings in the local pub chatting in his halting German to friendly 19-year-olds like himself, little knowing that very soon he would be a fighter pilot in the Royal Air Force, and that they would be taking pot shots at each other in the sky. He lodged with the Meyer family, in a house called 'Viere Winde', until his father sent a cable from London saying that he must return to England immediately, that war was inevitable and imminent.

With the family in 1983, it was ulcer-producing getting Jim to come on this trip. Although it was his idea in the first place, expecting him to keep to a schedule was stressful indeed. Our friend Theo Lorentz actually refers to Jim as 'Ulcerogenesis.'

Jim suddenly took a trip to Salisbury (Rhodesia) two days before we left. He and I and all four children were booked to travel and it was a last-minute rush filled with angst. He re-appeared at the 11th hour.

We flew Swiss Air to Zurich and then on another plane to Munich. Swiss Air

111

lost my suitcase. We then took a train from Munich and had to change three times to get to Kitzbuhel.

Anthony Ogilvie-Thompson, then at Eton with Bundy, was already settling into the Hotel Hofer when we arrived.

Jim went to the house 'Viere Winde' where he had stayed in 1938, wondering whether he could find out anything about the Meyer family. Anna, the daughter of the house, who was Jim's age, opened the door to him. A delighted reunion took place 45 years on. Anna was so thrilled to see Jim again and we invited her out to dinner. She told us she had been married to an Englishman named Peter Perfect, and was now widowed.

Jim and I walked round the Kitzbuhel cemetery where for Easter black-clad women were placing flowers on the graves – possibly those of their sons, who had been in the Luftwaffe and had died in the war. The graves of these young men bore photographs of them in uniform, with their names and the dates of their birth and deaths – they were all around 20 years old.

Being Easter in Austria there was pussy-willow every-where, tied into clusters like a "pudding of Monkeyboys", said Beezy, Monkeyboy being our grey kitten.

Jim was too bulky for Frazer Aitken's ski-suit which he had kindly lent us (I must add that Frazer has a figure like a thermometer), so Jim wore Julian's which was so big it looked like a pair of waders on him.

We all agreed to meet for lunch at Alpenhaus, a restaurant on the slopes. The boys insisted I bring my camera to Alpenhaus because of the barman. Beezy named him 'Das Phallus' because of the shape and size of his fingers. I was com-manded to photograph his hands, which may have seemed a bit odd to him, but Bundy explained to 'Das Phallus' that I wanted to be able to remember the people at Alpenhaus who had been so good to us.

Jim was already seated at a table when all seven of us trooped in to join him. There were two full glasses of wine next to Jim's, so the boys moved them to an-other table, and with much clattering of skis and boots and arguing about seating, we settled down.

Little did we know that Jim had picked up two gorgeous young girls and invited them to sit with him. They had gone to fetch their meal. They were a bit taken aback when they saw a great mob swarming into their places. There was much guffawing and teasing him about his 'pick-ups'.

Jim kept his woollen hat in a zippered pocket near his ankle. When I knelt down to fish it out for him, a man nearby remarked, "Checking on his wheels? I wish my wife would. She never checks my wheels."

We all started to ski on the nursery slopes with a textbook hunk of an instructor who, of course fell in love with Jess. We left after an hour or so, and the boys went full steam ahead and never looked back. Ending their first day on Black slopes no less. Squeezie and I were on the T-lift where one is required to keep one's skis absolutely parallel while the lift is in motion. Jim seemed incapable of doing this and caused the lift to come to a grinding halt on several occasions. Then he would fall and couldn't get up unless heaved by several sons. All the other people on the lift grew increasingly impatient with him, because it couldn't start again until Jim was dragged out of the way.

Luckily I can whistle with my fingers, which I did every time he fell, which was often. Bailey boys would arrive from every direction to pull Jim upright. Laughing made it much more difficult and Jim enjoyed himself greatly, even if all the other skiers were not amused. I tried to bribe one of the children to go on the ski-lift with him but they refused as it was too embarrassing. He was beginning to gain confidence on his skis when, typically, he suddenly left after a week and flew to London.

I got a bit beyond myself and skied down a Red slope (more advanced skiing than the Blue and Green ones) and I took a nasty fall. My neck hurt and seized up, and feeling sorry for myself, I told an instructor who took me straight to the hospital without a by-your-leave. There I waited for about an hour before an unsmiling nurse took me in to be x-rayed. Then another half hour and I was laid on a bed where a doctor came and injected my upper back and neck with about 10 little injections.

I was terrified. No-one smiled and no-one spoke English. When I tried to communicate that I wanted to phone the hotel to speak to my family, they paid no heed. I thought maybe they were trying to kill me. Nobody knew where I was. Maybe the entire hospital staff were Nazis and they knew about my Jewish blood. However, I was told I could leave after about another hour.

Not a happy afternoon. I trudged through the snow, which made a lovely crunching sound, longing to tell my children about my adventure and how terrified and brave I'd been.

I saw that Karajan was conducting at the Salzburg Easter Festival. Through various friends and contacts, I managed to buy two horribly expensive tickets for Jess and me. We heard the Berlin Philharmonic play the Brahms 3rd and 1st symphonies in that order. Neither of us had ever heard any orchestra like it. Total perfection for Brahms. Karajan wore black polished Nikes because of his damaged back. He limped onto the rostrum and begun the 3rd without a moment's pause. Oh God it was thrilling. He makes the minimum movement with his hands and wrists, and is otherwise almost motionless.

When I got back to South Africa, I told Bruce Attwood about the audience applauding for so long afterwards that they eventually turned the lights off in the Festspielhaus. Bruce said, "Why didn't they use tear-gas?"

My luggage never arrived so I spent the entire holiday more or less in the clothes I had worn on the plane. I slept in Jim's long-johns and vest, and borrowed various items from the boys and Jess. I was quite happy about it except for not having anything suitable for the Salzburg Festival.

Jess couldn't ski because of her ballet-damaged knees, so she slid down the pistes on her bottom and enjoyed herself like that. She wore pyjamas almost all the time, day and night. This was out of choice as she hadn't lost her clothes. Anthony very sweetly stayed with her at the hotel instead of enjoying himself on the slopes with the boys, when she needed to rest.

The Salzburg Festival must be one of the most elegantly dressed occasions on earth. Jess and I wore corduroys. Jess hadn't brought any smart clothes with her and I had no luggage. We procured the tickets so hurriedly that there was no chance to shop for clothes. I felt awful and apologised to two bejewelled Austrian women next to me. I explained that my luggage had been lost. They were very understanding and kind. For once, I really wanted to be dressed well.

When the concert was over, we wanted to creep out before anyone saw us. We were both high with the performance. A huge fat, florid man talked Brahms to me all the way up the aisle, an Englishman – he didn't notice our clothes at all, bless him. The final embarrassment for Jess, was hastening in to the men's loo by mistake, then making an even hastier about-turn.

I don't think we have ever laughed so much as we did at the Tyrolean evening at Pratzmayr in Kitzbuhel. A group of men and women – some in their fifties and sixties – yodelled to the accompaniment of a pianist and accordionist. They had to be seen to be believed. The pianist had plug-in drums and Jess mimicked his manner perfectly. He looked like an undertaker, throwing his hands up in despair, and his eyes to the heavens, not knowing whence the burden of his genius had come to him.

The accordionist was certainly in his 90s and sported a floral boater which he jerked up and down with his bald pate. The men wore lederhosen and had white legs with varicose veins, and the women wore dirndls, and were coy and girlish. They sang sharp with a pronounced tremolo. We were helpless with mirth and eventually Jessica and I had to be supported out of the hall. It was one the most enjoyable and memorable evenings for all of us.

26 MAY 1983 MONAGHAN

I cooked roast duck for a small dinner party to celebrate my birthday. Jim didn't come home until after 10 pm, by which time almost everyone had left.

25 AUGUST 1983

Extract from Beezy's letter from Italy:

"I woke up one morning to the sound of a goat that sounded like a person who couldn't make the sound of a goat trying to be funny 'beh-eh-eh-eh'. No wonder they cut their throats.

. . . We then returned to Venice which was as expected, a dream. Surrounded by kind of Eastern palaces, huge churches, the sun sets in mid-air, red, over the Death-in-Venice water, and the full moon rises out of mid-air, looking like the sun.

The art is fantastic, I felt dizzy with Bellini . . . We also went to the Peggy Guggenheim collection of superb modern art.

Beezy

115

The glass shops (endless) are nice but contain a lot of hair-raising Rococo hideosities. The masks are beautiful. . . . We didn't go in a gondola, the expense is not worth it without a lover.

Seven days left, and we go through Switzerland, Germany and France, then back to London where I set about becoming a rain-sodden, white, hardworking student, an important ingredient in the making of my career.

I'd just like to say, Jim and Bar, thank you for a fantastic 21st birthday present."

1 OCTOBER 1983
It's out of season and we had an illegal duck shoot. Over 1 000 white-faced duck cruising over feedlot. Eight guns, 78 birds shot, and Jim shot over half the bag! Deedle-dee! I made a curry, Jess did salads and we had an easy pleasant evening.

20 OCTOBER 1983
We had half an inch of very noisy rain and thunderous hail and we lay in bed revelling in it. We saw a hedgehog hurrying along the path to the library like Mrs Tiggywinkle. Full moon it was too – enchanting.

The 17th Hereford calf was born this morning. Lovely inspection of cattle while riding Kleintjie. Summer in full swing, Diedrick's cuckoos, Piet-my-Vrous, mosquitoes, green lawn – everything having babies.

Jess has finished 10 commissioned pictures for the baby book and so far the publishers are thrilled with them. She played the Beethoven G minor sonata and the Brahms E minor with Lamar Crowson and he praised her in a big way.

Beezy has started at the Byam Shaw Art School in London and loves it. When Thomas Pakenham and his mother Elizabeth Longford were staying with us on the farm, she told us that Princess Margaret had tried to get her son Lord Linley into the Byam Shaw and had failed. Beezy, without matric or A levels, did it on his own – we had nothing to do with it. He presented his portfolio and that was all. Very proud we are.

AND it has rained.

26 OCTOBER 1983 LONDON

At Covent Garden, John Amis said that if I found *Boris Goudonov* (Moussorski's opera) too much, I could go home at interval. He warned me it is very long and John had to write a review on it for a newspaper. Claudio Abbado conducted. It was so quintessentially Russian and so beautiful, it could have gone on for ever as far as I was concerned.

Launcelot Fleming and I went to a sung Eucharist at Westminster Abbey. Simon Preston conducted the choir for the *Missa Brevis* which he had composed. It was electrifying. We had a drink with him afterwards in his beautiful dwelling in the cloisters.

21 JANUARY 1984 PLETTENBERG BAY

Jim swam far out to spear fish, shot an elf, and unzipped his wetsuit to tuck the fish inside it so that he could reload and try and shoot another one, instead of having to swim back to the shore to do so. The elf bit him quite deeply on the bosom.

I asked Peter Berning if he should have an anti-tetanus injection. Peter said absolutely yes, and then asked me and Prospero, who was with me, when we last had anti-tetanus vaccine. As we live on a farm, he suggested we keep them up to date.

Prospero and I ended up having anti-tetanus jabs because Jim had been bitten by an elf. Jim, of course, wouldn't go to be injected at all.

My newly devised fishing method - wait for it - baited hook and line under water with goggles and snorkel.

Bruce Chatwin and I spend our time in the car driving in and out of town, he talking like his cousin who "went quite mad with a carving knife". Bruce is the best mimic I know, and the best raconteur. He is in the same league as Peter Ustinov, and that's saying something.

He and I went to a party given for Peter Wilson, the chairman of Sotheby's and a godson of Sir Abe, at the Cassirers. Reinhold Cassirer represents Sotheby's here in South Africa. As usual, Jim was away and asked me to go on his behalf. So I took Chatwin and we had a marvellous time.

There was one perfect remark by an owner of a Cork Street gallery in London. He had been all of three days in this continent and had been taken by Reinhold to see some exhibition at the Market Theatre, and said, "Why should blacks be expected to learn to paint on canvas when they paint so wonderfully on totem poles?" It needs Bruce to imitate his accent and style.

In London that year William and Rachel Douglas Home invited Jim and me to go to William's play *The Kingfisher* which was showing in the West End. We were to meet them for dinner and then all see the play together. We met at the restaurant, that is William, Rachel and myself. Jim didn't appear. I was like a hen on hot bricks going to the entrance of the restaurant to see if he was coming. I phoned our flat about four times and in all it must have been the most unrelaxed meal possible. We then went on to the theatre and I thought Jim might have misunderstood or forgotten the name of the restaurant and that he would be at the theatre. Nothing doing. No sign of him. I waited until the last bell was sounded, exhausted from constantly searching the audience which was finally seated and the play began. There was an empty seat next to Rachel.

Sir Ralph Richardson played the butler, Celia Johnson was the heroine. How I would have enjoyed it if I hadn't been so distraught.

When I got back to the flat there Jim was in bed reading. As Elizabeth Longford answered when asked whether she had ever considered divorce, "Divorce never; murder often."

APRIL 1984 PLETTENBERG BAY

Our Plett holiday was marred by the disappearance of our beloved Louis.[23] We waited in a frantic state for nine days until we heard he had been found dead, frozen in his helicopter, at an altitude of 23 000 feet on the lip of the highest volcano in the Andes.

I am sure that it was because he couldn't resist taking photos, and there wasn't enough oxygen for the helicopter to take off again. I don't know if this is the true reason but Louis endangered himself taking photos of charging elephants etc. – I don't think we'll ever know what happened.

Louis, what of your family who love you so?

I felt desperate in Plett running to the church and getting Father Sergel to pray for him and not letting him stop. I also bargained with the Lord at the Good Friday service by playing Bach and singing Mozart's *Laudate Dominum* solo, as a sort of bribe. All for you, Louis, and all in vain.

MAY 1984

Slingsby our ostrich is quite one of the family. He plays tennis, gardens, plays football on Sunday mornings on the lawn with Jim and the school kids, and loves coming into the kitchen. I found him sitting in front of Jessica's mirror in the bedroom, admiring himself. He devoured a Georgian silver salt-spoon off the table while we were dining. He has laid an egg! So he is now Mrs Slingsby.

When Prospero was 14 Jim gave him the only fatherly advice he offered. "Porky-boy, if you're going to be eccentric you must start early or people will think you're aging."

---

23 Dr Louis Murray, geologist for Anglo-American

The last time I ever tried to hit Prospero he took hold of my arms and held them down and said, "It's all over Bar. I'm bigger than you now." He was, and we did laugh.

Some years later when I had a proper set to with Prospero, he was 6'4" and I was carrying on like nobody's business yelling at him and he took me and put me on the top of our Cape Dutch armoire which is about ten feet high, and left me there. I didn't dare jump off in case it toppled. He left me there for about 10 minutes before he came back and lifted me down.

23 MAY 1984

Extract from Bundy's letter from Eton:

" ... on Friday we'll be in London and on the Monday I'm having my best time. I've been invited by another football-and-cricket-crazy friend of mine to go to Lords to watch the West Indies against England. Can you imagine how I will be in my element! Bar, it's like you going to see God conducting Bach!!!

I hope you saw that Liverpool finished top. The champions three times running. That's only been done twice before in history. They've won it seven times in nine years."

28 MAY 1984

Instead of going to the shoot at Rooipoort, all the Murrays and I went to Tessa and Julian at Klaserie. So sad to be without Louis. How heartsore we are for the Murrays.

We got stuck in the Land Rover in the blazing heat of the day, and Christopher O-T led us back to the house on foot, passing en route an enormous black mamba. Then we walked into a herd of buffalo in the river bed. Tessa and Julian make everything so easy and good. I love them.

B and Julian O-T at Klaserie

120

Joephas, the man who takes care of their property, keeps chickens, speckled and sort of tartan-patterned. The chicken hok is one of the most enchanting features of Klaserie. It is a corrugated iron box attached to trees and poles about 10 feet off the ground, and has a ladder up which the chickens are chased, flapping and squawking, in the evening. The door is then firmly shut to keep them safe from leopards, lions, jackals, etc. They range freely by day, and add to the atmosphere of woodsmoke and porridge cooking.

JULY AND AUGUST 1984

Went to all four concerts of Gundula Janowitz. I was in shock from the greatest singing I have ever heard and am likely to hear. Her voice is not of this world, it is like a beam of light, so effortless is it.

I wish Lamar Crowson had accompanied her Schubert recital. Very mediocre pianist she had. Her tour ended with Strauss's *Four Last Songs* and two Mozart concert arias with orchestra in the City Hall. One of the greatest experiences of my life. Never have I seen a South African audience respond like this. Thank God Jessica and Beezy were able hear her. Out of all whooping wonderful. I had John Amis on my right and Beezy on my left, both had tears rolling down their cheeks.

15 OCTOBER 1984

Extract from Beezy's letter from London:

" . . . I'm happier than I've been for a long time, due to being my own man, freedom in London is fabulous, I now ride my cloud machine, all the way to the Royal Academy where yesterday I saw Vermeer and de Hooch and contemporaries, and I discovered something very exciting in that they, especially Vermeer, were compositional geniuses. All abiding by such powerful rules of design as to subconsciously fascinate the viewer – it will affect all my work from now on.

I went to the Tate this afternoon where I was moved to tears . . . while looking at Picasso's Woman in a White Chemise. I reeled away from it.

. . . There was this Ghanaian guitarist of exceptional standard, and his group including two saxes, which sent purple rubber band-waves down the inside and back of my head."

OCTOBER 1984

Jim, Beezy and I went to Sam Jaff's fishing cottage near Machadodorp, which is one of my favourite dwellings. Sam has quietly become a very precious friend. It is possible to go to bed at 8 pm, have supper in pyjamas, etc. All the tedious social nonsense like keeping awake, talking, and the like, becomes unnecessary.

The rain on the iron roof makes a terrific din, and it leaks like all get-out, so that we have to put buckets and pots and huge zinc tubs at various key places all over the house to catch the water. And they have to be emptied regularly.

Sam Jaff

Beezy and Sam, 1984

There are countless paraffin lamps which are difficult to light and which smoke quite a bit. The wood stove takes ages to heat up so cooking bacon and eggs for breakfast takes longer than one can imagine. The bathroom is the warmest room in the house because of the stove for the hot water being there. So bathing is delightful and is a long, relaxed, drawn-out affair. All the wet clothes and socks and boots are laid out near the stove and there is a smell of river, and wood-smoke and paraffin and wet wool. I love it.

122

I had fetched Jim straight off a plane to take him fishing. He had in his suitcase a pyjama top, some bathing trunks, and lots of books. That is all.

The first morning he came in soaked to the skin, so that later he was seen casting along the banks of the river dressed in a red-and-white-striped pyjama top, with his green bathing trunks, and thick wet socks and heavy shoes.

While we were having supper there was a nasty smell and lots of smoke and it was discovered that Jim had put his shoes and socks in the oven to dry and they had started to burn.

4 JANUARY 1985
Papa died at 7 am this morning as a result of his 7th coronary.

We were in Plett and I couldn't get a seat on any flight to go to Mother. When I phoned Sam Jaff who was also in Plett, to tell him the news, he immediately found me a lift in a single-engine plane being flown within the hour.

I really hate flying in small planes, and when we stopped for fuel in Port Elizabeth, the co-pilot said to the young pilot, "Well done on your first landing!"
Papa, I hope you realise what I am doing for you.

At his cremation as he wished, there was only the immediate family attending, and no service of any sort. I thought it would be fitting to play a cassette of Jessica performing Couperin's *Piece en Concert*, with me on piano, which Papa loved. He loved Jessica beyond anyone, and was so proud of her music-making. We all stood while the coffin disappeared, listening to Couperin, and suddenly the music paused and Jessica was heard to say, "Oh shit," and then it continued.

10 FEBRUARY 1985
Extract from Beezy's letter from London:

" . . . I went to the De Kooning exhibition last week, and tears blocked my vision. Never have I seen such pure agony. His deep down feeling of dissat-

123

isfaction drives him into bounds like no other painter, so honest is he. Very inspiring.

My work still goes strong and John Lewis (studio head) is starting to see the value my 'side paintings' are having. While I slog on the model painting, I'll fly round like a high priest, and dab my brush over a waiting piece of board, from which another painting will emerge, putting zing into the painting from the model, and ping into the side painting.

... I went to the Chagall and Liz Frink exhibitions today. I love Chagall for his Russianness, Jewishness, use of colour and his awareness of life around him. Liz Frink freaked me out – she is the most powerful of all modern sculptors I've seen.

We are presently FREEZING. Snow and ice everywhere, we warm ourselves around the candle. I discovered a 10-foot long lavatory roll (inside cardboard piece) which was transformed feverishly between the hours of 9.30 pm and one in the morning – with a kitchen knife as my only tool, and paintbrushes – into 'Portrait of a rich white South African', complete with pink striped shirt, jeans, Gucci shoes, bow-tie, and grinning, frightened face."

14 FEBRUARY 1985
SQUEEZIE PHONED ME FROM HARARI – WOULD I BE HIS VALENTINE?
Would I! Oh garçon! Bien je jamais! Oh frabjous day! Jess says it's a miracle.

So you see they DO happen.

I had written to Jim, " . . . you give me a thrumming feeling in my discobolus – a highly sensitive organ as you wot."

16-18 FEBRUARY 1985 MACHADODORP
Fishing at Sam's with Sam, Prospero, Angela and the Fabians. We had every kind of perfect weather; sun, clouds, winds, storms. The best fishing, contrary to expectations was while it was thundering like crazy. I caught nine big trout and put back several small ones. Sam took two, Angela and Donald Fabian, one each. So I was the Angler of the Weekend. I caught all my fish on flies tied by Prospero. I have never seen the water so high.

I fished hard and was so happy. I was so deeply involved it was like being in a trance. I took a fish while walking stark naked down the middle of a pool. Then I found Angela and we both swam in Long Pool, floating on our backs clutching bouquets of wild flowers and singing, "willow, willow, willow". Angela was the more likely Ophelia because of her long hair.

Sam and I reacted identically when the lightning struck overhead. We were not together but admitted that we had flung our carbon-fibre rods as far away as we could, after the achtungs of the Piglet (Prospero).

Prospero and Angela were curled up under a cliff of Watsonia to keep out of the rain which was bucketing down, with much lightning and thunder. They were stuck there until it grew dark.

Anita Fabian, excellent botanist artist, drew flowers – a working weekend for her. I was sorry not being in the field with her to learn the flowers, but fishing took me proper and I fished my brains out. Prospero spent the morning with her, collecting and identifying flowers and loved it.

I love love love it at Sam's.

blue crane

3 MARCH 1985 MONAGHAN
Jim and I had a magic couple of hours at Mooiplaats. The day was bright and a wee bit autumnal. We visited the protea rupelliae in full bloom, and then in the last light of the day we saw a golden-breasted bunting and a chin-spot batis male. Blue crane breeding there as usual.

A peregrine flew over the garden and the bokmakieries are back, carrying on their varied and tuneful repertoire. A great joy to have them here after a long absence.

Jim offered to fetch me a cup of tea. I told him to use a teabag. He came to me with the tea. It tasted odd. I asked him to show me which teabags he'd used. They were bags of bouquet garni. Where did he find them?

21 MARCH 1985

Bach is 300 years old today and we didn't celebrate for several reasons. One was that the Bach choir was rehearsing the Matthew Passion so a lot of us were busy. And the worst has happened to our friends the Doughertys. Their rare and beautiful boy Mark has died aged nine. He had a massive heart attack while running in a cross-country.

Only a few months ago Rosa Dougherty and I were saying how intolerable it was for the Napiers to lose their child and how we could never live through such a loss – and now this happens to them. Why? I find the pain actually physical. What can they be going through?

So we didn't celebrate Bach's birthday.

20 APRIL 1985

From a letter from me to Jim:

> "I am at Zurich airport waiting for my flight to Vienna . . . I think and drink deeply of the vision of you playing at goals in between the oleanders, without your shirt, and your lovely head of hair flopping when you run, and wearing the shorts Beezy bought you in France, and all your beloved Lilliputians haring around, and little Eddy doing the odd cartwheel in his pink pants, and the bamboo at the reservoir waving in the breeze behind you, and the blue, blue sky, and the happiness. Now I am on Swissair bound for Vienna, and next to us is a Finnair bound for Helsinki. All very exciting."

APRIL 1985 VIENNA

Staying with Nora Herberstein. Brigitte Zaczek made it unforgettable for me by organising for me to attend all that was going on in the Musikverein.

Apart from spending all day and every day in the Musikverein, while Nikolaus Harnoncourt rehearsed Handel's *Saul*, I sang a few sessions with the Vienna State Opera Choir, under Nikki!! – thanks to the harpsichordist of the Concentus Musicus, Gordon Murray, who supplied me with a score that had come out of the archives in Graz.

I had no idea who the soloists were to be, so imagine my surprise and joy when Dietrich Fischer-Dieskau walked in. He was Saul. The others were Julia Varady, too much of an operatic voice for Handel I thought, she is married to Fischer-Dieskau. Paul Esswood, Anthony Rolfes-Johnson who is perfect for the part.

To go to the actual performance after attending 15 hours of rehearsal for the recording was very meaningful and satisfying for me; to watch how Harnoncourt so certainly makes it all happen the way he means to.

During one session in the Brahmssaal, while the soloists were rehearsing, I nipped into the main hall and Loren Maazel happened to be recording the Mahler 3rd with the Vienna Philharmonic, Agnes Baltsa and the Vienna Boys. What a choice for me! Brahmssaal or Grossesaal.

At the Mahler recording the piccolo was flat at the end of a movement and Gordon Murray who sat with me, wasn't amused. Gordon is a superb musician and a wonderful new friend. He has an incredibly finely tuned ear.

I was invited for drinks at a huge apartment in Vienna with wonderful paintings. The daughter of the woman who lives there is married to the son of Henri Matisse, so she has quite a few Matisses on her wall, amongst an impressive and varied collection of other paintings.

Gidon Kremer and Marta Argerich played Mendelssohn and Schumann in the Musiekverein. If I tried to describe it the page would go up in flames. I only wish with all my heart that Jessica will hear them one day. The audience wouldn't let them go after three encores, one was the last movement of a Beethoven sonata. I will treasure this evening for the rest of my life.

B and Gordon Murray playing Bach C major concerto for two harpsichords

Nora has been like a mother to me. There is an old Hungarian professor of architecture staying here with her. He has published a fascinating book which is called *The Power of Limits* and describes the proportions of examples of art, nature and architecture geometrically: every leaf, butterfly wing, human body, pyramid, shell, Stonehenge, countless paintings etc. etc. He has shown how mathematically harmonious almost everything that God and Man have produced. Not a new concept, but beautifully illustrated.

I lunched with Cecily, Nora's daughter, who is a beautiful and strong – an admirable person. I will describe Cecily later in this diary.

She is married to Axel Corti who is a famous film and opera director in Europe. He is attractive, very bright, high-powered and I would think impossible to live with. They have three sons: Sebastian and Severin – twins aged 18 – and Caspar, aged 15. All are over 6'3' and infinitely polite and charming. They sat paralysed throughout lunch because Axel is so critical of them and corrects them if they open their mouths. They get bellowed at if they close or open a door. I think we must borrow them and Axel can have ours for a bit. That would fix 'em!

Cecily Corti

Sinopoli conducted Verdi's *Macbeth* at the Opera House. Mara Zampieri is one of Brigitte's favourite mezzo sopranos, and I can hear why. She has a unique untamed wildness about her voice which is very powerful and beautiful.

128

ABOVE: *Anthony Clarke in 1958.*
LEFT: *The author aged 12.*
TOP: *My Auntie Vera, my granny and my mother,*
"Moo", aged four, in 1915.

ABOVE: *B and Jim with a piece of the Defiant aircraft in which he was shot down near Canterbury.*
RIGHT: *B.*
OPPOSITE: *Jim in Aunt Doods's hat, 1963.*
(Photograph: Murray Crawford)

RIGHT: *B and Jessica,*
1967. (Photograph: James
Fox)
BELOW: *Jessica, 1967.*
(Photograph: James Fox)
OPPOSITE TOP:
Beezy upon hearing about
the Wall Street crash.
(Photograph: James Fox)
OPPOSITE BOTTOM:
Beezy and Jessica, 1967.
(Photograph: James Fox)

Jessica and Bundy. (Photograph: James Fox)

TOP LEFT: *Jessica and Prospero: I had two sons and I told my nine-year-old Jess that if my fourth child was another boy, she could have him.*

TOP RIGHT: *Jess in Raymond Dart's top hat, taken by her future husband John Clarke when she was 15.*

OPPOSITE TOP LEFT: *Beezy looking creamy, 1972.*

OPPOSITE TOP RIGHT: *Bundy and Bimble, 1976.*

OPPOSITE BOTTOM: *Prospero dressed as Ganymede for Monkeyboy's christening.*

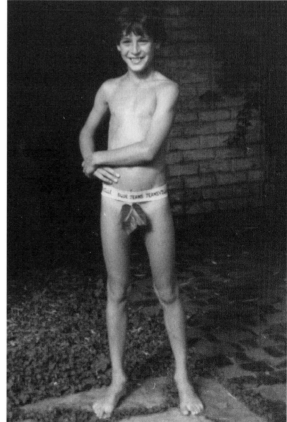

TOP: *B and her brood, 1977. Jess appears to be searching for lice.*
RIGHT: *Bailey family in hunting garb, 1979. (Photograph: Murray Crawford)*

TOP: *The jacket.*
RIGHT: *B and Clint.*

Malcolm Nay and Jess, 1988.

TOP: *Three generations at Jessica's wedding, 1985.*
BOTTOM: *Prospero, Bundy, Beezy, Jim and B at Jessica's wedding.*

TOP: *Bridget and Francis Orr-Ewing being throttled by Jim.*
BOTTOM: *Thomas Packenham and B at Thomas's book launch.*

TOP: *Pixie (Frederick) singing carols with B, 1989.*
BOTTOM: *Peter Townsend, Marie-Luce Townsend, B and Jim.*
OPPOSITE TOP: *Leaving Linden Gardens for Buckingham Palace - Jim's fly was being yanked into the middle. Try this while walking at a brisk pace.*
OPPOSITE BOTTOM: *Jim and Imogen, 1995.*

TOP: *B's birthday treat at King's College – with Emma and Steven Cleobury and Alexander and Max Baillie.*
BOTTOM: *Jim's 9th/75th birthday.*
OPPOSITE TOP: *B and Jim.*
OPPOSITE BOTTOM: *Jim learning heel and toe at his 9th/77th birthday.*

OPPOSITE TOP: *Life-long friends – Jamie Stormonth-Darling and Jim, both aged 78, at Lednathie in the Highlands, 1997.*
OPPOSITE BOTTOM: *Jim searching for a book, 1999.*
RIGHT: *Joan Berning keeping B warm on Murray Crawford's balcony, 1999.*
BELOW: *Imogen far too big for Jim to hold, 1999.*

RIGHT: *Prospero, Anna, Irene Menell and B at Prospero and Anna's wedding party, 2000.*
BELOW: *Jim at the river. (Photograph: Harold Gess)*
OPPOSITE TOP: *Prospero with Jim days before he died, 2000.*
OPPOSITE BELOW: *Jess and Beezy tenderly bidding their farewell.*

B in 2004 at Arthur's Seat looking over Edinburgh. (Photograph: Colette Douglas-Home)

In the foyer there was a notice saying that the bass was indisposed and that Nikolai Ghiaurov was taking his place. How lucky can I get? I had only heard his recordings and always longed to hear him.

10 May 1985 London

Beezy and I heard Murray Perahia play the Schumann with Sir Georg Solti and the London Philharmonic Orchestra at the Royal Festival Hall. I went to the rehearsal in the morning and Solti behaved like Hitler. He was awful – rude and really nasty to the strings. But his wizardry certainly works. Beezy was hypnotised. They did the Brahms 1ˢᵗ symphony and it was ravishing.

Most of the orchestral musicians I know find Solti unpleasant. Someone in the Philharmonia said they would open a case of champagne when he died. Is it rare to find such incredible talent and such wonderful wonderful music-making by such a person?

In a rather roundabout way, it is thanks to Isaac Stern, that John Amis and I saw the biggest firework display ever held in Britain.

It was the anniversary of VE Day and John had interviewed Isaac Stern in the afternoon. Stern had said he was very worried about his Royal Festival Hall concert, because the St Louis Orchestra, with whom he was due to perform the Mendelssohn E minor violin concerto, hadn't arrived from the States yet for the rehearsal. If they were late for the performance as well, then they would be competing with the fireworks display at 9.30 pm just outside the RFH on a barge on the Thames.

The orchestra arrived so late that they had practically no time to rehearse and the concert started late. John and I took advantage of the mishap and went out to enjoy the fireworks. It was thrilling. When the big rockets went up, the immense crowd went Oooooo! on a sustained rising note, and when the showers of stars fell down out of the sky, the crowd went Ahhhhh! on a falling note. People were jammed like sardines all along the banks of the river so I held

John's hand and his huge bulk made a path for me to walk behind him when we left.

The Festival Hall audience waited rather impatiently for over an hour for the din outside to cease in order to hear Isaac Stern. He was well worth it.

23 MAY 1985
Extract from Beezy's letter from London:

"Dearest Children and Hildegard, Jack Allen and the Magic Iron Dog, presents the forthcoming letter:
HELLO . . . Today I went to the Bacon exhibition at the Tate, a retrospective of over 150 paintings. Never have I seen such a powerful expression of paint in my life. I felt, at my reflection in the glass over the paintings, that I was in a fish tank looking out at another world, the depths of my soul screamed and all I could do was cry. Thank God for the real painters. How profound it is for a human – an old drunken queen, a reclusive weirdo – to produce such magic.
There was nothing in meeting him, there is quite often nothing in meeting famous people. Fame, after all, is a social illusion. He was just another person, very unhealthy, very intelligent, but to think he has this extraordinary gift with which to express his existence – that is exceptional.
There would be no point in trying to see him again, there is little or nothing left for words – all he can teach me is in his work."

31 AUGUST 1985
Jess married John Clarke in the barn here on the farm. About a fortnight before the wedding, Angela Lloyd asked me what I was going to wear. I told her I didn't know and wasn't actually thinking about it at all. I certainly wouldn't wear a dress! She insisted that I had beautiful trousers made and personally drove me to Nushka, a designer of repute and magical maker of clothes. It was a bit like taking our cat to the vet. I wasn't at all at ease. Nushka was so charming and wooed me into not minding quite so much. Angela chose the material and had it lined with silk.

I borrowed a cream silk shirt from my mother – who, I must add, never wears trousers so there were none to borrow.

Jess designed her own wedding-dress, mediaeval in style, as well as those of the flower girls. They all looked enchanting. Henrietta Hawson, Susie Dresner and Alexandra von Höne wore pale coffee-coloured sprigged smocks. All wore cream satin ballet slippers. Very countrified it was. Susie looked like a Botticelli.

Bundy asked me what he should wear. The others knew exactly what they would wear. Beezy hand-painted a silk shirt and jacket for the occasion; Prospero wore Bundy's Eton tail-coat with a loud candy-striped shirt. Bundy wore a smart pale-blue seersucker suit and borrowed a neckerchief from me.

Jess and John and their bridesmaids – Henri, Alex and Suzie

I was singing with the SABC Chamber Choir so I had a wonderful view of the wedding standing next to the hay-bale altar, instead of being part of the congregation.

Alan Solomon played Bach *Partitas* before the service. Lucky Jess and John having a violinist of that calibre playing for their wedding!

I had phoned Lanseria Airport and begged them not to have the Impala Jets flying over our farm during the ceremony, because we were recording the whole service. They complied.

Prospero and Bundy had filled the Land Cruiser with masses of buddleia picked from the sloot at Mooiplaats. With buddleia and plum-blossom we decorated the altar of hay-bales. The scent was heavenly. I had a team of angelic women friends who came and arranged all the flowers the day before. Barbie Lindop came early on the actual wedding day to fit Jessica's wreath of spring flowers which Barbie herself had made.

Jim dressed in Papa's clothes for the wedding

Every article of Jim's clothing belonged to my father, and he looked very handsome and good. I appointed no less than three people to make certain that he dressed in the clothes that I had prepared for him on the bed. It would have been very dicey if he'd been left to choose his own outfit. The dressers also saw to it that he was escorted in good time to the white-beribboned Land Cruiser, in which he and the bride were driven to the barn by Bundy.

Jim normally hated formal occasions, but he led Jessica up the aisle with great pride, and then stood alone at the front of the congregation with his feet together throughout the entire service. He was blithely unaware of hundreds of our friends sitting on the hay-bales behind him. He played his part of father-of-the-bride very earnestly.

At the end of the service, when he should have taken the arm of the groom's mother to accompany her out of the barn, he put his arm round my mother and walked her out along the aisle. We sang them out to a 13th century Allelujah accompanied by a tambourine. Jess chose Bach and Purcell and Orlando Gibbons to be sung.

Jess and her tall groom escorted by Maria Skosana and Lizzie Mafatle and our school children

The responsibilities of organising the wedding were many: flowers, marquee, seating, altar, choir, a horse-drawn coach, catering, the dance-band – and Jim. Jim was an exhausting 'job' because he so often disappeared at the crucial moment – usually to his library, but sometimes it was onto the farm, or elsewhere.

Our farm school children escorted the bridal pair from their horse-drawn coach up to the marquee, singing and dancing, wearing paper-flower garlands made by my mother.

Ready to leave

Abigail Kubeka sang wonderfully with drums and guitar while everyone lunched and then danced.

A press photographer asked me why every time she tried to take a photo of our three sons, they always jumped up in the air. The reason was that Beezy and Bundy were damned if they were going to let their 6'4" baby brother appear taller than they were in any photo. So every time a camera was aimed at them either Bundy or Beezy would be in the middle and lift himself high above the other two by hoisting himself up on their shoulders. The press lady was understandably puzzled.

Prospero, Bundy, Beezy – the three jumping boys

At about 4.30 pm the bridal pair left in the horse-drawn coach and soon afterwards the weather huffed and puffed and blew and grew into the first rain of the season. Lightning caused a huge power failure so that the disco that Beezy had organised to play had to be scrapped. The storm lasted so long that everyone had left by 5 pm. As the wedding had started at 11 am, and they would have danced on into

133

the night, I was very relieved to have no electricity, and went and collapsed on my bed.

September 1985

Quotes from a letter from me to Jim:

"I have a hollow ache in the pit of my stomach because you would love to be here so very much. What I find almost unbearable is, having caught a 2lb fish, I then expect to run to you wherever you are – and how I love to see you casting purposefully somewhere along the river – and show you my catch and be kissed and congratulated. And there is a mist and rain and the grass is slippery, great bunchy rich grass, and wild-flowers to make one's heart leap, and birds to make one's soul sing and such a sky in the evening.

It rained all day until about 5 pm and then suddenly the clouds were all swept away and the sun shone on a green hill with cows grazing. The water was as still as a mirror with pink clouds and spurwing geese, and hadedas, and stone-chats, and so much happening in the sky. The light was magic. The whole world was like a rainbow that had been absorbed by the wet air everywhere.

Then the steam rose from the water. And, as the sun went down, the first thrilling rise appeared. In the next half hour, I had three big fish on my fly, each for about a minute or two. The barb came off on one. But then I landed one – the 2-pounder – sitting in my waders on the pier to net it, praying to it, cajoling it, talking sweetly to it all the while, and lo, I landed it. And you weren't there! Anyway I stomped up to the house in the dark with freezing hands, cold so that I was shivering – and there was a roaring fire and a hot drink. Oh Squeezie what heaven! What is the use of going to bed when I've caught a trout and there is no Squeeze to cuddle and go on and on about how it happened.

How's that

134

I took another this morning. First cast and wham, it turned and took the fly as it hit the water. I only have to catch one more and I'll have enough for Pilly's birthday dinner. She wants trout and strawberries."

28 OCTOBER 1985
Extract from Beezy's letter from England:

"... I pass through cold misty landscapes of the English countryside while South Africa is on every page of every newspaper every day, and in each TV and radio broadcast. People are led to believe that all will be solved by sanctions, it is frightening to what extent the media has power. What progress has Jim's efforts for leaders to meet made? Surely it should tie in with the Commonwealth Peace Mission — something which I feel has little hope.

I met a very interesting artist who came to the school. Jazz musician, printmaker, painter and performer. Very inspiring and he came and gave me a tutorial afterwards, liked my work and very wisely suggested I should try repeating an image, so I can take it one step further and see what happens. He says I should tell people who tell me to channel in on one form of expression to fuck off. Picasso showed us that that is not so, it is also totally against my nature, all very well – but I find eternity in every medium, making it difficult enough to work anyway.

Pork[24] is having a whale of a time[25] and my belief that he'll grow into a fine young man is starting to happen. He's presently dirtying his hands on Patrick's farm.

We are having a Halloween party on Friday night for which I am going to make the masks. They want me to go on TV as an art student on an art quiz. If I do, I can imagine making a major balls-up. I am trying to find a florescent shocking-pink satin suit, which I can silk-screen to match my hair, which in

---

24 Prospero
25 at Bryanston School in Dorset

the near future is being dyed ultra violet, when it washes out pink, when it washes out green, etc."

9 NOVEMBER 1985

Bundy is 20 today. We celebrated his birthday dining at the Hertford – Jess and John, Jeremy and Sandra (Prinsloo), Bundy and me. I love John more every time we meet. Sad not having Jim with us, he is somewhere in Africa.

6 DECEMBER 1985

Jim and I, the Clarkes and Frank Berry, our doctor, went fishing at Driehoek. Mrs Clarke is pregnant. She wee-weed in an ashtray and Frank tested it and – yippee!

On Sunday the wind was high, water-ruffled, and Frank made a drogue out of a plastic bucket and it worked a treat. With a red setter I took five big ones in Loch Fillan.

3 FEBRUARY 1986

Extracts from Beezy's letter from Moscow:

> "I learnt more last week than any other week, about life – and art. The similarities between Russia and South Africa are vast. Same rulers, same police, same oppression, but the South Africans are free spirits. I encountered none here.

> The beauty of Leningrad knocked me down, like an endless Florence. The grandeur explains the reason for the revolution. The art collections put London's to shame. I managed to salvage from a mass of images, some basic rules of picture-making that are in common with the icons, Picasso, Matisse . . . "

This was the position of the members of our family this day. Jim was on a *Drum* trip and was in London for a few days. Beezy was at the Byam Shaw Art School and was staying in our flat in Notting Hill Gate, with Jim. Prospero was doing his first term A levels at Bryanston School in Dorset. Jess and John were living at Mooiplaats, our farm nearby.

Alaric, who had been away at school since he was 12, had decided to do a BA at Wits University so that he could live at home for a while. Unlike Jessica and Beezy, he had no idea what he wanted to do in life, so for the time being he decided that a general BA reading History of Art, English, History of Music etc. would be fun. It would be a combined effort. I would help on the music and art and Jim would write some of the English essays – hoping for better marks than he got when he wrote them for me when I was at school.

We had great fun finding relevant books for his courses in Jim's library, and on Friday Bundy went off to Wits to get his timetable, starting on Monday. He and I had been alone together on the farm for 10 days. He had been very sulky with me. He'd recently left his love, Claire in Durban and had chosen to come back to live on the farm while he was at Wits. He was so moody and bad-tempered that I had a Big Talk to him, explaining that I couldn't help not being Claire and if he were going to live at home, he was to be pleasant about it. Thenceforward he was a pleasure and we enjoyed each other's company.

Every morning it was his wont to come across the courtyard when he woke, and climb into bed with me where we would have several cups of tea together before we started the day. He loved Bach and he had been lying on the sofa the evening before, listening to me playing the G Major French suite, and he said, "Play it again, Bar. I love it".

On Friday night I went to bed leaving his food in the warming oven. It wasn't that late but I enjoy reading in bed, so I didn't give him another thought. He had spent the months between writing his A levels at Eton in June and the start of the University term in South Africa in February working at the stock-exchange. With his earnings he bought an old red convertible Alfa Romeo Spider, which needed work on it. He and our farm manager were going to spend the weekend fixing it.

The police came to my mother at about 9.30 pm on Friday night. There had been an envelope in Bundy's car with my mother's address on it. On his way home the steering wheel had come clean off and he was killed instantly.

I knew nothing of it until about 7.30 am on Saturday when I went in my pyjamas to the kitchen to make our usual pot of tea. I saw my brother Richard's car parked outside and in it were Richard, his wife Jenny, my mother, and our beautiful doctor, Lesley Wentworth. Bundy had always tried to be ill enough so that he could see Lesley Wentworth – alas he didn't get round to it.

My first thought when I saw them was whether I had enough bacon for their breakfast? I was excited and pleased to see them as Richard hardly ever came to the farm. I didn't suspect anything untoward because Jenny sometimes brought her Girl Guides out on a farm project. So I thought they'd made a party of it.

When I ran barefoot in my pyjamas to greet them, Richard was out of the car first, white and silent – he was normally flushed and grinning. I ran into his arms.

"What is it?" He shook his head and couldn't speak.

"Bundy, is it Bundy?" He nodded.

"Is he dead?" He nodded.

I remained with my arms round his neck, hanging on to him while the others followed us into the house.

I said, "Thank God he's not maimed. Thank God."

Jim had described his knees knocking in the cockpit of his Hurricane on his first scramble. Until then he had believed the expression to be figurative. My knees were bruised black and blue for about a week. When I sat, Richard held one knee and Lesley the other and I had no control over them whatsoever. If they let go, the knees went klonk klonk of their own accord and it really hurt.

Shock is weird. My first reaction was to act the hostess and offer tea and breakfast. Then I sat at the piano and played Richard's favourite Bach gigue that he made me play every time he saw me. I couldn't help myself. I also began to shake and couldn't stop.

Richard offered to do everything there was to do. Besides Jessica, the only ones I wanted to phone were Jim and Beezy. Thank God Jim was in the London flat with Beezy. He might have been somewhere in Africa and out of communication for weeks.

Jim flew home that night.

I told Beezy to make sure he was with Prospero when he was told. I didn't want to tell Prospero at all. He was 17. It was his first term away from home in England. I spoke to his housemaster, who was kind and wise. I suggested we didn't tell Prospero until the end of term in three weeks' time, so that he could finish his work and not have the shock and horror of the news. His housemaster said he must be with me now, and me with him, and he would put him on the next plane, and that the next three weeks did not matter in the least. He could make up the work next term. I asked the housemaster to allow Beezy to break the news to him personally.

That night Beezy and Prospero slept in each others' arms before flying home the next day.

Richard offered to identify Bundy and told me it was better for me not to see him. Too damaged he was. Richard took on all the arrangements and protected me in every way he could.

At the memorial service the family sat in the front of the church with no pew to lean on so we sat on the floor in a heap, holding each other. Jessica played the sarabande from Bach's 5th cello suite for Bundy. She was barefoot. She played superbly and then collapsed.

I was in no state to think what music to have at the service, but Richard and Susie Cock and many members of the chamber choir sang, and quite a few musicians from the orchestra played. The oboist had a broken arm in plaster, yet he came and somehow managed to play.

It was curious, but I could sing the hymns. It turned into a festival of love. I felt buoyed up by the warmth of our friends.

Ingrid von Hone, in her huge generosity, gave a get-together at her house after the service, making lovely eats. She did adore Bundy.

This is all nearly 19 years ago and it is the first time I have written about it – or thought about it in such detail. Not easy, no I am not over it. No. When I started to write about Bundy's death, what I wanted to write was how valiant my mother was. She was told by the police coming to call on her on Friday night. She told them on no account to contact me. Bundy was dead, I couldn't help him – I must be allowed to sleep the night and she would tell me when I woke.

It is a strict rule in our family never to impart bad news of any sort at night. Sleep is essential before dealing with problems. In this case it was remarkably selfless and thoughtful of my mother to keep it from me. She told Richard and they together planned how they would be present to support me next morning.

Extract from Prospero's letter from Bryanston, Dorset, September 1985
" … I have problems working. I am so utterly devastated by the Bundy affair. When the shock wears off I miss him. Half my life seems to have gone with him. We were so close and had no need for verbal communication. I can't stand it sometimes. I see his face at night when I roll over and I go mad!"

Beezy, who was 24 at this time, held us and kept us all afloat. He was so philosophical and wise in his attitude to Bundy's death, and he proved a tower of strength to me.

Bundy's ashes were delivered to the farm in a little cardboard box. That evening Jim drove home with Prospero. They had bought a crate of drinks. I had hidden the box of ashes in the drink cupboard and Jim was calling Prospero to carry the drinks in and put them away.

I didn't want Prospero to see the box, so I sat at the piano and played Beethoven and insisted that Prospero should come and sit with me and listen. He explained that he must help Jim with the drinks. It took a lot of sign language to Beezy to go and help Jim. I so wanted to protect Prospero, and he thought I had gone nuts with my Beethoven. It was comical in its way.

We took the ashes up to a place near our sacred tree on Mooiplaats, and Beezy held my arm in his muscular warmth and we flung the ashes together in a wide sweep over the veld grasses and indigenous bush that we all love so deeply.

Then Jessica, Beezy and Prospero collected some biggish well-worn rocks from round about, and made a little cairn. This was not planned, it was extempore, and it is still there. Jim was not part of this little ceremony. I think it was too much for him – he declined. Bundy's cairn is in the centre of a Stone Age circle with a very low crumbling stone wall.

Years later when Prospero and I were at Gloucester station together, he said, "I hate this station. This is where I waited for two bloody hours for Beezy to come and tell me that our brother was dead."

I am superstitious, mostly thanks to Benny who had a huge fund of complicated rituals which have certainly rubbed off on me. I still feel I have to worry about someone to keep them safe.

Eighteen years later I read aloud about Bundy's death to a creative writing workshop. I couldn't finish reading. I told Beezy about the evening at the writers' workshop, and asked him about how he reacted when I told him of Bundy's death. It is the first time we have ever really talked about it. Two points that I found most interesting were firstly, that when I phoned him in the flat in London and told him the news, his knees knocked. Secondly, after he and Prospero had spent the night weeping in each other's arms and were on the train back to London in order to fly home, Beezy had a moment, a flash of normality, which in his case, is joy. And he decided at that moment that he had to hold on to this joy and take it back to us all. That is whence his strength came and which he gave to us.

Beezy also told me that when he told Jim, who was in the London flat with him, Jim's eyes brimmed and he paced round and round the flat. He couldn't speak about it.

APRIL 1986 PLETT

It is six weeks after Bundy died and we are at Bimble's House, our house in Plett. Jessica is pregnant and lives in her pumpkin suit. Everyone is so kind to us. It is sore. So sore. I feel raw, peeled, like a naked nerve. I dread seeing almost everyone.

Beezy brought with him Camilla Battis. I didn't know her before but she proved to be gentle, thoughtful and sensitive and it was a pleasure to have her in the house. There were more young girls staying that I wished were not.

I had a phone call from a friend who was sailing his yacht round the Cape and was due in Plett. the next day. He had a girlfriend with him and he asked if he could spend a few nights with us. There were nine in the house for starters and I didn't want more. I told him we had a full house. He said not to worry, they had sleeping bags and rucksacks and they would camp on the floor of the living room. I said it wasn't a good time. They came.

About 7.30 every morning before anyone else was up and about, Jess would check that the coast was clear, and I would creep out and go down along the beach, up some stone steps and into Dries and Sandra Botha's bed where I would snuggle up and be cared for and where no demands were made. What friends they are!

The thought of every meal with a party of people was beyond me.

I will treasure for always what Jessica did for me. One afternoon the yachtsman came into my bedroom to chat. I was lying reading on my bed – Jim had gone back to the farm – and Jess passed by just as I was telling the yachtsman that I really did not want to see anyone in my room. Jess suddenly started screaming at him, "Get out! Get out of my mother's room! Leave her alone for God's sake!" – and more that wasn't polite. Really yelling like a banshee she was. She was like a tigress protecting me. Normally Jess is quietly spoken and rarely raises her voice. That she did this on my behalf was one of the most warming and loving experiences of my life.

JUNE 1986 LONDON
I went to Mahler's Symphony 2, *The Resurrection* at the Albert Hall with Beezy and John Amis. Had to be carried out into a taxi and put to bed with hot-water bottles. Mahler is not a good idea at this time. He is emotionally dangerous. I am still missing several layers of skin. Everything is too much for me.

6 AUGUST 1986
Frederick James Alaric Clarke was born to Jessica and John at 6.35 pm. The birth of this baby is so welcome. A new life for us all – what a timely gift.

The syringa trees are still bare and I love to lie under them and see the berries the colour of caramel, against a blameless blue sky. It is one of the many pleasures of our Highveld winter.

1 NOVEMBER 1986
I was to fly to London in the evening and I went in to visit Helen and Mozie Suzman during the morning. Mozie asked me why I was limping. I didn't know why – I had probably banged my leg on something. I wasn't worried about it. Mozie examined my leg and said it was a deep-vein thrombosis and I was to go straight to hospital after he had given me a heparin injection. Do not pass GO and do not collect 200. I said, "I am going to London tonight" and he said, "no you are not,

142

neither are you going home to fetch anything. Someone must bring your things and meet you at the Sandton Clinic."

Thanks to my father being a doctor, I have been given a private ward almost every time I have been hospitalised. There were no private wards available, so I was put in an eight-bedder.

I was in excellent health and I was told to lie on the bed and not walk around. Again I wore Jim's pyjamas, no slippers, no dressing gown. I was ordered not to get up to go to the loo but use a bedpan, and I was surrounded by women who had been together for days, if not weeks.

I rang the bell for the bedpan, no-one came, so I raced to the loo and raced back, and dived onto the bed which collapsed because the base had been raised for my sore leg. I was given absolute hell by the sister in charge of the ward. The other patients were dying to talk about me but their beds were too far apart for any private gossip.

The ward spokesman eventually couldn't keep herself from quizzing me, "So what's wrong with you?"
    "I have a thrombosis in my leg."
    "When's your op?"
    "I'm not having an op. I am just having treatment."
    "This is a surgical ward. You are having an op."
    Silence for a while. Then she told me what operations each person in the ward had had, in detail. She said she had had a gastrectomy. I said, "oh dear."
    She said, "Do you know why?"
    "No."
    "Because my gas tube was too short."

Every morning after breakfast, the spokesman spent at least 45 minutes curling her hair with heated rollers, and making up her face with an assortment of lipsticks, powders, mascara, eye-shadow and goodness knows what. I thought she must have a husband or lover coming, but no-one ever came to see her. Once she had completed her preparations, she sat bolt upright and fell asleep with her mouth wide open, snoring very loudly.

Jess came to visit and we rolled about in fits of giggles.

Two lovely young girls came in one night to have varicosities operated on the next morning. They chatted ceaselessly when they got into their beds. The spokesman said, "You had better do all your laughing now, because you won't be laughing tomorrow."

Opposite me was a 93-year-old granny, who, the spokesman said, was dying. The first night I spent there confirmed this. Doctors were in and out all night, screens were placed round her bed, various drips and cylinders were brought in, and altogether it was impossible for me to get any sleep at all. I did not know about the others. In the morning, I suggested to the sister in charge that it would be more thoughtful to put someone terminally ill in a private ward to die. It was not very encouraging for the rest of the patients. In the morning they did wheel Granny out to a private ward.

Her daughter, aged about 65, arrived from Durban. The rest of the patients in the ward knew her and said what a shame it was about Granny. She told them that the family were on their way up on the Greyhound bus for the funeral. There was general commiseration but considering Granny's age, it was all for the best etc.

At lunchtime, Granny sat up and consumed no less than three plates of soup!

I will never opt for a private ward again. I wouldn't have missed this for anything.

Christmas 1986 – Where are Jim's trousers?

CHRISTMAS DAY 1986
In our Nativity Play, four-and-a-half-month-old Frederick played Joseph dressed in a white nightie, a Harrington square on his head with tinsel as the headband. Monkeyboy, our cat, took the part of baby Jesus asleep in the manger, which was a doll's cot. Beezy, wrapped in a blue tablecloth, was Mary.

While Prospero was filming the scene, Monkeyboy jumped out of the doll's cot. Prospero giving the commentary, added, "And the Christchild jumped out of the manger – the first Miracle!"

I sat and worked the wind-up gramophone and Beezy in a top hat, tails and floral shorts, with Boogeyman, our dear friend Rowan Torr dressed in the family tutu with a rose between his teeth, performed a very hectic tango. Rowan is a beloved friend and an hilarious addition to our family antics, which he enjoys whole-heartedly.

JANUARY 1987
Clyde Berning, aged six, said to his mother Joan, "I don't know whether to go and play with Jim or go and play with Kevin [aged five]." More music to Jim's ears.

Jim said that the Bernings cannot go to heaven, they are in heaven already. Their farm must be one of the most beautiful sites on earth.

APRIL 1987
Beezy had an excellent exhibition at Karen Mc-Kerron's gallery. He took an entourage of eight farm schoolchildren with him. They were bare to their waists and Beezy had painted colourful designs on their bodies. Beezy wore Jim's mother's bowler hat which she had worn hunting. On either side of it he had tied real vultures wings and had painted them in vivid colours. Lady Mary Bailey would have writhed around in her grave like a lathe if she could have seen it. His outfit was a Beezy humdinger, Ndebele apron etc. Mary Slack opened the exhibition and in all it was a very good evening.

Mary Slack opening Beezy's exhibition – he's wearing Lady Bailey's bowler with vulture wings

In March he had a successful show in Cape Town.

145

I spent about 14 hours in total listening to Sinopoli rehearsing the Mahler 2nd with the Vienna Symphony Orchestra. It is still an emotionally draining experience but hearing it being worked like this helped me grow really familiar with it, and not react so violently to it.

I went to the actual performance with Lili Schoenberg and she cried before I did. She invited me to her flat on the Schwartzenbergplatz where we played duets, one of which was the Schubert F minor Fantasia. Lili told me that Schubert had dedicated this work to her great-grandmother and great-grand aunt. They were the Esterhazy princesses, Schubert's pupils.

She so enjoyed playing with me and I suggested to her that she played with Gordon Murray with whom I was staying. She said she would never dare ask Nikolaus Harnoncourt's harpsichordist, and a professor from the Hochschule to play with her! When I told Gordon that Lili Schoenberg would be so glad if he'd play duets with her, he said he wouldn't dare suggest playing duets with a princess.

Such is Vienna snobbery. And because I am South African I cannot be slotted and therefore have the pleasure of playing with both of them. I thank God.

Brigitte took me to Durnstein where Richard Coeur de Lion was imprisoned. Durnstein is made of shiny black and treacherously sharp rocks pointing up from the Danube, looking like an illustration out of a frightening Grimms brothers story. The Danube is wide and fast-flowing there, and Russian barges passed us bearing coal. Next time I am in Vienna, Brigitte suggested that we go by boat to Budapest which is only three hours from Vienna.

Nikolaus Harnoncourt with his baroque band, Concentus Musicus, did Handel's *Te Deum for the Peace of Utrecht* and three Purcell anthems I went to all the rehearsals. The counter-tenor was completely bald and when I told John Amis about a 'boiled egg' singing beautifully, he laughed and said, "That's Christopher Robson. He's not bald, he had to shave his head to be in John Cage's minimalist opera, *Akhnaten*." Harnoncourt electrifying as usual. I adore him.

146

Cecily Corti had a dinner party where I met Fritz Molder. He was sentenced to death by Hitler and spent many years in prison. He was in the Foreign Office in Vienna when Kurt Waldheim applied for his first job – wearing lederhosen!

JULY 1987
Prospero and Jim went to the Ogilvie-Thompson's shoot at Rooipoort without me.

They shared a room, and Jim brought out a book he had with him. It was Chairman Mao's *Little Red Book*. He gave Prospero a wry smile and muttered something about it being an antidote to their present surroundings. "I think it's appropriate reading," said he.

4 OCTOBER 1987
Jim purchased Tweefontein, a game-farm near Monaghan, and 12 of us celebrated there with a feast of freshly-caught trout, and strawberries and cream.

We saw eland, zebra, ostrich, hartebeest, impala, and fold upon fold of hills and thick indigenous bush and it is beautiful – beautiful, and it is ours!

22 NOVEMBER 1987
Michael Snyman, Jessica and Albie van Schalkwyk played the Mendelssohn D minor trio to raise funds for Michael to study in Vienna. It was a huge success and Michael is off to learn with Gerard Schultz, the 2nd violin in the Alben Berg Quartet. All thanks to Brigitte Zaczek who heard Michael play and because she teaches at the Hochshule. She arranged everything for him.

DECEMBER 1987
Prospero brought Woo Dick-Read and Mark Freeman with him from England to spend the Plett. holiday with us. There were seven males and me. They ate enormously.

The sea was warm and clear and Jim speared eight mullet one morning off Beacon Island rocks, and almost every day we had fresh fish for breakfast. I do wish he wouldn't put his freshly shot fish inside his wetsuit. He then comes and lies on the bed with me with scales on his chest, smelling of fish.

Dominique Botha and I made friends with three spear-fishermen on a rock below Murray Crawford's castle. They asked if Jim represented the Transvaal at spear-fishing. Yet more music to his ears.

Suddenly we had a huge party – about 70 people. It started at 6 pm and they left at about 2 am. Tony Berman looked interesting in Beezy's gold lamé cocktail frock and his black high-heeled Voortrekker shoes. I bought these shoes for Beezy at the Vryberg cattle sale. Simon Wilson, Prospero and Woo were with us at Vryberg. The minute I saw the shoes I knew they were for Beezy. Simon, who also takes size 9, offered to try them on for Beezy, removed his huge trainers, kept his thick football socks on, and tried them. The salesman was open-mouthed. So were all the people, black and white, that had gathered to watch.

Beezy in his gold lamé

That cattle sale was memorable for the fact that it was the only time Jim has struck me. We had flown from Lanseria in a six-seater plane and I felt so ill that when we came in to land at Vryberg, I looked down at a graveyard and felt I would have preferred to be under one of the tombstones.

At the cattle sale, it was terribly hot, boring, and lasted seemingly forever. It was held in a sales ring and some pigeons flew over fairly low, and I took aim, as it were, with an imaginary shotgun. Jim hit me hard on my arm. I immediately burst into tears. I had been dreading the plane journey home and it was all I needed to set me off. Jim apologised profusely and explained that he was only preventing me from bidding for 40 awful-looking cattle that were circling the ring.

148

Back in Plett the Kingwills came to stay, and we took Dominique Botha, aged 13, and Paula and Doë Kingwill, much the same age, up the river in a boat for a picnic. We were swimming in the middle of the river and I told them to pretend to drown when boats came past, to see if we could alarm the boatmen. The girls were giggling and 'drowning' alternately. A boat chugged towards us and Dominique was heard to yell at Doë, who always reacts very slowly, "Drown, you stupid arse!" They are all in their first year at supposedly smart girls' schools. So much for teaching them to be Young Ladies.

JANUARY 1988
Jess has been asked to lead the cellos in the Transvaal Chamber Orchestra. She is enjoying it more than she thought she would.

14 MARCH 1988
Beezy had his show in Cape Town where he painted the entire exhibition during the opening in front of TV cameras and it was a success.

Prospero and Woo went off to the Virgin Islands where they are working as waiters at the Last Resort, which is a much sought-after restaurant situated on an island of its own. Prospero earns extra by collecting the garbage off American yachts that are anchored in the bay. He arrives in a little rowing boat and they have no option but to pay him whatever he charms them into handing over. He has earned enough to go and visit Venezuela with Barnaby Logan.

Excerpt from Prospero's letter from the Virgin Islands:

"The Last Resort is very hard work, which I am enjoying. Every third morning at 8 am I do the garbage run which involves taking a small boat to all the yachts in Trellis Bay and charging Americans extortionate amounts to remove their trash.

I have done the garbage this morning . . . I've learnt to suss out exactly at what point to break the news that the service is not free so that it's too late to give the trash back. It varies, but the people fall into categories and there are lots of little quirks that I play on. Sometimes I give an arrogant chuckle when they refuse to pay thus embarrassing the tight bastard . . .

. . . The American people are so much friendlier, easier and more outgoing than the Poms we get in here. The Governor [of the Islands] came last night. What a nermal. He made very sure we all knew he was the Governor.

Please find me a place to stay in France that is very very beautiful – in deep country – no grape-picking – beautiful daughters – good cook etc."

MAY 1988 ENGLAND

James Fox and I drove to Oxfordshire to see Bruce Chatwin who is so terribly ill. He looks even more beautiful being so thin that the bone structure of his face is hauntingly visible. He hardly has the strength to talk, but is still amusing and was very excited about my speaking to the composer, Kevin Volans.

He telephoned Kevin in Ireland and handed me the phone. Bruce was insistent that we should meet each other, and raved about Kevin, and played me a tape of the music he has written for Bruce. Bruce miming ecstasy, eyes to the heavens, gasping, shaking his head slowly from side to side while we listened to the tape. When I was leaving, he pulled me to him. I kissed him on the lips and he whispered, "I'm HIV positive." This was early days for AIDS and he had tried to keep it secret until very recently.

24 MAY 1988

On the morning of Beezy's exhibition in London, the telephone rang and a foreign voice asked for Beezy, who was still asleep, so I asked if I might give him a message. It was Ziggy, the milliner who said, "I am finishing Beezy's hat. Ask Beezy if he would like 3/4 inch bells, which sound like this: (ting-a-ling) . . . or 1 inch bells, which sound like this: (pling-a-ling) . . ." I chose the sound I preferred and a little later, Ziggy arrived on a bicycle wearing a very dashing panama which he had fashioned into a sort of boater, and a pair of yellow braces. He had a charming delicacy and lightness of touch. He brought Beezy's hat, which was a blue-and-yellow tricorn jester's hat with the 3/4 inch bells.

I asked Beezy wasn't it very expensive and he said yes, but he is bartering it for a painting. Ziggy chose his painting, bade us farewell and rode off down Linden Gardens with the painting tied to his basket.

We all walked to the exhibition, my 77-year-old mother on Beezy's arm, and he in his tricorn hat, and a flowing gold cloak.

He had organised a wonderful opening at Vanessa Devereux's gallery. Eliot and his Zulu Dancers leapt about and beat tom-toms outside the gallery on kelims spread out on the pavement. Blenheim Crescent had been

Beezy and Granny at his Notting Hill exhibition

blocked off for the occasion, and a big crowd of guests were enjoying themselves having their drinks in the road.

Woo arrived having crossed the Pacific in a 52-foot yacht. He was unwashed and unchanged, straight from his expedition.

A pretty little girl of about 10 climbed onto a table in Vanessa's gallery and struck up quite beautifully on her violin. Apparently she lives in Blenheim Crescent and enjoys playing at functions in the area.

In all it was a very lively and successful evening.

Went to Glyndebourne with John Amis. Willard White sang Osmin in Mozart's *Entfürung,* and for me his was the only outstanding voice. The production was charming and I do love Mozart opera – *Entführung* was enchanting.

I took Prospero and Phillida to see Maggie Smith in Peter Schaffer's play, *Lettice and Loveage* which we all adored. Hilarious and brilliant is Maggie Smith.

29 May 1988

Since Bundy died I have frequently had very disturbing dreams about him. Often ghoulish and the effect lasted through the following days. There have been times I have feared to fall asleep. Then last night I dreamt the most wonderful dream. I dreamt I was singing with Richard's Chamber Choir on the fields near the river on Monaghan, and while we sang, a flock of big white birds flew over us. Someone asked me what kind of birds they were. I told them they were European storks. Then one dived low and flew straight past me – and it was Bundy, looking golden and smiling radiantly, more radiantly than he ever did in life. He flew fast and joined the rest of the flock. The sight of him was so vivid and filled with joy.

I knew I would never worry about him again. I have not had any bad dreams about him since.

5 June 1988 Johannesburg

Jess played Couperin's *Pieces en Concert* with Alan Solomon conducting the orchestra. It was superlative and she played flawlessly and looked enchanting in the mushroom pink dress I had bought for her in London. Alan is a genius.

August and September 1988 Monaghan

It is the most beautiful spring I can remember. Early rain, snow on the mountains, crisp and thrilling.

Prospero is in France staying with a family who cannot speak a word of English. At first he was lonely and so frustrated at not being able to gabble that he wrote to me every week. Now I have a letter about every fortnight because he is beginning to speak French more readily. He has learnt most of his French from three-year-old Balthazar because he speaks slowly enough and his vocabulary is suitably limited. I take my chapeau off to Prospero for persevering and not copping out by going to Maxine who is very near by. It must have been so tempting to stay with her and speak English.

He is now fluent enough to sell the vegetables they grow at the local market.

He also ploughed a field with a hand plough, and watched a tractor doing the same job in the neighbouring land. He told me they rarely eat meat because they are not well off enough to buy it. I reckon this is a good year off for him before going to Warwick University. He is using it well.

Extracts from Prospero's letters from France.

". . . on the train from Bordeaux, there is a small French biddy who is giving me poisonous glances from across the carriage bless her. I think it's my feet."

". . . well, it's raining. This means two things: I am not weeding, and my tent is floating around the garden. So, every cloud has a doff lining."

"I planted 800 cabbages in one and a half hours last night. That's 23 minutes faster than the world record set by Carl Philip Emanuel Botha in 1733. I don't think I'll disclose it though – there's bound to be paperwork. It's thundering and just like a day of rain at home. I would so love to be eating sherbet, reading Tintin and lying under the piano while you play."

". . . M Robbins looks like a very fit undisciplined monk and he works like a Duracell battery – all day every day. When we are working on the same piece of land, he talks constantly which is very good for my French, but quite hard work."

"My comprehension of French is improving but so far my ability to talk has met with blank incomprehension on the part of the listener. Still, it's only been two weeks. It seems like a year though.

I'm in the middle of a Herculean task at the moment. I have to cut, dig, rake and move an entire field of peas which have vrekked. Unfortunately I can't see what I'm doing due to hayfever . . . Some bastard who owns the field next door did exactly what I'm doing in one hour with a tractor."

"This French business is really very challenging and I expect very good for me. I find I talk to myself a great deal. The only book I have in English is a 940-page *The Making of the English Working Class*. It is very very heavy-going but a good desert island book. All the food on the island would run out before one finished it." [In preparation for reading History at Warwick University.]

"Last week I went to help Frances . . . She also does someone's garden in Villeneuve on Thursdays. We arrived at this hideous nouveau-Spanish-villa-vomit-maison-dream mit swimming pool and toys of all kinds all over the place. The man, who looks like Mr Ruck, appeared and directed us to the back of the house, treating us like servants, which we were. It felt quite weird. He gave me a weed-eater and pointed me in the direction of a hedge, which I began to demolish. Unfortunately the weed-eater promptly died on me. Mr Ruck seeing the smoke and hearing the explosion, marched over with rage burning out of his eyes. I shat myself but thought I'd first see what he knew about the machine before blinding him with bluff.

He knew nothing. I suddenly knew everything there was to know about weed-eaters. I knelt next to the smoking ruin and traced various pipes, pushed various knobs, talking very quickly in English all the while, my voice showing contempt for a machine that could break with such ease in the hands of someone as expert and experienced as myself.

It worked. I could see his expression changing from rage to confusion to understanding and eventually as I ripped a pipe off the top of the machine in triumph, to contempt for his machine. I almost laughed out loud with relief.

I handed the pipe with instructions to acquire another and declared the weed-eater unfit for use.

He now had a certain respect for my mechanical knowledge and so became slightly less forbidding. He even offered me the use of his pool while he went off to buy a new pipe. I swam until he returned without the new pipe, thank God. Then on finding that I was South African, he said that when in Mauritius he had had a SA wine which was quite excellent. I told him I thought SA wines were a lot more interesting than French wines – whereupon he frowned and invited us to lunch.

He produced four different bottles of delicious wine and the meal lasted for about three hours at the end of which we were fairly drunk. We had also become firm friends. He asked if I played billiards and I said that I did, and that I loved the game. So he took me into his study where I spent the rest of the afternoon learning French billiards, which is a totally different game from the one I know.

Strange day, arriving as a nervous gardener and ending up drinking his wine in his study."

8-24 SEPTEMBER 1988 MONAGHAN
Pixieboy[26] is staying with us while Jess and John are in London. In spite of having German measles he is angelic. He must be the dearest two-year-old in the world. He only cried once when the Land Cruiser wouldn't start.

Bedmates – Frederick and Brevis

Jim and I took the whole farm school to the circus. It was great fun and they loved it. I drew the pianist while we were there and Jim was paralysed with mirth. She had arms like thighs, a very severe haircut, and her playing matched her appearance.

10 DECEMBER 1988
Prospero came home. I hope he stops growing, he is now 6'4". It is bliss having him back and we all went fishing with Sam. It was heaven. It rained and Beezy lay on one bed and Prospero and Emma Tremlett and I lay on the other bed and talked nonsense and giggled. It was a scene of such sweetness that Beezy said it should be obligatory for Maggie Thatcher, Ronald Reagan and Gorbachov to lie on a bed and giggle and talk rubbish and there would be hope for peace on Earth.

CHRISTMAS EVE 1988
We sang carols at the Hertford and it was very bad except for Barbara and Susan Tom's duet.

26 Jessica's son Frederick

Pixieboy loved opening presents and was very keen for everyone to receive theirs and didn't want them for himself. Later there was a huge cloudburst and we ended up having to move inside and have our Christmas dinner on tables we'd set in the living room near the piano.

In the middle of the meal Gilbert, son of Masilela, arrived covered in blood having been stabbed above the eye. We called an ambulance which magically came fairly promptly, and they took him off to hospital. His own brother Edward had stabbed him. Twenty years ago their father, Masilela, arrived at our front door in a similar state. A sadly alcoholic family.

Jim has asked me to give him some coaching in doing cartwheels. The reason being that 'Countess Mouse' (alias Nadya Botha), his eight-year-old friend, is not impressed with his cartwheels. She phones to make dates with him to meet on the beach to play noughts-and-crosses in the sand, and to practise cartwheels, at which she excels.

Jim received a hand-delivered letter from Nadya Botha which reads:

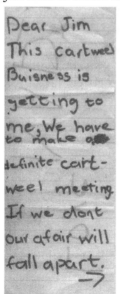

She was very excited to be invited to dinner with us. She arrived wide-eyed with Dominique, her elder sister, and I asked her what her normal bedtime is. She said, "During term-time I go to bed at 8 o'clock."

Her 16-year-old sister exclaimed, "Liar!"

Nadya, the Countess Mouse, smiled sweetly and said, "It doesn't matter."

156

17 FEBRUARY 1989
Imogen Louise Clarke was born.

MARCH 1989
Extracts from a letter from Prospero in Moscow:

"Dear Jim and Bar,

Please forgive me for not writing to you for so long. Lots of excuses spring to mind but I'm not convinced by any of them.

We had the most exciting adventures in Russia . . . I was busy about 20 out of the 24 hours a day, looking and learning and swallowing as much as I could of this other world in the short time I had.

We flew to Moscow where the snow was swarming like bees. Snow makes me very excited. The airport was hideous and frightening – full of intimidatingly dressed soldiers, long grey coats and red and gold stars, unsmiling.

We were hustled onto an iron bus which skidded towards Moscow. There was a full moon, tall, tall pine trees – and ice. The roads are enormous – 16 lanes wide, but we had arrived late and the streets were completely deserted. It was strange not being able to read the road signs, and I felt very far from home. It was cold, there was snow, tramlines, an impossible alphabet, and a feeling that we had flown back into the '50s – the snow covered cars from another age. There was no neon, no litter, no plastic bags to add colour to this moonlight stage-set. God I was excited.

The actors appeared on this set the following day. Moscow is a big busy city. There are 10 million people who dress much like Jim does in London; layers of nylon in various shades of dinge. Everyone wears a hat – either woolly like Jim's or proper fur hats that prove one's in Russia. It is incredibly noisy, as all the trucks and cars seem to have lost their silencers.

We (four from England and one from Iceland) formed our own tour group and decided against joining any of the official bus trips around Moscow offered by Intourist. We used the metro, which is vast and grand, with chandeliers and marble everywhere. It's about three times as deep as the deepest London tube and the escalators move at running pace. It costs a fifth of a pence to anywhere, and the big green trains arrive every minute.

157

Intourist offers tickets to the Circus at £18. We found our way there and bought them for 35p. The Bolshoi is officially £20, we paid £1 for tickets ...

Red Square is beautiful especially with a full orange moon rising behind it. St Basil's – that church that looks like Hansel and Gretel's house, with lollipops and liquorice etc ...

I bought a rabbit-fur hat. It was bizarre. I had arranged to meet two birds at the metro near out hotel at 11 pm in order to sell them some jeans. They didn't turn up, but I was soon approached by three Russians, one of whom handed me a note which read 'Would you like to buy fur hats, military watches, military belts, perestroika badges, etc.?'

I said, 'No thanks, I'm waiting for some friends.'

They then handed me another note, 'We're deaf.'

I spent an hour bargaining with these three deaf Russians. Every so often the one watching the metro doors would flap his arms and I'd have to disappear into a telephone booth and pretend to be phoning while the police walked past. Then back we'd go, the 'spokesman' hastily scribbling notes to me in perfect English while the others looked about warily, arguing about the market price of a pair of Levi's in USA and the UK, discussing the size and condition – on and on.

They were 'talking' to each other in sign language all the while. God it was strange; snow, night-time, and this clandestine marketeering with three deaf guys. Eventually we did a deal, and went off smiling. The deal had not been helped by the fact that our pen stopped working all the time – a kind of deaf person's stutter. As it gave out mid-sentence, one of them would shake it and then burn the end of it with his lighter which gave it another lease of life. Apparently the deaf mafia is big here.

When we were completely lost we resorted to taxis which cost one packet of cigarettes to go anywhere. The drivers were all marketers and spoke enough English to tell us that they thought Gorbachov a dangerous communist shit, up to no good.

Everyone queues for everything, everywhere. Very sad, as often the people at the back of the queue don't know what they're queuing for. People were incredibly kind and friendly. We stopped a rushing commuter to ask our way in the impossible underground. He grabbed my arm, about-turned and marched up the mile-long escalator, out the door, round the corner, across the

158

street to another metro, handed us the four 5-kopek pieces we would need for the train, and disappeared before I could hand them back or thank him.

An artist at a gallery told me that he wished more than anything for the return of Tsardom, then embraced me and gave me a beautiful painting that I was admiring. Looking out of a window at the winter palace after being stunned and exhausted by the Hermitage from a room with tons (literally) of gold on its walls, Leningrad spreading into the white distance, gold turrets glinting in the sun, people walking alone or in pairs across the vast square immediately below, walking carefully in their black coats and hats so as not to die in the cold – I had tears in my eyes.

We went to the Pushkin museum, the Russian and perhaps most spectacular of all, to the Armoury where the treasure of the Kremlin are housed. We were told it was impossible to see the armoury without paying £20 and going on an official tour. However, we managed to pay just 30p each and pushed into the middle of a crowd of Germans who were on such a tour.

Our Icelandic friend was too nice and hesitated and got caught, so we all stopped and turned ourselves in to the guard at the Gate of the Kremlin. We pleaded and smiled sweetly and after 10 minutes or so, he relented and organised us new tickets for us. He had put himself on the line, we discovered later. The treasures are breathtaking.

Prospero trying on clothes in Moscow

We also looked at the east end of Moscow, which like most European cities was the poorer part, the west wind being the prevailing wind. People's faces were coarser, and they looked very surprised to see us in their tatty crumbling streets.

We smuggled ourselves into the University, a giant Stalinist skyscraper designed to make one feel completely insignificant. Its architecture epitomised his entire regime. We talked to some students who made us desperate with their pessimism. They believe that the inertia of an entrenched bureaucracy will guarantee its continued survival and their continued misery, despite perestroika and glasnost.

McDonalds recently opened a restaurant in

159

Moscow. Six months later there is still a two-hour queue outside it. 35 000 people applied to work there. Capitalism comes to Moscow and with it the most revolting side effects – burgers which cost thousands of acres of rain forest, plastic bags, disposable everything, TFC producing cartons – the hungry consumer monster ...

...The simplicity of the Muscovite's life – albeit enforced and hideous for that – still held certain values and beliefs about society that greed has totally eroded in the West. I am well aware of the awful inequalities in Russia, the inefficiencies of industries and the wastes in defence – but for all that the people have a naiveté and a purity that we have completely lost ..."

26 MAY 1989 VIENNA

Spent my birthday in a paradise not far from Vienna. Ernst (first French horn in Vienna Symphony Orchestra) and Maria Mühlbacher invited me to spend the weekend at their fishing chalet in the mountains where I woke to see miles and miles of fields covered in lily-of-the-valley, forget-me-nots, daisies, speedwell, campion etc. So thickly spread are the flowers that the grass is barely visible. There are birch forests on the near horizon, and the Alps in the distance are still covered in snow.

The river is bristling with trout, and fast-flowing. Ernst challenged me to take a trout from his stream. I crept up on it and dapped and a big one took my fly immediately. He was impressed, and I took it back to Vienna where Brigitte cooked it expertly.

Brigitte took me to *Il Viaggio a Rhiems* (Rossini) in the Opera House where Ruggiero Raimondi sung and acted supremely well. Abbado conducted. Samuel Ramey terrific. It was a wildly imaginative production and I am very lucky to have been there.

A rehearsal of Nikolaus Harnoncourt conducting Mozart's *Lucia Scilla* with Gruberova and the 18-year-old Cecilia Bartoli. Brigitte said to watch out for her – she will go far. The whole rehearsal was thrilling beyond words. Brigitte took me plus all my luggage into this rehearsal, and then drove me to the airport.

Went to Trevor Pinnock's rehearsal of Haydn and Mozart. He is a wonderfully exciting musician. Harnoncourt is a hard act to follow and Pinnock does fine. But I went to a performance of Handel's *Saul* in the Queen Elizabeth Hall with John Amis. John Eliot Gardiner was conducting and we walked out. It was too polite, the choir too perfect – no balls. After Harnoncourt's Handel, it was lifeless.

Perahia played the Beethoven 4th with Solti and made it the most original and beautiful Beethoven performance I can remember. John introduced me to Brian McGee and Isaiah Berlin. I wish Jim had been with me. I bet he does too!

Pinnock rehearsals all day. What energy he has. Superlative musician conducting from the harpsichord.

October 1989

Jamie Stormonth-Darling and his sister Nancy[27] came out from Scotland and we took them to Londolozi. We saw 119 different birds in two days, including a grey cuckoo shrike and a Nerina trogan really close up. Jamie deserves his knighthood for being a very parfit gentyl knight.

B and Jamie Stormonth-Darling

6 November 1989

Extract from Prospero's letter from Warwick University:

"I've finally settled in my house which is actually really horrible. I enjoy it in a masochistic way though. It is made of that brick that you see all over England that looks as if someone's drawn it and then coloured it in with the last Koki chalk that works – the horrible orange one that outlasts all the others.

---

27 She was married to Jim's brother Derrick

161

If I look out of my window, the Rottweiler in the block that provides the visual extravaganza from my viewpoint, begins a five-minute German tirade, obviously celebrating the fact that its visual monotony is briefly relieved by the appearance of my head. It makes me realise just how lucky we are to live where we do . . . The Rottweiler will probably live there all its life.

I'm doing a course called Europeans in Africa and Asia. I think our professor could do with a copy of your case against Columbus, Jim. Another course – Landscape and Society – is taught by a wonderful man who pushes himself along the table on his bum, perches on the top of his chair-back, and is contagiously enthusiastic. It is all about the *Doomsday Book* and the Romans and the plague and is fascinating.

French is getting very difficult now but is taught by an excellent man. The main History course I am doing, is Europe 1500-1725. I am knee-deep in Ottoman life at the moment, and loving it . . ."

11 FEBRUARY 1990
The miracle has happened. Nelson Mandela is a free man. We watched the television for hours and saw him leaving the prison. Jim walked round and round the room saying, "Thank God this has happened while I am alive to know it."

20 FEBRUARY 1990
Yesterday I went to Judy Finch, an astrologer who had my birthday details and was told nothing else about me. I had never been to an astrologer and was nervous.

Deep restlessness, my chart says, which I must accept as a river that moves and is ever-flowing. Still water is stagnant, unproductive. I must realise this restlessness is my way of creating and I must use it in its many diverse ways. That is what I am here for.

I told Judy that I have always felt one must excel at one thing and therefore, because I try many different art forms; I am no good at any. I am a flibberty-jibbet. Judy said, no, it is my way of creating – to do many things. She said I have an abundance of energy coming out of the earth through me and I must use it. She

162

said I must put my thoughts down in writing to enable me to change into what I really am. All my life I have played a role of disciple to someone and I must stop. Not stop loving him, but stop living through his creative ability. His link with me is so old and that is why I am sticking with it.

He was a scholar in the library at Alexandria before the fire. I was a warrior. I loved him then and was not allowed to because of our different stations in life. Here we are again. He is a scholar in his library. He cannot love in the way I know love and by loving him I have denied myself life. I have sacrificed myself for him. I must understand this and try to have self-regard and find my role. Our link is terribly strong, but if I want to become my true self, I must consciously break it.

She said, "What I see as pain in your life is the ultimate martyrdom, ultimate sacrifice of the whole aspect or purpose of life, which is love – to feel it, to express it, to let it flow out of you. You must be careful not to be drawn by an intellect or mind that you wish to express but only allow it to be expressed by someone else, in sacrifice to your real self. You are and always have been the promoter of the stardom of those around you."

When I told her Jim's date of birth, she said, "He lives in his head. When life gets too painful, he escapes into his head, into books. The whole purpose of his life's existence is to give the truth of the past to the world. He cannot emote – and he's going to uncover the past to make man understand the present.

"You are the one who has to take all the action. Before he goes, you must honour yourself. You have to stop living on his behalf. Paint, write, make music, or whatever. This is very very important. You have to live for the glory of who you are – not be here for the glory of this man. If you do not, you will repeat this role of service to someone else. The more I look at both your planets together the more I see an incredible closeness between you. But it is a master-disciple relationship.

"When he dies you will be free for the first time in your life. You have worked whole-heartedly at loving, and learnt pain, hurt, joy, hate etc., which you would never have known without him. You will be rewarded for loving him all your life. You must start your adult role while he is still here."

163

Judy was sure he would die within two years. This was a huge shock to me at first and then in a way, it taught me to move on with my life.

I found this reading gob-smacking to say the least. Whatever one's view of astrology, it is phenomenally accurate. Judy had never met either of us.

I had no intention or idea of writing. Thank you Judy for sowing the seed.

MARCH 1990

I think my farm school is becoming more and more important to me. It has nothing to do with Jim. It has been my creation and my doing. I am making it something special. It is so important to the kids on this farm and in this area. Charles Nwaila is a born headmaster and we work very happily and positively together. Charles is a wholly dedicated teacher and these kids are blessed to have him here. He christened Imogen in the font/birdbath in the courtyard outside my bedroom.

*Charles Nwaila christening Imogen
in the birdbath*

APRIL 1990

I sang in the *St John's Passion* with the Chamber Choir under Simon Preston and loved it. It has been a wonderful experience singing Bach under a great musician and I wish so much it could happen more often. What music! Singing Bach makes me feel well, and wholly fulfilled. On occasions when I am playing Bach, I feel that Bach is playing me and I momentarily lose my self totally. These moments are possibly the true meaning of bliss.

MAY 1990 LONDON

I was on the tube going to St Paul's for evensong and a man in working overalls sat next to me doing a crossword. I peered at it and he had spelt 'ashes' 'ashs'. Eventually he put his ballpoint back in his breast pocket, sniffed and folded his paper.

I turned to him and said, "two across is 'preamble'."

So he got it out again and said, "how do you spell it?"

So I told him and then I said, "two down is 'poster'."

He passed me his pen and the paper, and the train had passed St Paul's! I was very put out and the people opposite us who had watched it all said, "It serves you right for doing the crossword!"

So I got off at Bank and crossed over to catch the return train. On it was a group of nine-year-old wolf-cubs from Lancashire. I was so busy enjoying them I very nearly missed St Paul's again.

Frank Longford took us – Jim, Prospero and me – to the House of Lords for lunch. His daughter-in-law Val Pakenham describes it as a crèche where one can drop them off in the morning and fetch them in the afternoon, knowing that they have slept and been fed and well cared for. Frank Longford introduced us to our waitress, Penny, and told us that Penny came from Castle

Lord Longford

Pollard, which is the Longford's village in Ireland. Penny smiled and as soon as she was out of earshot, Frank said, "She does nothing of the sort. She was heard telling another waitress, 'Lord Longford likes to think I come from Castle Pollard'."

165

26 May 1990

John Amis took me to Glyndebourne. Peter Hall's production of Britten's *Albert Herring* was visually utterly enchanting. The sets were so detailed and charming, I feasted my eyes and concentrating on the music was almost an effort.

In one of the London broadsheets, Reuters published a little piece headed, 'Not Plum Crazy'.

"Linz: A four-year-old Austrian boy was so disgusted by his grandmother's plum dumplings that he dialled emergency services for help. Police asked the boy to give the dumplings another chance. He agreed."

20 JUNE 1990 MONAGHAN

After weeks of hard work to organise a benefit concert at the Market Theatre to celebrate Chris McGregor's music, I have stopped carrying on like a loon without cease.

Diana Cowen came out and together we learnt by heart WH Davies' 'Leisure'. We 'stopped and stared' and lay under the Chinaberry trees on the most perfect still day. Jim was in Cape Town and the day was slow and unpressured. We wrote letters and sang duets from Bach's cantata, *Christ Lag in Todes-banden*. We walked up to Maria Masilela's house over our boundary and saw beautiful Ndebele dancing and singing. The day rolled gently by. Di rubbed my back with almond oil and I felt deeply content. It was a day of peace and beauty and home, and no-one could ask for more. We even had garlic in the salad! (Jim wouldn't allow garlic in the house).

B and Diana

166

JULY 1990

At our shoot at Monaghan, Basil Hersov's shoe came adrift and he said, "Jim, do you have a hard-drying adhesive?'" Jim heard it as, "Jim, do you have a hotline to Jesus?"

8 JULY 1990

Diana celebrated her birthday here on the farm with some young Greek friends. They were warm and sweet and natural and I was very happy to have them here. Di, Grant and I sang the trio from *Cosi fan Tutti*. And after eating delicious Greek thingies, they did Greek dancing, which I love. I am useless at it, but I am so at home with people who sing and dance. I must try and keep such company more often.

10 AUGUST 1990

It is exactly 50 years ago that Jim's father Abe died and there was a ceremony at his grave at St James. Jim gave a good speech. It rained, and all the Baileys that were present went to Rust-en-Vrede afterwards for drinks. It is a Baker house with a marvellous view of the sea and where Abe had spent his last years. He had had both legs amputated above the knee because of a disease which affects the blood circulation. During that time he loved being taken on his yacht in the bay and often invited the coloured kids who were on the jetty longing for a ride. Abe got a great kick out of it. Like father like son.

When I got back to the farm that night at about 10 pm, I phoned Gran and raved – as I could only do about myself to my mother – about how marvellously I had played Bach, Mozart and Schubert with Neil Solomon on two pianos at UCT College of Music. I was high on playing better than I knew I could, inspired by my beloved Neil. Granny was happy for me and chatted for a while, and bade me good-night.

The next morning at about 7.30 am, Jessica and John came into my bedroom while I was still in bed, to tell me that Richard had been killed in a car yesterday. Which means that my mother, knowing her only son had died that day, had kept any

inkling of it from me that night, so that I would
sleep. I had detected nothing whatsoever in her
voice. I was so thrilled with myself with our
music-making, and she let me be.

She had had a coronary when she learnt of Richard's death that morning. This was only diagnosed
later. Quite extraordinary strength and thought-
fulness.

Richard

Richard believed in nothing and wanted his body
to be used for medical study at the University. So I phoned Philip Tobias, Professor
of Anatomy at Wits, and having commiserated, he asked how Richard died. I told
him and he said it was unlikely that they could use his body because there would
have to be an autopsy. He told me to ring the man who runs the dissecting department and ask him what he thought.

I phoned Mr L and he said, "Mrs Bailey we'd love to have your brother but you see
they never put the organs back nicely after an autopsy, and they don't stitch nicely.
I am sorry because we would love to have your brother." Richard would have split
his sides laughing.

They did an autopsy and found that Richard had had a massive heart attack and was
already dead when he rolled the car. This made a huge difference to our reaction. It
was all too much after Alaric killing himself in a car. Heart attack is more accept-
able. Richard ate and drank and smoked himself into it. Papa warned him he wouldn't
make old bones. Richard said he was happy living the way he did and didn't mind
dying.

14 AND 15 SEPTEMBER 1990 LONDON
The 50th Anniversary of the Battle of Britain.

Beezy said taking Jim to Moss Bros. to fit him out in a morning suit and top hat, was
like bathing our cat. He was very otherwise until Beezy had a brainwave and told

168

him that he looked like Fred Astaire, and that he should try some steps. Thence-forward a total change of attitude from Jim.

Jim must be one of the only men on earth that didn't know he had six medals besides the DFC. I had to find out what they were from a secretary in the offices of the RAF, and then have them made up at Spinks. Jim looked stunning in his grey topper and tails with all his gongs.

For morning tea, I gave him about a teaspoonful in case he may want to pee during the ceremony. We had to be at Buckingham Palace at 10 am. We needn't have worried. Prince Philip came over before the flypast and addressed those that had flown in the Battle of Britain. Most of them were 70 plus. He said, "If anyone wants to pee, do so any time you like over there in the Guards' loo." A chorus of sighs of relief.

When the Spitfire and Hurricane flew over us and did a slow roll above the palace, I felt I was going to pass out. It was so hugely moving.

As we walked out of the gates of Buckingham Palace, Jim immediately removed his topper and put it on my head. There was an old woman in the crowd we passed who recognised the DFC on Jim's jacket and almost wept and said, "Thank you, thank you for saving our country!" God, I was moved – and so so proud of him. Growing up in South Africa one

Two toffs leaving Buckingham Palace

has no idea of the valour and heroism of the fighter pilots who fought in the Battle of Britain, and what they meant to the people of Britain. Here I was, walking next to 'One of the Few' that was still alive, *and* he was my husband.

Off came the tailcoat, his shirt sleeves were rolled up. Jim had had enough of formality.

Next day was the Memorial Service in Westminster Abbey. The BBC televised the whole ceremony and I have a copy. It was certainly one of the most moving experiences of our lives. I felt very privileged to be there. The entire Royal Family was present, and we were seated near the front between the choir and the altar, so we had a very good view of it all.

The Archbishop of Canterbury gave an inspired sermon, and ended it by saying: "Greater love hath no man than this; that he lay down his life for his friends. We do not sentimentalise those who died in the Battle of Britain if we salute them with those words of our Lord. We do not romanticise those who are still with us, who fought then and were ready to die. We simply remember with the deepest thanksgiving what those few gave and did for us."

CHRISTMAS 1990 JOHANNESBURG

Christmas lunch at Mary and Hank Slack. We brought them a little red pig for a present. Duroc pigs are deep russet-coloured and very sweet. There has been a bad drought and it broke today with miraculous skies, rainbows, clouds and every sort of light.

31 DECEMBER 1990

New Year's Eve at Glendirk with the Menells etc. Hugh Masekela played with his band and it was a good party. The Menells' parties always are. But I don't really like parties enough if dancing isn't allowed. I enjoy myself for a short time, and then I long for bed.

28 MARCH 1991

I rode down to school to see Charles Nwaila. I rode Kleintjie without stirrups – excellent exercise. A black eagle flew over me enjoying a thermal.

I remember buying Kleintjie outside Kok's store. There was a notice there saying, '2 kattens, 2 horses and 1 spotted pig'. You had to take the lot, so I did. Kleintjie has been a great success and I have worked the cattle on him for long years now.

170

Charles Nwaila is a dream of a headmaster for our farm school. A born teacher and a deeply caring man. I wish we could work together forever. One can see the children blossoming under the guidance of Charles, and Fanie Masilela our neighbour. Fanie has made our school choir one of the best in our area. He is as gifted a

Fanie Masilela and his choir

teacher as he is a singer and dancer and between Fanie and Charles Monaghan Farm School is excellent. Fanie also runs the sports and we have a boy that runs cross-country for the province. We only have about 100 pupils in total between Grade 1 and Standard 5, and yet we win football matches and athletics competitions against schools five times as big.

27 MAY 1991 LONDON

Pinnock conducted Purcell's *King Arthur* at St John's, Smith Square. It was electrifying. After the performance I went backstage and he took me in his arms and flung me round and round – so he was certainly aware of the magic he had made. I took M who said it was not her sort of music. I must be alone or with like-minded company on such occasions. Ruinous to be with someone who is not enjoying it.

John Amis with Jess and her two bairns

John Amis took me to Mozart's *Cosi fan Tutti* at Glyndebourne. Trevor Nunn's production. Beautiful 30s scenery and costumes on board an ocean liner. We went down on the train with Imogen Cooper and her husband, John Batten. David Hockney was there wearing a bright-green shirt and a red tie. He was the only person at Glyndebourne who was not in evening dress.

We had a happy journey back to Victoria with Simon Rattle, who had conducted, and he had his sister and parents with him. His sister is slightly retarded. Interesting that Simon is anormal and the sister subnormal. They are equally not like other people. He was very caring and sweet with his family. Imogen, John and Simon, John Amis and I took up the whole section of the coach and had a bottle of wine and much good chatter, with Simon relating all the backstage gossip.

JUNE 1991
At a dinner party I sat next to Laurens (van der Post). Someone mentioned something astonishing and I muttered, "Well, slaan my met 'n vuurhoutjie!" and Laurens was nearly crying with laughter.

I was lining up at the Wigmore to congratulate Imogen who had given a wonderful recital, and I met Colin Deane and Andrew Vishnevski. I had been sitting behind them and felt I would so love to know such a lively and beautiful pair. Andrew's Polish profile with cheekbones of great beauty, and Colin's joy was irresistible. We then found ourselves in the queue for Imogen after the concert and started to chat.

We left the Wigmore together and as it was raining, they offered me a lift in the Yellow Dinosaur – a battered kombi. First they had to deliver some shelves in Swiss Cottage. Then we were hungry and didn't have enough money between us to buy much food, so I said if they would take me home then Andrew could meet Jim and question him on the origin of the Greek myths, and we could have something to eat. Andrew was directing a play on the subject of the Greek Myths.

As we drove into Linden Gardens Colin said, "There's Jim!" Jim was wandering along in the rain. Colin recognised him from a description which I didn't even remember giving. I was perched on a sort of plank between the front seats of the kombi, and when Colin said hello to Jim, Jim greeted him warmly although he had never set eyes on him before. Par for the course for Jim.

Andrew and B

172

I leant over and suggested that we all go up to the flat and have a drink. Jim explained that he was locked out of the flat. He had gone out to breakfast at a Notting Hill café at about 10.30 am and had been locked out ever since. It was now about 4 pm. He wasn't fussed about it in the least. I had no key. I was relying on his being home when I arrived. Luckily Beezy was staying with us. He had a key, and even luckier, I knew where he had gone for Sunday lunch.

So we all went to a coffee shop in Notting Hill and while Andrew quizzed Jim on the Greek myths, I telephoned Beezy and asked him to come home and let us in. As I returned to our table, Andrew kissed his fingers and threw them in the air to tell me how marvellous he thought Jim was.

This was the start of a precious friendship for me. Colin I see every time I go to England and we spend many hours swooning over music together, chiefly over Gundela Janowitz of whom Colin has every recording and many private ones that Janowitz herself has given him. Sadly Andrew is usually working too hard, teaching at RADA and directing his company of players, The Cherubs, to be able to join us as often as I'd like.

Colin Deane and B

At Oxford, at the Christ Church Gaudy, Jim looked beautiful in his gown, and there was a service in the cathedral. The anthem was a modern setting of a John Donne poem and wonderfully sung. Jim was reunited with his friend Bill Symons and enjoyed that, but found it otherwise a bit dull. I felt about 19 with all the old fuddy-duddies and was delighted not to dine in hall with them, and skipped off up St Aldate's.

31 August 1991 Johannesburg

The newspapers are full of Beezy. Photos of him on the front page of the *Sunday Times,* and a huge piece on him in the *Cape Argus* headlined, "Inverted art racism, says Beezy – The National Gallery boob over 'domestic worker' Joyce's linocuts?"

Beezy entered three paintings under his own name for the Tri-ennial, which is considered to be the most important art exhibition in South Africa. He also entered a triptych of three linocuts under an assumed name, Joyce Ntobe, a domestic worker from Khayelitsha. He used a fake Woodstock address and gave his own telephone number as a contact number.

The National Gallery bought Joyce's triptych. His own work was turned down.

When Beezy revealed that he was Joyce, it infuriated certain people, because 'white guilt' was at a high level. The anger was compounded by his being a grandchild of a legendary colonial gold-mining magnate. "Yet," as Helena Kingwill reported in *The Sunday Independent*, "the joke played itself out on its own, like a circle of dominoes accidentally toppled." She added, "Bailey has systematically kicked down all the sacred cows he could find and has consequently created so much controversy, that the mere mention of his name raises mixed reactions and cynical smiles. Few understand however that, to him, these have been brave efforts to break down barriers that hold humanity separate and disempowered."

A large painting under his own name was bought by the National Gallery soon after this incident. Since then, from time to time, Beezy has shown as Joyce Ntobe. She has had small rooms of work attached to larger exhibitions of Beezy Bailey. Joyce lives on.

29 SEPTEMBER 1991

Laurens van der Post organised a trip for us to go to Botswana with his daughter Lucia and her family. Of course Jim had 'other things to do' so Beezy, Prospero and I went. How wonderful it would have been to have Laurens himself with us! Lucia van der Post was to write about our trip for a London magazine. She had been commissioned to write about the country, the flora and fauna, but sadly our trip did not include a meeting with the San people with whom Laurens had formed such a loving and renowned relationship.

We were to meet the Van der Posts, we were told, at Gwetha, an airstrip in the middle of a large expanse of nowhere. We flew in a Cessna single engine and I wasn't sick. We landed at 11.40 am and no-one was in sight. The sun was high and hot and the only shelter was a tiny strip of shade by an iron half tank. After we had been sitting there for about an hour, a black man appeared and opened the half tank, in which was stored a fire extinguisher, a rake, and some cans.

174

I made a bed out of all our jackets, and lay in the tank and read. Prospero strode off in the midday sun in the direction of a cluster of huts we had seen from the air. Beezy got some paper and charcoal out and was perfectly content. We all were. We had one small Liquifruit between the three of us, but it was an adventure and when it cooled down towards evening, we would make our way to the huts to beg or buy food and drink. We went through a list of people who would have gone crazy in the same situation and had a lot of fun.

At 3.30 pm David Dugmore, who was running our safari, arrived in a Land Rover. It was a relief to meet him and be able to drink water. Then a plane landed bearing the Van der Posts, who had waited at Maun for us. Lacked communication, we did.

We all went to the Magkadikadi pans – vast expanses of saltpans, we were told, covering as large an area as Switzerland.

The most memorable part of our trip was meeting Jack Bousfield. Jack has lived here alone on the edge of the pans for long years. He is burnt by the sun and resembles a piece of biltong. He wears a kikoi, which looks like a mini-skirt from afar, and he is slight and wiry. His speech is quiet, understated and humorous, and he has many a tale to tell. Jack is mentioned in the *Guinness Book of Records* for having killed 43 000 crocodiles. He has crashed seven aeroplanes, four of which were total write-offs. Shortly after our trip, Jack killed himself in a microlite.

Laurens says the stars are so near to us that we can *hear* them. He describes them saying "tsa" like a hunter to his hunting dog. We sat in a row of canvas chairs to witness the sun setting every evening. Tall Ilala palms against the vastness, slowly becoming silhouettes. The stars were too exciting for me to sleep easily. I knew if I looked out my tent, there they would be. Always and forever.

Jack took us all, driving a fleet of 4-wheeled motorbikes, to find the best and most beautifully made Palaeolithic hand-axes I have seen. Alas, the most perfect one I found will go to the Botswana Museum and not to Jim.

We went on to the Delta. The Okavango River. Sunset with Constable cows drinking, wonderful avian traffic, with the scent of potato-creeper, and the sound of robins, bou-bou shrikes, Egyptian geese, babblers etc. – yet another heaven.

While walking to our tents after supper, David told us to shine our torches if we went to the loo during the night because hippo, hyena, lion, elephant, etc might be around the tents. I was terrified.

Frogs were making a lovely tinkling noise without cease all night and I asked

Prospero what kind of frogs he thought they were. He said, "Tent-penetrating killer-frogs." They were bell-frogs. I shared a tent with him and we laughed so much when we were in bed that the others shouted across to us to shut up.

It's Friday again. It has been Friday for three days running. The party of eight split and Beezy, Prospero, David Crichton-Miller (grandson of Laurens) and I went off for the day to a shallow part of the river where we could swim without the danger of crocodiles. The water was crystal clear and we swam and splashed around for ages. Then Beezy decided we should have our lunch in the water, so he brought the fold-up table down the bank. We all laid the food on it and sat on the cooler boxes, in water up to our waists. David and I shared a cooler-box and if David stood, I wasn't heavy enough to hold it down. Beezy knelt stark naked, and we had our meal with shoals of little squeaker fish swimming round us. Prospero and Roger tried to catch some by feeding them bread and trapping them in a plastic bag. They failed. It was bliss in the heat of the day to spend so much time playing in the cold water. On the way back to camp, we saw crocodiles, buffalo, hippo, letchwe, giraffe with babies, zebra, kudu, and ground hornbills as big as turkeys.

On Sunday we went for a two-hour boat trip on gin-clear water. I saw a biggish fish and oh for a rod! We landed on an island where we whiffled through the tulgy vegetation up to our thighs in mud, to seek the setatunya, a rare buck, which we did not find, but I did see my first pratincole, a bird I have longed to see since I was at Cape Town University.

We watched yellow-billed storks building their huge messy nests and the plumage under their lace-like wings was flamingo pink. They carried twigs and branchlets in their beaks and put on an impressive show. In the night a hippo did a poo right next to our tent and it stank so strongly it made me feel sick. We heard hyena, lion and hippo. I didn't sleep enough and was too afraid to go and pee. So at 4 am I woke Prospero to come with me to pee. Which he did.

9 OCTOBER 1991

This must be visually the most wondrous evening of my life. We were at Sarondella on the Chobi River. At about 5.30 pm we drove on the plains near the river over miles and miles, the sun a cerise balloon gently sinking over about 2 000 buffalo on the one side, and about 200 elephant on the other. There were two main herds of elephant and the matriarchs of each herd 'talked' to each other across the plain. It sounded like microphoned borbarigmy. Eventually they ran towards each other, weeping with emotion. When they met, they smelt each other's breath, linked trunks, huddled, like loving family friends.

Meanwhile on the sunset side of us, a pair of cheetah waited for something to kill. We watched them for about 15 minutes and one chased after a waterbuck. It didn't chase seriously, but to see it run was beautiful beyond belief. A pair of kori bustards was mooching about near us – they are the largest flying bird on earth.

The moon was a sliver and the baboons were shouting at the roosting guinea-fowl. I saw an African skimmer who flew along with its lower bill in the water skimming for food, hence its name.

When I was home again, I phoned Laurens in his flat in London to tell him about this perfect evening in detail. I rattled on waxing lyrical, and there was a long silence. I thought we had been cut off, and I said, "Laurens, Laurens are you there?" After another pause he said, "You have made me weep."

NOVEMBER 1991 MONAGHAN
Jamie and Mary Stormonth-Darling came and stayed. I took them down to the farm school and having shown the children and their teachers where Jamie and Mary lived in Scotland on the map of the world in the classroom, Charles, Josephine and Gloria, three members of the staff, sang *Loch Lomond* in three parts.

Prospero drove them through a violent storm in which three trees came down over the drive and the road was washed away.

Thomas Pakenham came and stayed and Jim and I and all the children went to his book launch at the Inanda Club. It was terribly hot so afterwards we swam in the big Club swimming pool. Beezy, Nicci and I had our swimming costumes with us and Jessica didn't, so after watching us cavorting around in the water she jumped into the pool in her very pretty dress and swam with us for ages.

23 NOVEMBER 1991
Beezy and Nicci were married by Charles under the sacred kaffirboom (we are not allowed to use that name now, *erethrina lysistemon*, I think is the official name)

Beezy and Nicci's wedding   *Beezy and Nicci at his birthday party*

at Mooiplaats. Two singers, Petrus Mofokeng and Isabella came and we sang *Soave si il vento* because Beezy and Nicci were going to Bequia for their honeymoon, thanks to Mary and Hank. Bequia is a small island in the Caribbean. The Mozart was apt. The words mean, 'May the winds be gentle, the waves tranquil, and all the elements respond benignly to our desire'.

Nicci's father longed to walk his only daughter down the aisle, so Beezy made one out of stones. The going was very tricky and the ladies laddered their stockings on the aloes and tripped over rocks. But an aisle it was, even if it was in the middle of the bushveld.

The African Jazz Pioneers played for the bash in the barn at Monaghan afterwards.

DECEMBER 1991
The Magic Flute was being performed at the State Theatre in Pretoria. The Korean soprano, Sumi Jo was singing the part of the Queen of the Night, and Clint van der Linde, aged 14, was one of the three boys taking part in the opera. I was told by Richard and Susie Cock that Clint could sing the Queen of the Night aria, and indeed he mimicked Sumi Jo and did it so brilliantly he practically outsang her.

I went to a Drakensberg Boys' Choir Christmas concert, went backstage at interval and asked their conductor, Bunny Ashley-Botha, if I could hear Clint sing the aria. He said I could come to their hostel the next day and hear Clint, as he hadn't the music with him. Clint was standing near by and said, "Sir, the music is in your brief case." So, after the Christmas concert, we went to the practice room in the Linder Auditorium and I brought a ghetto blaster on which I taped Clint. It was a mind-blowing experience.

I sent this very scrappy tape to John Amis, who played it on BBC2 in a programme he presented called The Singer not the Song – along with Caruso, Galli-Curci, Callas, Gigli, etc. etc. Clint was the only boy's voice he used. It was a two-hour programme and John announced that it was the most beautiful boy's voice he had ever heard.

JANUARY 1992 PLETT and the sea is warm
I flew up to Johannesburg to sing at Anthony Ogilvie-Thompson's wedding, then flew back to Plett the next day, where our family, the Bernings and the Orfords were having supper at a restaurant on the beach. I kissed everyone but especially Jim, and the people seated next to us at the restaurant thought I'd been away for months or even years. Someone asked, and when Prospero told them I'd been away for the night, their reaction was amusing.

15 APRIL 1992 MONAGHAN
The BBC World Service came and filmed me with my Farm School for the Referendum. Fergal Keane is terrifically supportive of the school and comes with his delightful colleague Milton Nkosi to many of our school functions. Fergal and Milton represent the BBC World Service in South Africa.

I phoned Fergal while he was still in bed late on Sunday morning and asked him how his wife, Ann was. He said, "She's lying here next to me with a face on her."

26 MAY 1992 LONDON
Had a wonderful birthday party in the flat in London. I had in my luggage eight avocadoes that Beezy had bought in Swaziland. I made avocado soup, and had a chicken and mushroom and ham pie from Mr Lidgate.

Alice Thomas Ellis came. Her real name is Anna Haycraft, wife of Colin who owns Duckworth Press and knows Jim. I was longing to meet Anna because I love her books. She is like a beautiful gypsy, long dark hair, wild looking, smokes and drinks red wine without cease. She kissed me warmly on meeting but sidled in through the other guests and then sat next to me at table and hardly spoke for about half an hour. She had a notebook and wrote in it from time to time. When she did speak, she spoke quietly and begun a wonderful tirade on David Lodge. She is as amusing as her writing. Her husband is exactly right for her and is brilliantly anarchistic.

At my dinner I proudly told Nicholas Shakespeare that we had a Fourth Folio of The Complete Works dated 1685. He was silent for a few seconds and then said, "We've got a Second." Nicholas is a direct descendant of William Shakespeare's brother. He was his usual bubbly self and charmed everyone. He is writing a bi-ography of Bruce Chatwin and came to interview me on Bruce, which is how we met.

I spent a huge amount of energy trying to get Jim's Bronze Age opus magnus published. It looks as if Simon & Schuster are taking it on.

JUNE 1992 IRELAND

Jim and I spent a dreamy week starting with the Pakenhams. Thomas inherited Tul-lynally which is the biggest castle in Ireland. It is June and cold. God knows what the castle must be like in winter. The gardens are paradise and while Thomas was showing us round we hid from tourists every time we saw them.

While Jim buried himself in their library, Val and I walked in the rain and saw purple bugloss, buttercups, speedwell, forget-me-nots, campion, columbine, and valerian. It was like fairyland. They have the greatest beech tree in the British Isles, and the biggest oak in Ireland. Thomas is obsessed with trees.

There is a very good organ – a Bevington – in the huge stone hall at Tullynally, with superb acoustics. There was no sheet music so Val took me to the priest in Castle Pollard who provided me with some and I had a good morning playing the organ.

When Prospero was staying with Thomas and Valerie some while ago, he came downstairs one morning to find that a large bowl of flowers in the hall had been knocked over. There was the broken vase, flowers all over the place and puddles of water on the stone floor, on which lay the Lord and Lady of the House, fighting for the cloth to clean it up, and yelling at each other furiously. While this was going on, a busload of tourists arrived to see the castle. Thomas and Val roared with laughter – as did Prospero. This lot of tourists are unlikely to forget their visit.

The cook – very Irish – whom Valerie says is mad and a very bad cook, put 10 plates on the warmer for lunch for the four of us.

We boated on their lake Darravara. Val had a long swim. It was much too cold for me, and even for Jim. We saw tiny purple orchis, wild violets, herb robert, meadowsweet, eggs-and-bacon, and fields – miles of fields – of buttercups and daisies. The lake is stunningly beautiful and I was impressed with Thomas's handling of the boat – he was unexpectedly efficient. Jim would never have been able to start a boat engine.

The Pakenhams took Jim and me to lunch at the Desmond Guinness's, who live in another castle near Dublin. They were giving a huge lunch party where three Russian gypsies played violins and a guitar in the dining room while we ate. They were truly terrific fiddlers and had settled in Kilkenny, travelling to play all over Ireland.

At table I sat next to an incredibly attractive man who really appreciated the music and we talked intensely afterwards finding much in common. We went off together to look at the portraits of all the Mitford sisters, Diana Mitford being Desmond's mother. This man whom I thought was such a dish, has a Russian wife much younger than himself, and a little boy of four who is the image of his father. They were charming, and they asked us to come and visit them in their home in County Carlow. By this time I was rather in love with the man. I was gob-smacked when I discovered he was John Hurt.

I hurried over to where Jim was deep in conversation with Paddy Falloon, to tell him how I had fallen in love with John Hurt, and pulled him over to meet him.

Jim hadn't a clue who any actor was, except maybe Laurence Olivier. He never watched films and never went to the cinema. He was sweetly amused by my passions. I often pleaded with him to watch Nikolaus Harnoncourt on video, and went on and on how wonderful NH is, and how I love him. Jim would laugh and say, well done! And go off and read.

I do not know Harnoncourt personally and do not wish to. I love worshipping him for his musicianship – from a distance. Yehudi Menuhin was another passion for most of my life. Jim being uninterested in music, for some reason liked the violin and understood my love for Yehudi.

Jim's passion, true passion was for books – he didn't have passions for humans. That is how he was. I remember wishing sincerely that I could be a beautifully leather-bound volume, held in his hands.

Once when there was a terrible winter fire on the farm and it crept towards the library, I knew that if his books went, I would seriously consider killing myself. I couldn't conceive how he would react.

Paddy and Jane Falloon had us to stay in their beautiful Palladian house in County Kildare. Jane runs it superbly and is an excellent cook. She loves doing The Times crossword and playing scrabble, so we are great mates.

We all called in at the Hurts on our way down to fish in Waterford. The Hurts live in a lovely country house which belonged to Cecil Day Lewis and where he lived for many years. The house was beautiful but somehow empty of energy. John Hurt did a bit of painting as a pastime, but I felt he came alive when he was either at a party, or when he was working on set. I left feeling sorry for him in his lovely country house, isolated and slightly lost and bored, until his next film was being made.

We went to Christopher and Judy, friends of the Falloons, in Fethard County Tipperary. Judy is as warm and thoroughly Irish as Benny was. Their thatched cottage, Tullow, Connemara ponies and the mountains of Morne on the horizon, make it heaven. We dried our rain-sodden socks on the Aga and it was so congenial I wanted to stay forever.

Tullow

Sadly, the Blackwater was too muddy to fish – such a pity for Jim. It rained steadily, which the Irish call 'a soft day'. We stayed at the Keanes in Waterford. The kindness and friendliness of our hosts all over Ireland has been very warming.

When we met in London, Jane and I hastened to the local video shop to look for films starring John Hurt. We couldn't wait to see him in some of them and spent an afternoon on my bed watching *The Field*, and *Champion*.

When I arrived back in London, Jim had flown to Ghana and I was on my own and thinking of going to bed, when I read in The Times what was showing at the Haymarket. I phoned and booked a ticket, being told there was one return, and off I went to see GBS's *Heartbreak House*, with Paul Scofield, Vanessa Redgrave, Felicity Kendall etc. and directed by Trevor Nunn. God what acting!

This is the benefit of being alone. I'd never have been able to get two tickets, and I can decide to go on the spur of the moment, and move fast.

Took the 31 bus all the way to Camden to deliver Jim's book to Colin Haycraft. Anna was sitting in her dark kitchen with her cats and cigarettes and the inevitable bottle of wine. We chatted happily for ages. She unfolded slowly into marvellous puckish company.

Simon & Schuster phoned to say they are publishing Jim's book in April!

John Amis took me to Monteverdi's *Return of Ulysses* at English National Opera. As John said, too much recitative and not enough harmony. Like eating hors d'oevres the whole bloody evening when you long for bread and steak. Anthony Rolfes-Johnson was superb, and now this morning I hear he as been awarded the CBE, and so has Trevor Pinnock. Well chosen awards methinks.

Phillida and Colly – Beezy ate the still life after he had painted it

Colin Deane came with me to Bath to organise something in Granny's flat. It was a bit spooky without Granny there. Weird being in a home of your own family when they're not there. Photos of us all everywhere. We went to Matins on Sunday in Bath Abbey, which is so lovely and built in 1499, the last of the Gothic in England.

Colly and I had a delicious lunch in Pulteney Street just over the road from Granny, and then walked to Sydney Gardens and then to the Pump Room. When I told Prospero he said, "Ah yes, that's where Jane Austen went to joll."

14 JUNE 1992

I went to the Wigmore for Schubert's C Major quintet, the Lindsay quartet plus Sandy Baillie on the extra cello. Peter Cropper, the leading violinist, pulls such faces when he plays it is hard not to watch him. Sublime performance of sublime music. This was my first meeting with Sandy and the beginning of a precious friendship. Then in the afternoon I went to the RFH for rehearsal of Bach B minor with Sir David Willcocks. Seven hours of music today. Heaven.

15 JUNE 1992

Imogen Cooper invited me to lunch and then asked me if I minded if she played me the entire 80-minute recital she was preparing. Did I mind???? Schubert G major sonata, *German Dances op.33*, and then Schoenberg. Imogen's cleaning lady hoovered throughout her playing, just outside the door. I asked Imogen didn't it drive her dilly? She said she always does it if someone is with her. She gets jealous.

When I was in the bath the phone rang six times and I gave up trying to get to it. How unrestful can anything be!

184

19 June 1992

Worked all morning on Jim's publishing with Colin Haycraft, Giles de la Mare, Peter Robinson and Michel de Breteuil. Left in the drenching rain to fetch Jim's briefcase that he had forgotten somewhere in Denmark Street. Posted it to South Africa, then sped to the Civil Engineer Institute where Roy Goodman was rehearsing the Hanover Band.

I took Clint's tape. At the break, I played it to Roy Goodman. He said, "I want to record with this boy. Bach's cantata no.51. No boy in the world has ever recorded it because it is too difficult."

Roy himself was probably the greatest soprano of his day when he was a King's chorister. He said he had never heard any boy sing like Clint. He told me to ring Hyperion and make a date for a recording. I was so excited I almost ran through London. Roy Goodman is an exciting and hugely energetic conductor and his Hanover Band is tops.

I ate a kebab in a Cypriot café with the freezing rain spatting in the doorway and I was poured a soup-like cup of builder's tea. I had walked through the pee-ridden Tottenham Court Road tube station lined with drunken beggars, and then on to the gold pillars and crystal chandeliers of the Hall where Roy was conducting. A very London day.

I copied a tape of Clint for Hyperion as soon as I got home, and when I telephoned them they said the first date they could give Roy was in September. Clint was now 15 and his voice had shown signs of breaking for good. It was really a case of great urgency to make this recording. I pleaded with Hyperion to no avail. God what a disappointment.

23 June 1992 France

Staying with Maxine in her 15th century moulin in Lot-et-Garonne. I am sleeping in an attic on the very dusty floor under a piano. I have to climb a ladder to reach my bed. Beezy and Prospero are here which is bliss and heaven.

Last night there was a dance and bonfire for St Jean in the nearest village. So at 11 pm we drove there. Miriam, a friend from South Africa drove with Beezy and Prospero shouting conflicting directions at her and saying "Christ!" in a German accent every time she screeched the gears. We were in hysterical laughter while we drove round and round the village where absolutely blow-all was happening.

185

There were a few people standing about and a lone mouth-organ player. Miriam hooted, screeched brakes and we drove the winding narrow roads home where we played 'Oh hell!' until midnight.

I went with Beezy into a field near the moulin where we did pastels of the countryside. I really enjoyed it and it enabled me to get an inkling of what hard work it is to concentrate like Beezy, and how damn good he is. My second attempt was of the moulin and its very complex surrounding of trees – too much, not a success. But Beezy and I sat in the wheat field and spent a very precious time together. He is kind and encouraging about my drawing.

On Thursday the 26th we all went to Monflanquin to lunch at Le Jardin. This town is built around the big church on a hill, like Chartres. It is a very old walled town of mediaeval buildings, sprinkled along cobbled streets with quaint shops. I bought a pretty straw hat with a blue ribbon for Jessica.

We went to exercise the horses for Titi and Jeanine in the Perigaud area. Huge forests, vineyards, fields of Flanders poppies mixed with purple vetch, ripe wheat and barley. We rode hard for two hours past mediaeval farmhouses and galloped flat out through a huge oak forest on a soft bridle path in single file.

Maxine's house is full of cobwebs and dust – thick dust – and the whole house is dark and smells of dog though there isn't one.

On Saturday, she drove me to the station at Tonneins. There had been a strike and the train was actually an earlier one that was three hours late, and it was just leaving for Bordeaux. Big Maxine took my case in one hand and me in the other and literally flung me and my case onto the train as it begun to gain speed. I landed on the floor in a heap with my luggage and was as apologetic as I could be, in French.

On my way to Heathrow to fly home, I spent an hour or so with Laurens van der Post. He looked well and sent such loving messages to Jim re: his book. Poor old Ingaret[28] is losing her marbles fast.

On the flight I hesitated over a second piece of toast and the steward said, "A bit risky, isn't it?" What joy to hear Englishness!

28 Sir Laurens' wife

Beezy, who is in London, will be 30 on 21st July. He has just learned that his bio-
logical father is Denis Kiley. He was lunching with Kiley and having seen him
regularly over the years, he realised he looked like him, had the same speaking voice,
hand movements, highly original humour, etc. etc. They spoke of the possibility of
being related and so it was revealed.

That evening Beezy phoned me from London and told me he knew. I asked him
not to tell anyone until I had broken the news to Jim – then he could tell whoever
he liked.

Jim's response to this fact was typical of the man he is. I hardly slept that night
and at dawn I took the book he was reading out of his hands, removed his spectacles, and said, "Listen. I have something very important to tell you."

No answer. I repeated it.

He said, "Let's have it."

I said, "Kiley is Beezy's father." There was silence. I died twice.

After about a minute, which felt like ten, he said, "I've always regarded Kiley as
a genius who has never used it to the full." He then replaced his spectacles and
continued to read his book.

In 1979, when Kiley married for the 4th time, he wrote: "I've been marrying a more
cheerful type of wife this week. Her name is Yuriko and she is smallish and yel-
lowish and puffs. She has short healthy legs which come right up to her knees . . .
When she is late for work she shuffles rapidly to and fro in that instant shuffle
which Japanese ladies have and which makes them look as if they are running on
little wheels . . ."

SEPTEMBER 1992 SEYCHELLES

With Phillida. For starters we missed the early plane from Mahé and thus spent a
beautiful morning on Beau Vallon beach, swam to Fisherman's Cove, where we
found on the verandah two green coconuts full of their delicious milk, waiting to
be drunk. They were placed on a table obviously ordered by someone who hadn't
come down yet. We drank them and swam back to catch the plane to Praslin. The
flight took 15 minutes.

There we were driven through the primeval tropical forest, which is more or less as it was in its virgin state. The granite is pre-Cambrian, i.e. 650 million years old. There are several waterfalls and marvellous tangles of Tarzan-type growth. We had a short swim at Anse Lazio and were stung by microscopic jellyfish which made it a little unpleasant. The game fish I saw are ghostly silver-grey or whitish, which is their camouflage in these conditions. We picked branches of cinnamon and chewed them.

We were dropped at the jetty an hour and a half early for the ferry to La Digue. Of course we couldn't resist unpacking our swimming gear and snorkelling off the slippery steps of the jetty. The sea is gin-clear round these islands, and ridiculously brightly coloured little fish are everywhere. They look as if a child has used the brightest koki chalks and coloured them in.

In the prow of the ferry sat the La Digue under-15 volleyball team. They had just beaten Praslin and were very pleased with themselves and very noisy. All the paying travellers sat in the comfortable seats at the stern. Phil and I started off sitting on the front deck but as the sea became wilder we got so wet that the team invited us to sit up with them. We squeezed in amongst them and they sang or rather screamed, "We are La Digue team . . ." No rhythm or tune. After about 20 minutes the waves were seriously huge, spraying all over us. The girls were so noisy and happy that they prevented me from feeling too sick and terrified.

Oh was I pleased to see the island! Disembarking was a great relief. Viva la Stugeron[29]. We were taken to the lodge in an oxcart driven by Teddy who said he was 18. We thought 13 or 14 more likely. It took ages to reach the lodge because Teddy kept meeting friends and stopping to chat to them on the way.

It truly is paradise. One could understand using cowrie shells as currency here which they did not that long ago. The pace is *molto adagio* in every way. We take books to read at meals because the service is tortoise-like, the dining room floor is the beach, the roof is of palm leaves, so there is a wonderful quietness.

We snorkelled off a white, white beach, 10 minutes bicycle ride up the road and we were alone. The coconut palms bend at beautiful angles and the takamaka trees are huge and fragrant with blossom.

Each palm hut is provided with bicycles every morning, and off we go on expeditions. The taxi is an ox-cart and there are no cars on La Digue. We passed the cemetery which is jolly and colourful and sun-washed and I felt it would be a delight to lie there when my time came.

---

29 pill for travel-sickness

Last evening we rode through a forest to a copra factory, stole fresh coconuts, saw giant tortoises, and huge bats the size of yellow-billed kites which are here in great numbers. There are fairy terns like little spirits, and glossy black paradise fly-catchers. The sea is more turquoise than one could think possible. We felt naughty stealing coconuts until we realised it is like stealing blades of grass, so abundant are they.

The spider-lilies are fascinating as is much of the flora here. The banana tree out-side our hut looks like a peacock's tail, two-dimensional.

Creole music makes Boeremusiek sound original and sophisticated. It is dread-ful. It almost puts me off going to dinner.

The sunsets of wondrous beauty, gold and silver are over too quickly. Some of the other islands are visible from here and I am especially fond of Silhouette be-cause I learnt its name when I was a child and thought Silhouette in the Seychelles sounded as romantic as anywhere could be.

In my mind all the while deep down is the worrying thought of the half-hour I have to spend on the ferry going back to Praslin. I did feel sick on the way here.

We were introduced to the 'English bird expert'. He is an American cretin. He has been here a year and knows practically nothing. He showed us the black para-dise flycatcher, which we had already seen nesting. He knows no other bird. Cre-ole is sort of kitchen French. I saw a sign for the toilet. It read 'twalet'.

A fat old bus like something out of *Rupert Bear* goes up this volcanic hill of an island at 4.30 pm every weekday, taking the workers from the lodge back to their dwellings. The stuffing is coming out of the seats and all the metal is worn smooth. Dripping with seawater, we dumped our bikes against a hedge and caught the rickety old bus up to Bellevue. We never got there because the engine petered out near the top. So the passengers climbed out and walked the rest of the way. We rode back on the bus, whose engine started again on the downward slope.

People here live well. If they are jobless they get 40 rupees a day. The unem-ployed must sweep from 7 to 11 am, so the island is spotlessly clean and there is no litter.

We met an Englishman who lives here and says he cannot employ labour be-cause of the government arrangement of the 40 rupee dole. La Digue is drier than the other islands so he irrigates his banana plantation. One banana sells for the equivalent of R3 so off one tree you can make a comfortable living. There is enough fish and fruit here to live on very little indeed.

Hyacinth took us in his glass-bottomed boat. We saw hundreds of brightly coloured fish with extraordinary patterns, and wondrous coral caverns. I felt seasick so I dived off the boat and swam back to the lodge. We went on the bus again, which was driven by a drunken man with an external strabismus called Simon. He shouted very loudly at passers-by, one of whom was a fat mammy who handed him a shopping list and money and when he tried to refuse it she reached up and hit him. There was a box of fish under our feet that stank. I saw one was a cordonnier. The box was handed to a man in the road on the return journey.

I was singing French songs, and various parts of a Mozart mass and Simon being Catholic recognised the words and wouldn't let me stop and was so pleased that he took us off his normal route to Grand Anse to see the "huge" waves. Compared with the Cape waves we know, these were tiny. We sung 'Au clair de la lune' and Simon joined in and the whole busload had a rollicking time.

Simon told us there was a wedding on La Digue that afternoon and showed us where the reception would be. He was quite willing to drive us to the church but we jumped off at the corner to walk to it.

We were in time for the beginning of the wedding service. There was a whole row of little girls at the front, all dressed to the nines in bright neon colours and with masses of ribbons and clips in their hair. The church is huge and was decorated with tropical flowers, candles were burning and it was lovely, but the singing left a lot to be desired. It was harsh as are most Creole voices I've heard when they sing.

Chickens are totally free-range on La Digue and they have the right of way. How they stay alive is a miracle. Chickenhoks are forbidden.

Mercifully the sea was much calmer on the way back and I felt fine.

JANUARY 1993 MONAGHAN
The little pastel I did in France in the field with Beezy is framed and hanging in the living room. Jim looked at it and said, "Um, this is not quite up to our Beezy's normal standard is it? Let's move it shall we?" When I told him that I had done it he was mortified and so sweet in trying to undo what he had said. It is now in the storeroom.

Charles Nwaila left to become principal of Magaliesburg School. It has been a terrible blow to me. It has added to my general lowness in health and will take a lot of digesting. I cannot imagine finding anyone like Charles again to be as excellent an influence on our children here. They were very blessed to have him and so was I.

I sent a copy of Clint's tape to Simon Preston and he woke me by phoning me at nearly midnight in Plett. to say that if I didn't make a CD of this voice, he would never forgive me, and I would never forgive myself.

So I got Clint to come to Plett. from George where he lived, to give a fundraising concert to make a CD. His father drove him over, and when Clint arrived in our house, he immediately sat at the piano and played and sang Gounod's *Ave Maria*. I burst into tears. The quality of his voice was such a shock for me. What was more of a shock was Jim's reaction. He didn't like my attention focused on Clint.

And focus I did. We needed R50 000 to pay an orchestra and recording costs. It was not easy. I had the music faxed from the Drakensberg Choir School and the fax was soft and grey and not very legible. I read the music for the first time the day of the concert and it kept sliding off the piano.

I collected as many people as I could who might want to sponsor the recording and Clint sang like a dream. Luckily Hilton Appelbaum was there and he was hugely impressed. He suggested I play the tape to his father-in law Donny Gordon the next day and Donny eventually agreed to sponsor the whole thing.

I bullied my friends to form an instant orchestra and the CD was made. There was need for haste. When Clint spoke, it was evident his voice had broken, but he could still sing treble. It would be a matter of weeks – maybe a month.

Jim was visibly relieved when all this musical effort was over and I could spend all my time on him.

FEBRUARY 1993 PLETTENBERG BAY

Paddy and Jane Falloon and Thomas Pakenham came to stay in Plett. Thomas gave a talk on his book, *Scramble for Africa* at the Community Hall to over 500 people. Jim introduced him. I was agog to see what they would both wear. Jim was almost perfect, his socks matched – but his shoes didn't. He had one velskoen and one leather shoe. Then Thomas came on in shocking pink socks and sandals, his shirt crept out in front and a large part of his stomach showed. He had pulled his sweater off mid-speech and dropped it onto the floor.

Speech a huge success.

8 MARCH 1993 JOHANNESBURG

Clint sang with the Transvaal Chamber Orchestra at the Linder. Eight hundred people and the orchestra gave him a standing ovation, and made him repeat the Queen of the Night revenge aria. After this encore, Richard Cock who conducted it, announced to the audience that if Barbara Bailey hadn't phoned him about 10 times to have Clint singing in this Baroque concert, they wouldn't have heard him.

Clint sang in Cape Town with their orchestra and I had the same trouble nagging them to accept a boy soloist. They refused, but then my beloved Gerard Korsten was conducting a concert there and when I told him about Clint, he agreed without having even heard the tape. Clint was a raving success.

MARCH 1993 MONAGHAN

I have had pneumonia and don't remember ever being as ill.

There was a ghastly accident with the swing-bridge. 30 schoolchildren were on it without supervision, jumping up and down as hard as they could over the river which was in full flood – hugely swollen with the rains. A cable gave way and they all fell into the river.

One girl of 18 was drowned. She was epileptic and must have had a fit. Another little one of four drowned. The others managed to scramble out onto the banks. It was too awful. Hysterical mothers were reunited with their drenched children. I felt hopelessly useless because of being laid up with pneumonia. It was raining, and I had John fetch as many as he could to come and get dry and have hot drinks in the house.

We had the police and helicopters searching for the two that were missing. Their bodies were found after two days. New stringent rules about crossing only three at a time and always in the company of an adult.

21 MARCH 1993

Clint has recorded the Bach Cantata *Jauchzett Gott*, and he came to the farm where I had 30 of my friends to hear him and thus celebrate Bach's birthday. They had only completed the recording of the first movement with orchestra, so I had to accompany him on the piano for the 2nd and 3rd movements. And then we did Mozart's *Exultate Jubilate*.

B and Clint

I made everyone leave by 5 pm so that I could go back to bed. It was a big effort for me. Well worth it though.

APRIL 1993

Six solid days of rehearsing the Bach B Minor Mass with the chamber choir and Simon Preston. I was so worried about not being well enough. I DID IT. And the performance was one of the most exciting experiences I have had.

I wish so much I could sing Bach under such a musician more often. I am so deeply myself when I do. For me it is like a devotee taking communion.

8 JUNE 1993

Jim's book launch of his *Flying Verse* at the War Memorial was a great success and he gave a beautiful speech. What a poet he is.

I have been poorly for long months and I am trying to put on weight and get stronger.

SEPTEMBER 1993 FRANCE

I went to Maxine in Lot-et-Garonne and it was gentle and relaxed. Maxine is such a generous spirit. I played the piano for two or three hours a day without interruption.

Then on to Paris to meet Jim. He was happy to be there and spent almost all his time at the bookstalls on the Seine. Eventually I went my own way and enjoyed being alone.

I was thrilled at the thought of Jim joining me in St Severin's, a 13th century church where they were reconstructing the funeral service of Charles III. Jim said it sounded wonderful and he'd meet me there. He didn't turn up. I waited and waited and was so disappointed. I tried to practise detachment – not good at it. He came back at 11.30 pm to the flat where we were staying. He said he'd lost his way to it. I wish I didn't expect him to come, then I wouldn't mind so terribly.

Jim went on to London and said he was sorry I wasn't going with him straight away. He said, "It would be very useful – there is so much for you to do for me."

23 SEPTEMBER 1993 IRELAND

Staying with the Falloons in their house in Kildare. Jim has gone to New York. Jane Falloon, Christopher Horsman and I walked to Clungow's, which is a great Jesuit school in Ireland, where James Joyce was educated. The school drive is about a mile long and we walked in the wet cold shade of the oaks. The graves of past monks are under cypresses so old and so cold – the exact opposite of the graveyard at La Digue in the Seychelles.

The Falloons drove me up to West Meath to Eliza Pakenham's wedding at Tully-nally. A fairytale wedding.

I wore my mother's tweed suit with full-length skirt and her stylish black velvet hat. My outfit was spot-on for an Irish country wedding and Elizabeth Longford told me how grand I looked. It was good to feel well-dressed. Such a change! I shudder to imagine what I might have worn if it were not for my clothes-mad mother.

They married in the church in Castle Pollard their local village, and returned to Tullynally in the Longford coach drawn by two black horses with flowing manes. To see the coach winding its way up the road inside the grounds of Tullynally was as romantic as can be. And for that short while the sun shone!

Thomas's sole contribution to the organisation of the wedding was to leave the keys of the only car that goes properly in Dublin – arriving two nights before the wedding. He also asked Eliza the bride, two hours before the wedding, to see that there were enough umbrellas for the guests in case it rained.

Lord Longford, Eliza's grandfather, spoke well, and then Thomas in his speech said, "Eliza asked me to promise I wouldn't tell this story. When she was about eight years old she came running in to me saying, 'Daddy, Daddy, I know all about sex! And I can't wait!'" Eliza stood behind him blushing deeply.

There were about 200 hundred guests for the dinner. I was seated next to Thomas. We sat down at 9.30 pm and only started to eat after 10.30 pm because the lights had fused.

Candles were lit and while we nibbled bread and drank wine, somebody whispered to Thomas that there was a rumour the house was on fire. "So I am doing nothing, acting on the grounds that either it is or it isn't." It transpired that something had caught fire in the kitchens.

We finished dinner at nearly 1 am and then most people went to dance, but we drove back to Kildare.

B and Judy at Tullow

28 SEPTEMBER 1993
Spent a few nights with Christopher and Judy at Tullow, the sweetest thatched cottage on earth.

Christopher and I climbed up the mountain of Morne behind Tullow, and looked down on Ireland – walking in heather and bracken and along a boreen[30] with blackberries and hawthorn and holly.

Then I went on to John and Maura O'Shea (Fergal Keane's mother) in Cork. They live in a house that looks onto the harbour. John is learned and thoughtful, and he listens.

The bath! One tap isn't, I mean there is no cold tap. The hot tap has to be turned on and off with a spanner. I nearly boiled.

In the morning I walked to Passage to post letters. The lady in the local pub said

30 lane

it was half a mile away. It was 2 miles. It was raining gently, 'a soft day', and having posted my letters I was wet enough so I hitched back with an old man in a clapped-out little car. He asked where I was staying. I told him and he said, "Any friend of John O'Shea has a personal claim on me." This man was a carpenter, and went on to discuss David Copperfield.

I went back to Tullow on my way to Dublin. It poured with rain all day and cleared in the evening. At about 6.30 pm we walked to the flooded river and the sun shone weakly over the bridge, sheep grazing, and an 8th century ruins of a church. There were clouds, a Queen Anne house in the distance, freshly rained air, mud, and beauty whichever way you turned.

When I helped Judy put the horses away at about 10 pm it was starlit and very dark. The smell of the horses and the clean clear air was exhilarating. Their kitten trotted along with us. I walked along the boreen with old stone walls and robins and wrens and wet leaves and flowers and moss in the walls, and the fresh cold wet clean air. How I love it.

18 OCTOBER 1993 OXFORD
Staying with Deb. She has been my close friend for 40 years, and Shirley vV for 36. Shirley and I were reminding each other of the long, long hours we used to spend in the bath, she drinking brandy and ginger-ale, I ginger beer. We were armed with a jar of pickled onions, and a jar of crystallised ginger, and there we lay soaking in the steaming water and chatting. We decided it was far more comfortable and hedonistic than sitting on a sofa in the livingroom.

Shirley was a very keen tennis player and often went to Wimbledon. She once had tickets and invited me. We started driving to Wimbledon, the traffic was heavy, and we looked at each other, turned round and went back to her flat, ran the bath, lined up our gastronomic delights, and having soaked for a while, went and lay on her bed and watched Wimbledon far more comfortably.

OCTOBER 1993 LONDON
I am doing everything in my power to help Jim with his book-publishing. He does love me for what I am doing for him. And I love being able to do this. I must recognise this and not want him to give something of which he is incapable.

196

John Amis invited me to the last ever recording of *My Music*. I took Shirley. To be listening and looking at John, and Frank Muir and Denis Norden and Ian Wallace . . . it was like being at a party with my best friends. Dear John.

19 November 1993 Monaghan

A bee stung me at the back of my knee while I was sitting in the kitchen. Very thin skin over lots of blood vessels. By the time I had given myself anti-histamine injection, the itching had started furiously in my palms and the soles of my feet. I phoned Arnold the local doctor, went back to the bathroom to find cortisone, and passed out. I was carried to my bed, having wet my pants. Arnold arrived bare-foot and worked like a one-man-band battling to find a vein. They were collapsing. He gave me adrenaline into my belly and put me on a drip after hunting for a vein in about six places. My bp was 50 over 10. My feet were blue-white, and Arnold was also white, saying, "shit, oh shit." I thought at the time I must remind him about his bedside manner, and I was very worried about the drip being hung on the Augustus John drawing above my bed. I stopped caring about myself I was so far gone.

He put my legs right up the wall to try and get blood into my head. I had rigors for about two hours. The ambulance came and put me on another drip, and sped me off to hospital. I vomited hugely, and was freezing.

Arnold told me afterwards that I had between 5 and 10 minutes to live. Thank God he was at home to be called. The effect of all this lasted 10 days.

December 1993

Nelson Mandela together with FW de Klerk has won the Nobel Peace Prize.

Over 30 years ago Jim foretold that it would finally be up to black and Afrikaner nationalists to find a solution for South Africa. Jim was particularly pleased it was De Klerk who had the honesty and courage to abandon apartheid values, and because he had won the Abe Bailey Scholarship as a youth. Abe established this scholarship to enable Afrikaans students to study in England. He was committed to encouraging Afrikaans and English South Africans to mix and work together.

Abe lived from 1864 until 1940. Now Jim, born 1919, has been trying to do likewise with the black and white people of our country.

It was 1984 when Jim finally sold *Drum* and his other local publishing interests to Nasionale Pers, the Afrikaans publishing house. He was widely criticised for 'selling out' to Afrikaner interests. He had tried to sell it to the English press here and to what he called "the limousine liberals", but to no avail. They were not interested. By the time he sold *Drum* the political climate had changed to a large degree and he had some faith in Nasionale Pers. It was a very hard decision for him after 40 odd years of honourable battle.

11 January 1994 Monaghan & Cape

Peter and Marie-Luce Townsend arrived to stay for three weeks. We had a week on the farm, a week in Plett and a week in Cape Town. They have been easy and delightful houseguests.

I had a racehorse on appro for a week to see if I wanted to buy it, and I asked Marie-Luce if she would like to ride with me. She shrugged her shoulders and said OK. It is nerve-racking riding out with someone when you don't know what sort of horseman they are. So many say they can ride but have only ridden a horse once in the mountains with a group, and have no idea how to control a horse and often have no feel for it.

Marie-Luce and B

Marie-Luce chose the racehorse and I rode Kleintjie and kept looking back at her to see that she was all right. I was nervous for her throughout the ride. Afterwards I asked her if she had enjoyed it and she shrugged and said she had.

Later Peter told me that she had represented Belgium as an equestrian in the Olympics.

Peter had a fall walking up some steps in the dark, cut his forehead and had to be stitched. We were on the farm when the stitches were due to be removed. I have removed stitches on many occasions so Peter was pleased not to have to be driven to a doctor, and happily trusted me to do the job. Frederick and Imogen, aged

198

eight and six, were with us and wanted to watch the procedure. Fred carried chairs to have ring-side seats, made little tickets for the audience of two, and Peter lay on the sofa in the livingroom. He didn't mind in the least and a sweet little tableau it was and easy-peasy.

Jim said it was a pity Peter didn't marry Princess Margaret because he, Jim, would have had a very well-placed pad to stay when he was in London.

Larry and Viv in love
January 1994

31 JANUARY 1994

We lost five cows and three calves. Killed by lightning! Wonderful huge rains since September. Our giraffes, Larry, Viv and Joan are very happy and hopefully Viv and Joan are pregnant. The zebras have bred and the veld is more luscious than ever before, because we are understocked.

MARCH 1994 PLETTENBERG BAY

Jess and John went abroad for three weeks and left Frederick and Imogen with us. We did a lot of Keurbooms River fishing off the jetty with line and tiny hooks, and often had our supper there. Imogen was in charge of the food. She prepared our sandwiches by pressing the slices of bread onto the fish-scale-covered boards of the jetty. She would then take the knife we had been using to gut the fish, butter the bread and stick the knife into the marmite or jam to finish them off.

Imogen on the pier

At this time, Imogen aged five was at a Catholic school and was going through a period of religious fervour and wore little crosses and holy trinkets on her wrist. At night when I had put them to bed, I stood outside the door to hear her warbling, "O Sacred Heart of Jesus, I give my soul to Thee . . ."

They were so good and such a joy that when they were flown back to their parents, I watched the plane disappear in the sky and sat down on the tarmac and wept.

I had taken my own children on exactly the same fishing expeditions when they were little. It was wonderful for me to share these same delights with my grand-children.

26 MAY 1994 LONDON

At the flat we had a meeting with Andrew Best and Tony Harold, who want to publish Jessica's book of children's poems that she selected and illustrated.

Then I went to the dress rehearsal of Mozart's *Figaro* at Glyndebourne. Haitink con-ducted the LPO. The official opening of the new theatre at Glyndebourne tomor-row is to be televised in every country in Europe, so that they were thoroughly rehearsed and played like dreams. It was too much for me and I began to weep at the opening bars of the overture. But then I usually do.

When Fritz Busch conducted *Figaro* he said, "It is too loud." The concertmaster said, "But maestro, we haven't started playing yet." So Busch said, "Yes, but when you do, it will be too loud."

Haitink was superlative and I am sure would have pleased Busch. It was cold, windy and raining at Glyndebourne.

31 MAY 1994

John Amis took me to Tchaikowski's *Evgeny Onegin* at Glyndebourne. It was a crisp beautiful sunny cold day. *Onegin* was magical. Andrew Davis conducted, Gra-ham Vick produced it. Prokova was Tatiana, Yvonne Minton, Lorinda. The peasant chorus was enchanting and as for the party, I would have loved to step onto the stage and join them to do the *Polonaise*. A brilliant production and Glyndebourne at its best.

2-9 JUNE 1994 ITALY

As I flew over the north east coast of Italy it looked like the Okavango swamps –

little landmasses on the edge of the Adriatic. Then, as we flew lower over one of the islets, it transformed and became a city. Venice.

The first night we I stayed in a nasty little pensione just off St Mark's Square. It was very noisy, in addition to which the bells of St Mark's donged very very loudly every hour.

Kev and Shirley in Venice

So next morning I phoned for help to Randy Mickelson, a friend of the Fergussons, who had urged me to contact him when in Venice. He found us a charming little pensione, next to a church with fragments of Mantegna frescoes – badly bombed by our bombers, shamefully.

He was teaching Manuela Custa and for the entire week we sat in on her lessons at Randy's invitation. I learnt a good deal.

Randy lives in the Palazzo Brandolini. His living-room is where Wagner wrote the 2nd act of *Tristan*. His apartment is on the piano nobile and faces onto the Grand Canal. He taught Federica von Stade and Marylin Horne among other great singers, and must be one of the most sought-after singing teachers in the world. Manuela is very young and is already singing at festivals all over Europe and is a joy to hear.

Every afternoon Randy takes us to see the treasures of Venice. He enjoys this and we could not have had a better guide. He shows the Queen of The Netherlands around Venice and all sorts of dignitaries are sent to Randy to be their guide. His knowledge seems limitless, and his enthusiasm is catching.

He took us to the Frari to see Titian's *Assumption of the Virgin*, which over the centuries had many layers of varnish and was almost black. Bellini's triptych of the Madonna is in the side-chapel. At Rocco we saw Tintorettos and what I loved best there – Giorgione's *Christ on the Cross*.

We went to the Palladian Villa Foscari outside Venice. It was closed to the public but Randy phoned Barbara Foscari who invited us to visit privately, so we saw the kitchens and were brought coffee in the drawing room. Heavenly peaceful house. Huge grandeur outside, cosy inside, kitchens very similar to the great Cape Dutch houses, which were based on Palladio's ideas. Serenity extraordinary. The villa is also known as Villa Malcontente – a not very encouraging name. I must ask Randy why. Goethe wrote *Kennt du das Land* here.

We went to Padua where Giotto's frescoes make the Capella degli Scrovegni look like an angel's jewel-box. I was moved to tears.

Still in Padua, we then walked to what Randy says is the best food shop on earth. The food in Venice he finds inferior. He bought prosciutto, cheese, and then went on to show us the shrine of St Antonio, 800 years old. St. Antonio's relics include his tongue, his pharynx, his jaw with teeth, his hair – all horrible, black and shrivelled. An extraordinary form of worship.

We went to hear Margaret Price sing in the Fenice. It is the prettiest opera house I have seen. I had no smart clothes, so I borrowed Manuela's silk trousers and black shoes, which were a tad too small. I walked to the Fenice in my trainers, carrying the black shoes in a plastic bag to change into. They pinched my toes, so I thought what the hell, and put both pairs of shoes in the plastic bag, and entered in my bare feet. The carpet was deep pile and I was happy.

Margaret Price disappointed us in the first half. After interval, she sang like her superlative self. Maybe she had a swig of the hard stuff at interval. We have heard this may be so.

Randy filled pepperoni. Capers, breadcrumbs, garlic, tomato and olives were fried in olive oil and then stuffed into the pepperoni and stuck into the oven. The quality of the olive oil makes all the difference. I salivate at the thought of it.

Randy's partner Franco and I are becoming well qualified on the perfections of the various flavours of gelato in Venice – and make pigs of ourselves.

21 JUNE 1994 LONDON

I went to St Paul's Cathedral for evensong and unbeknown to me they were celebrating the Annual Festival of Friends of St Paul's. It was full of very smartly dressed people and I went and took a seat in the 3rd row from the front. I was wearing my usual jeans and jumper and felt a bit out of place.

The Queen Mother aged 94 arrived. She looked twenty years younger than that. After the service, she came and shook hands with the men at the end of my row, i.e. three people away from me. Group Captain John Constable was next to me – his name was on his seat. I apologised for my garb and told him I was married to one of the six Hurricane fighter pilots who defended St Paul's during the Battle of Britain. He was overwhelmed by this information, told his wife and friends, and invited me to join the dinner after the service. He pleaded with me to get Jim to come as well. I told him Jim was supposed to meet me here and that to find him would be would be well nigh impossible. I could hardly join them for dinner with the Queen Mum accoutred as I was.

But it was a happy meeting and a beautifully sung service.

10 JULY 1994 MONAGHAN
Nicholas Dougherty, aged 14, shot his first eight guinea-fowl here, and got a right and left! A remarkable feat for his first shoot, but not too surprising for a son of Simon Dougherty. Simon has shot with us every year for over two decades. The bag was 82 guinea-fowl and seven francolin. After the best rains for eight years there were more birds than we have ever seen on this farm.

SEPTEMBER 1994
Sir Ian McKellen came and lunched with us after looking at the *Drum* Archives. He is helping Marie Human who runs the Archives to organise an exhibition of *Drum* photos at the Barbican next year. He loved the photos of the Cape Moffies all togged up in drag. He is very charming and has lovely legs!

27 OCTOBER 1994 LONDON
Back to London for a thoroughly Beethoven/Nikolaus Harnoncourt fortnight. Spent almost all day and every day in the RFH at the rehearsals for all nine symphonies Harnoncourt was recording with the Philharmonia. The orchestra didn't take long to be bewitched. Many of them said they didn't want to play Beethoven with any other conductor again. These are hardened orchestral players who don't often get excited about any conductor.

In a London review, Barry Millington wrote under the headline, LIKE NO OTHER CONDUCTOR ... "Nikolaus Harnoncourt drew electrifying performances from the Philharmonia that exhilarated the players no less than the audience. Harnoncourt's highly personal conducting style was evident from the opening bars of the Second. Fixing his players with a demonic stare, he launched into the first chords with a sudden physical jerk that suggested he might have been struck by lightning. Certainly it galvanised this orchestra into playing Beethoven as they play him for no other conductor . . . These performances were as revealing as they were thrilling. Harnoncourt's decision to work with a mainstream symphony orchestra is paying handsome dividends in this cycle. For players and patrons alike things may never be quite the same again."

Kevin and B

4 NOVEMBER 1994
Kevin Volans wrote the music for a ballet and he and I went to Sadlers Wells where it was performed. Dear Kev is a genius. So is Sylvie Guillem who danced. Kevin's music is perfectly apt for her style of dancing. He writes sparingly and his music is uncompromising and honest. I love the whiff of Africa in his earlier compositions but more and more his works are losing any trace of his South African origins. He says he was moulded by Morton Feldman who cautioned, "just because you come from somewhere, doesn't mean to say you're interesting." Kevin himself says, "I'm nothing if not logical. What really interests me is finding ways of writing music which doesn't involve compositions at all."

7 NOVEMBER 1994
John Amis gave a pre-concert talk in the Royal Festival Hall. It meant so much to me to hear him speak of Beethoven walking along the streets of Vienna, talking very loudly to his companion, then stopping and taking a pencil and paper out of his coat-tail, and passing it to his friend to write his response.

11 November 1994
Imogen Cooper and Wolfgang Holzmair did Schubert's Song Cycle *Winterreise* at the Wigmore. He has a superb voice, but in my opinion not enough passion. Imogen perfection as usual. I think she plays Schubert better than anyone – including Brendel who taught her.

13 NOVEMBER 1994
In the RFH at Nikolaus Harnoncourt's Beethoven 9th with the Philharmonia, I sat next to Alfred Brendel. When Till Fellner, aged 22, played the Beethoven *3rd Piano Concerto*, Brendel's fingers performed it on his knees and he kept trying to stop himself by tucking his hands under his arms. At the entrance of the soloist in the last movement

Nikolaus Harnoncourt

of the *9th Symphony*, he sang a dreadfully sharp note forte. I turned to Brendel and looked at him cross-eyed. He got the giggles. At interval, he put his hands on my shoulders and said, "And how are you getting on?" in his heavy Viennese accent, not having a clue who I was.

16 NOVEMBER 1994
I took Thomas Pakenham to Rohan McCullough's performance of Beatrix Potter in St Mary Abbott's where B Potter had her wedding service. Then we went to Rohan and Hugh's party afterwards. Rohan is incredibly beautiful.

Rohan McCullough

8 DECEMBER 1994 MONAGHAN
Richard Marlow brought his choir of Trinity College Cambridge to Monaghan Farm for the day. Thirty-one undergraduates, girls and boys, studying various subjects at Trinity – not all reading Music for their degrees. One young girl was an Egyptologist and Jim relished showing her his beautiful collection of prints of the drawings of Champollion.

It was a typical summer's day and they gambolled like puppies, swam, played frisby, ate a huge lunch, slept and then were taken to view animals at the Game Farm. There was a terrific cloudburst and the rain came down in buckets. They were driven in open bakkies and were drenched to the skin. That evening they performed at the Hertford. Richard Marlow announced that this must be the first time the Choir of Trinity College Cambridge had performed wearing no underwear.

205

They had arrived like drowned rats and it was most fortunate that they had their black-tie outfits to change into.

Kevin and Clare Pakenham with their children are in Cape Town for the Christmas holidays. Dominic Pakenham is nearly six and his list of the most important things in the world is: God, then Invisible (being dead is invisible and he loves it), then Freedom, then Food, then Leggo.

He wrote a Valentine to his father Kevin that reads:

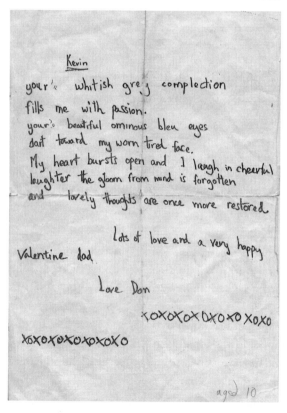

31 December 1994
New Year's Eve and Jim and I were in bed by 8.30 pm. Sucks to New Year's Eve. Since Bundy died, New Year's Eve is too emotional for me to celebrate. I hate it.

It reminds me of all the wonderful ones we had with Nicky and Glennie Behr, dancing until midnight with all the children, under the stars, the lambs roasting over the coals – without Bundy it is not to be contemplated.

7 JANUARY 1995 PLETTENBERG BAY

Kevin Volans and Phillida Kingwill came to Plett. A huge school of dolphins swam into the bay and stayed there for many hours, consuming large quantities of elf. Phil had gone surfing at 7.30 am and came up to the house in a great state of excitement. We all sped down to the beach and swam with the dolphins for as long as we had the stamina. At one point I was further out to sea than they were and so close was one of them that I had eye contact. I saw the scratch-marks on its face. They were in the bay until about 1 pm. It was like being allowed to cavort with the gods.

Kevin is working on a concerto for piano and wind instruments, commissioned by the BBC for the 1996 Proms. It is being dedicated to me!

31 August 1995
Celeste, our little Chinchilla cat – a child bride of but 10 months old – gave birth to Zubin, Pansy and Japonica in an old leather hatbox. My mother has knitted a blanket to line it for the occasion. It was at the foot of my bed, and I helped Celeste with her confinement. Birth is thrilling beyond description. We are keeping Zubin and Pansy.

Zubin

When she was old enough, Japonica was flown to Beezy and Nicci in Cape Town. Jim had to go there on business, so we doped Japonica, put her in a comfortable box and Jim took her as hand luggage. When he got to Beezy's house, he put the box on top of the piano and forgot about it.

She started mewing. Mercifully Nicci heard her and rescued her.

OCTOBER 1995 IRELAND

Kevin and I drove from Dublin to Tipperary to stay with Christopher and Judy, and then on to Cork to the Frahars. John Frahar is Professor of Anatomy at Cork University and Kate is a GP. John and I walked in Kinsale where the harbour is like a toytown dream.

John Fraher

Kevin and I stopped at a beautiful country house hotel in Birr on the way to Kildare. There was a roaring fire in the livingroom, where one of the other guests was sitting reading in an armchair. A 15th Century mass was playing on a tape machine. We were served tea, and the guest introduced herself as Lady M. She told us she was from Wiltshire and was on her way to Galway to play Scrabble with her niece. She had a sort of shelf made up of what appeared to be one single large well-upholstered bosom. Kevin suggested that she and I should have a game of Scrabble before supper. We did, and I beat her. She did not like that at all and hardly spoke to us again.

Kevin and I shared a room to save expense and we got into one of the beds to do the *Times* crossword, to which I am addicted. Discussing the events of the evening we laughed so much that someone knocked on the wall to shut us up. Mr Volans and Mrs Bailey caused a fair amount of alarm sharing a room without the additional problem of making such a din after we had gone to bed.

An Irishman, on hearing a lady say she had turned 40 and had never been able to find a husband said, "When you get over the disgrace of it, the life is more airy."

Irish motto: "Never tell a lie except when the truth won't fit."

OCTOBER 1995 MONAGHAN

David Bowie has been painting in Beezy's studio and they did some combined paintings, which will be shown in Europe and America.

A photographer from American Vogue came here to take pictures of Bowie's

model wife, Iman. While she posed, Celeste the cat grabbed the attention of the photographer to such an extent that he took countless photographs of her and she positively upstaged Iman. I wasn't here at the time, but how I wished I had been!

Above: Iman's nemesis
Right: Celeste sunbathing

Kevin, Beezy, Jeremy Crutchley and I went to the Johannesburg Biennale at Newtown. Beezy made his debut appearance as Joyce Ntobe – his alter ego – in a striped dress, high heels and a 'doek'. Jeremy, an actor highly experienced in the art, did Beezy's make-up and rendered him unrecognisable.

Jeremy was snazzily dressed in a fake leopard-skin waistcoat, tailcoat and Beezy's top hat, and described himself as 'King Pretentious Fuck the First of Fake Leopardia'. No-one recognised Beezy. One well-known artist who shall remain nameless, treated him as if he were a Coloured tart, and was rude and dismissive towards 'her'. When he learned it was Beezy, he was all over him.

13 NOVEMBER 1995
Jasper Alaric Sebastian Bailey was born to Nicci and Beezy.

Joyce Ntobe, first public appearance, with Jeremy at the Johannesburg Biennale

209

Sean O'Connor, who is running the Farm School now, produced a very good Nativity Play. It was funny and moved fast and was a great success. Sean is uncommonly gifted. The Angel Gabriel was a large fellow with huge white wings attached, who rushed onto the stage flapping his wings and yelling at the top of his voice, "I bring good tidings etc." leaping up and down and flapping throughout his speech, grinning broadly. The sun was a large orange disk at the end of a long stick, which rose behind Mary's bed, and wobbled up and down quite violently. Sean is doing such valuable work with the kids. May he be with us for a long time. Quite a few people from the British Embassy came to see the play and were impressed. The Embassy is very supportive towards our school.

I was stung by a bee. Prospero helped me with the injection of adrenalin and stroked me to keep me calm. He phoned the local doctor who was on his way prestissimo. Prospero carried me from the kitchen to the livingroom. While I lay on the sofa trying to breathe, Kevin played an arrangement of an aria from Bellini's *Norma* so exquisitely that if I had died I would have been quite happy. Watching Prospero's face while he listened to Kevin's playing is something I won't forget. Kevin's gift was as healing as the adrenalin. "Nothing like a hangman's noose to make a man concentrate marvellously."

January 1996 Plettenberg Bay

Plett. with Jim and Kevin. We have just heard that Jim is being awarded the CBE. He says it stands not for Commander of the British Empire, but for Champion Banana Eater.

Simon & Schuster are publishing his huge tome on the Bronze Age, *Sailing to Paradise,* after procrastinating for three years. He has spent so much time on this work, thank God it is happening at last. Whoopee for Jimothy!

31 May 1996

Here is a quote from the letter that Desmond Tutu, one of the nominators for Jim's Honours Award, wrote:

. . . James Richard Abe Bailey's must be the single most important individual British contribution to magazine and newspaper publishing for Africans throughout the continent. For years DRUM magazine was unique in the spread of its circulation across Africa. In recent years we have seen the richness of Mr Bailey's photographic archives reflected in a number of books tracing Africa's history during the years of its decolonisation.

God bless you,

Yours sincerely,
Desmond Tutu.
Anglican Archbishop of Cape Town.

Laurens van der Post wrote to Mr Burnett of the Nominations Unit:

Dear Mr Burnett,

I shall be grateful if you would allow me to add my plea to that of Sir Jamie Stormonth Darling to nominate James Richard Abe Bailey for an Honours Award.

By now you will have heard, I am certain, the several diverse reasons why so many of us feel that Jim Bailey should be recognised in this way. I feel that in his own personal life he as deserved more than sheer military recognition for the role he played in the battle for Britain throughout the war, and by the example he as set in his personal life ever since. There is no braver and better record from the world of Southern Africa than he started to earn in the Battle of Britain, and continued all through the fighting thereafter. I think that the book he wrote in that regard is in itself a public service as a history of that time.

And then there his outstanding work as pioneer in providing the black people of Southern Africa with the means of literary expression. It is difficult in these days of heady emancipation, to visualise the achievement and value of such a pioneering enterprise at a time when South Africa was caught up in the worst passions and excesses of the apartheid government. *Drum*, the

211

magazine which he initiated for black writers and their supporters, was like a mobilisation call among one of the indigenous nations suddenly morse-coding in what had been the profound and sultry silences of Africa. The number of people who as a result learned their trade of writing, who saw a future for African literature in English in Africa, at a time when few had even [openly] dreamt of it, was colossal.

Even when *Drum* was no longer published [by him], the research that Jim Bailey has done archaeologically and culturally into the ancient heritage of Africa is of world significance, and I hope it does not seem presumptuous on my part to suggest that the award of a Knighthood in recognition of sustained pubic services over the long random years would not be too high.

Yours sincerely,
Sir Laurens van der Post CBE

Beezy, Prospero and I went with Jim to Buckingham Palace to watch him receive his award. Prince Charles was doing the Investiture instead of the Queen and it was very touching seeing our darling Jim being honoured. He and Prince Charles giggled about something and when we asked Jim afterwards, he couldn't remember what it was either of them said. They did discuss Laurens.

A chamber orchestra of students from the Royal College of Music played baroque music before it started, and for the duration of the rather long in-between periods during the Investiture.

To begin the proceedings four Beefeaters, i.e. Yeomen of the Guard, came with great poles and banged them on the floor in unison. All part of an historic ritual. Then the Prince came on to the stage looking rather red in the face as if suffering from a hangover. Maybe he was.

The reactions of Beezy and Prospero were interesting. They found the whole procedure hilarious and said it was of Jim's tribe and not theirs. They consider themselves to be African and this ceremony was foreign to them. I love all the traditional pomp which the English do so well. I was intrigued to hear how the boys felt about it.

Above: Jim with Anthony Sampson
Right: Jim with James Barnor, ex Drum
photographer from Ghana

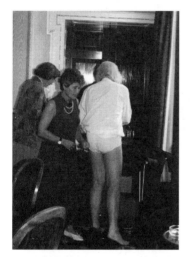

Above: Jim Bailey
Left: Jim thinks he's invisible whilst changing –
Mary and B helping

Jamie and Mary Stormonth-Darling organised lunch at the Caledonian Club after-wards and we invited all the old *Drum* staffers in London to join us, among whom were Anthony Sampson, Anthony Smith, James Fox, James Barnor, Denis Kiley and Deb Duncan. The trouble and thought that Jamie put into this day is immeasurable. He brought an entire Scottish outfit all the way from North Berwick – kilt, sporran, tam-o'-shanter, etc., for Jim to change into before dessert. Being Jim, he changed in the diningroom and here he is in his y-fronts mid-change. He had his back to us, and like an infant couldn't see us ergo we couldn't see him.

213

The S-Ds had left North Berwick at 4 am to do this for Jim. It meant a great deal to Jamie that Jim was getting honoured too. It was a lovely celebration.

20 JULY 1996 MONAGHAN

Jim and I invited to a grand birthday lunch for Nelson Mandela in the gardens of the Union Buildings in Pretoria. It was fun and we sat with John Kani whom I find good company. Lots of African music throughout, which was a delight. But I was ill and we left early. Jess and John brought Frederick and Imogen who were so thrilled to be near the great man.

I have been very ill. Glandular fever diagnosed, high temperatures and vomiting.

29 AUGUST 1996

Sherborne College Swing Band spent the day with us on the farm. They are touring South Africa – schoolboys and girls from Dorset, and delightful. They played in the big barn and our farm schoolchildren danced throughout the concert. They all had putu and sous for lunch and although they exchanged few words, their common language was music, so the day was a great joy for all concerned.

9 SEPTEMBER 1996

Lying in my bed at 6 am. I heard a very tuneful bird, imitated it, and it came right into the celtis tree at my bedroom door. It was a Kurrichane thrush.

Jess and I went to take a birthday gift to Maria Masilela who turned 100 today. Her son, Fanie gave her a big party Ndebele-style – an enormous pink birthday cake and much singing. Jess drove me because I am still stricken with ME or whatever depletes me of energy. The Masilela family have been our neighbours ever since Jim bought the farm. They were here long long before we were, in a beautifully painted Ndebele collection of houses, just over our eastern boundary. Mud and dung floors and walls, clean-swept low-walled front yards, chickens running free, children galore, old women in Ndebele blankets and bead-work that they themselves make. Lovely smell of cattle and veld, wood-smoke – gentle good neighbours they are.

Nightstar and Mars Bar[31] think they are house pets. They come into the bedrooms and the library, eat the sugar off the coffee tray and make a lot of mess. They haven't pooed in the house as yet. I bought these horses for Frederick and Imogen and neither of them likes riding much, but I ride them often and they are perfect for my purposes. I love them.

My little courtyard is full of flowers and butterflies. I have been confined to my bed on and off since the trees were bare in July. Now it is mid-September and they are in full foliage with the masked weavers weaving their multiple nests and making a huge mess all over the courtyards. The males build and build nest after nest in the same tree, and then Mrs Weaver takes her pick and lays her eggs.

John Clarke, who is on crutches having snapped his Achilles tendon poor lamb, found a sunbird's nest in the rough oak near the garage. She is sitting on eggs.

Frederick, who has just turned nine, won a silver medal for karate so he and Jim had their photo taken wearing their recent awards, Jim with his CBE, and Fred in Jim's RAF jacket with wings etc. and his silver karate medal. When being photographed Jim is always self-conscious to the roots of his follicles.

Jim then invited Fred and Imogen into his library for coffee. Imogen put 14 spoons of sugar and the whole canister of coffee into her cup. Jim didn't even notice. Fortunately she threw the whole lot out behind the bushes. The two of them then locked Jim into his library and were a bit disappointed when once more, he didn't notice.

---

31 horses

I asked Imogen if she had managed to get Jim to practise his ballet part for Romeo and Juliet. She said, "I'll force him."

I had discovered Imogen giving Jim a very fierce ballet lesson. She was singing the Montagues and Capulets theme from Prokofiev's ballet which she had watched Fonteyn and Nureyev perform on video about 30 times. She had put eiderdowns all over the floor and was trying to get Jim to walk like Nureyev by pulling his foot to point outwards. He was trying not to split his sides. When I came in, she commandeered me into singing the music while she partnered him.

19 SEPTEMBER 1996
The Oxford Schola Cantorum visited us on the farm. They were charming, their singing beautiful, and they were so taken with Clint's CD they bought six of them. They sang Byrd and Stanford at the Hertford concert in the evening after we had taken them round the game farm. All a great success.

26 SEPTEMBER 1996
It is cold. There is snow on the Cape mountains, yet from my bed I can see black-collared barbet, Cape white eye, Cape thrush, Kurrichane thrush, Cape robin, bul-bul, puff-back shrike, turtle-dove, grey loerie, black-throat canary masked weaver – telling us all there is a boomslang slithering along the high branches of the white stinkwood tree.

20 OCTOBER 1996
Clint sang his first solo concert as a counter-tenor. Malcolm Nay accompanied him, and Jess played the cello with them for *Es ist Vollbracht* from Bach's *St John Passion*, with Malcolm at the piano. When he sang Handel's *O had I Jubal's Lyre*, Malcolm started the introduction so prestissimo that I held my breath. Clint sang it miraculously.

Clint was awarded a full scholarship to Eton for a year, thanks to Ralph Allwood, the head of the Music, and Dick Haddon who happens to be in charge of the over-seas intake for A levels. I wrote a long letter to Dick Haddon saying why I thought

217

Clint would benefit from being at Eton for a year. Extraordinary coincidence that Dick was Bundy's tutor. He wrote back and said how unusual and helpful it was to have a reference from someone who was known to him.

I also told Nicholas Welsh the head of the English department at Eton all about Clint. I have known and loved Nicholas since he was four years old. Clint's English was poor at this stage, and he certainly was not ready to take an A level in this subject. Nicholas said he would teach him to love English through music, through the poetry that was written for music, and he would not be required to write the exam.

And this genius of a teacher did just that. He nurtured Clint and made him feel secure in those very exacting and foreign surroundings. Nick opened his heart and his home to Clint and made his time at Eton very different to what it might have been.

Ralph Allwood had heard Clint when he (Ralph) came to me in South Africa. He invited Clint to his Eton summer choral course, where Clint excelled. It was Ralph's suggestion that he should try for a scholarship.

23 OCTOBER 1996
St Mary's Standard 1 girls came to Jim's 9th (77th) birthday party. I am still too weak to do much.

I couldn't go to Wits in the evening where Jim was awarded the English Academy Gold Medal for services to English Literature. Marcia Leveson, Professor of English at Wits and Chairman of the English Academy, nominated him for this award.

Jim learning to dance

5 NOVEMBER 1996
Roy Goodman and the European Union Chamber Orchestra came for the day. They all swam and then bought quite a lot of CDs of Clint. Roy presented me with a copy of Bach's *St Mark's Passion* which he has recorded with this orchestra. It is a thrilling performance and I think the first recording of this work. It is a

compilation of Bach's music, fitting new text to it, which was customary in Bach's time. It was performed at St Thomas's in Leipzig in 1731. This recording is a reconstruction. Roy's music is as alive and as satisfying as Harnoncourt's, and that's saying something!

13 NOVEMBER 1996
Kevin arrived to stay. I am not well, and keep mostly to my bed.

I am reading TE Lawrence. Curious man he must have been. Winston Churchill described TE Lawrence: "Despite all his profound dislike of publicity, he had a remarkable way of backing into the limelight." Jim's elder sister Cecil typed *Seven Pillars of Wisdom* for TE.

25 DECEMBER 1996
Only the immediate members of the family came for Christmas. It was so relaxed and we all decided we should always spend Christmas together. When there are no outsiders we behave and talk in a so free a fashion that we cannot imagine why we shouldn't live like that forever.

We went to Plett. and I stayed upstairs and everyone else lived downstairs so it was peaceful and very restful for me.

27 FEBRUARY 1997
Alexander Baillie is in South Africa with John Eliot Gardiner as part of a workshop with Busk Aid. Rosemary Nalden is doing excellent work with street kids from Soweto, teaching them stringed instruments. She organised for JEG to bring part of his orchestra to this country to play with Busk Aid and do workshops with them. They performed together at the Linder Auditorium and Sandy Baillie was soloist playing a Haydn cello concerto superlatively.

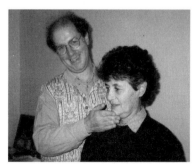

Alexander Baillie giving B a lesson on Alexander technique

219

Sandy and Crystal his wife came and spent the day and it was as good as a day can be for me. "The Lord couldn't make a better, I'd say, and if he could, he never has done." I played the orchestra part for Haydn's *C Major concerto* – Sandy plays like a dream. Then we did the Beethoven *G minor sonata*. What a treat for me to be able to do this with him! Then a lovely supper at the Cradle[32] with Prospero.

5 MARCH 1997

Wettest March in history. The bridge over our river was washed away with the floods. There are floods all over the country.

15 MARCH 1997

Cecily Corti came from Vienna, bringing her son Sebastian. Then Thomas and Valerie Pakenham arrived. Strange mix it was.

Then Ralph Allwood and 38 choristers spent the day at the farm. Eton
College Chapel Choir was touring
South Africa and they rehearsed in
the livingroom for two hours. Clint
was a member of the choir, and
there was a wonderful meeting of
Monaghan Farm School Choir and
Eton singing Zulu songs together
with Etonians trying some Zulu

Choristers of Eton rehearsing in our living room

dancing. Ralph had me beating the skin drum for their Zulu number. He has a rare gift for understanding and dealing with adolescent boys. They are natural and polite and thoughtful with Ralph at the helm. Various masters at Eton who have had troublesome boys and even wanted to expel them on occasion, send them to Ralph. He seems to work magic.

One of the choristers, Dominic Passmore, has a beautiful voice. He is 13 and he and I are in love. He won a scholarship to Eton. He is delightfully uninhibited. When

---

32 Prospero's restaurant on his game farm which is part of the Cradle of Humankind.

Dominic Passmore with B

I went to Eton and was walking from the Music School, I passed a rowing Eight plus their cox, the lightly-built Dominic. They were all clad in white blazers with their team colours, and seeing me on the other side of the road, Dominic raced across to me and jumped into my arms, his legs clinging around my waist.

Later, when I was at Ralph's house with about 10 members of the choir, singing through a Mozart mass, Dominic walked in. He came straight to me where I was sitting on the carpet and sat himself in between my knees so we could share my music score.

From Ralph I was to go to the Welshes for supper. Dominic immediately said he'd come too. I explained it was a bit of a grown-up dinner so he offered to escort me there and placed my arm firmly through his. Nicholas Welsh opened the door and I introduced Dominic by telling Nick we were going steady. Dominic broke in and said, "Oh no we're not! We're sprinting!" Nick invited him in for a drink.

MARCH 1997 PLETTENBERG BAY

We all went to Plett. and the Eton Choir came and performed in the Community Hall. Ralph asked me to find a drum, which I did, and then had me play it with the choir in front of 500 people. I was also asked to introduce the choir, which I found terrifying. Thomas and Val came and Thomas was so kind giving me advice. He is so used to public speaking he would have done it with ease. I wish he had. I was monstrously tired.

10 APRIL 1997

Flu and high fever. We saw four snakes in one day. It has been unseasonably cold and they came to fill their bellies before hibernating. The sun is very welcome at present because it has been so scarce.

I Fagiolini, a choral group of six singers from Oxford who are touring SA, are recording a CD with a Soweto group of singers and it is a wonderfully sensitive mixture of European and African styles of music.

They came to the farm for the day. Roderick Williams, the bass, sang Russian songs at the piano, and they all sang in the livingroom for Jim and me – lovely group of musicians. Roderick is a darling and has enormous talent.

Prospero took me as his first passenger in his Kitfox. This tiny aeroplane was assembled by a dental mechanic, and looks like a toy. Surprisingly I enjoyed it and wasn't sick. We flew very low over Hartebeestpoort Dam and a water-skier got quite a fright but then waved to us. As Prospero says, everyone there is playing, either sailing or windsurfing or fishing so they don't get cross when he dive-bombs them.

Jim not sitting pretty in his kilt, 1997

28 April 1997

Our beloved cat Daisyboy went missing – never to be seen again. Because of the unusually snaky season Jess thinks it could have been a snake. Daisyboy was 14, and may the next world be as good to him as this was. My mother always says that if there is such a thing as reincarnation she hopes to come back as one of my cats.

10 May 1997 Europe

Stayed with Cecily Corti in her beautiful flat, like an eagle's nest high among the trees. Being with Cecily is a joy. I am so at ease here and so comfortable. I don't feel in the way or strange. Cecily gets on with her life and I with mine. A rare gift for a hostess. I feel very fortunate to be here.

Cecily told me something enchanting. There was a young mother pregnant with her second child. She explained to her two-year-old that she was about to give birth. When the new baby arrived the two-year-old pleaded to be left alone with the new-born infant. The mother finally relented but kept the door ajar and witnessed her two-year-old bending over the crib whispering, "Tell me about God – I have almost forgotten."

At 7 pm the first evening, we discovered that Nikolaus Harnoncourt was rehearsing the Chamber Orchestra of Europe in the Konzerthaus. It was Mendelssohn's *Midsummer Night's Dream*. It was as magical as it was meant to be. The opening string passage was like gossamer. Only Harnoncourt can sustain an unaccented pianissimo like that. I was transported. Oh, what he does with an orchestra!

Jim phoned me here in Vienna yesterday and I was thrilled. His secretary dialled the number for him! Again I long to help him with publishing Abe's and/or Mary's biography. I feel so good when I can offer to help and when I get to London I will go flat out at it.

Harnoncourt conducted two Schubert operas. I found it claustrophobic in my seat in the stalls and during the first half, I noticed the second box on the left was empty. In the interval I met up with Phillip Bell, a musician friend. He and I went upstairs before the beginning of the second half and found the door of the relevant box locked. So we went into the next box and climbed over the partition, which meant being suspended over the auditorium and possibly being spotted and sent out, or possibly breaking our limbs or our necks.

All was well and Philip and I sat on the floor of the box until the lights were dimmed for Act 2 when we sat up and gazed on the Chamber Orchestra of Europe and enjoyed the rest of the evening. I am good at corrupting my friends.

Cecily took me to lunch with the grandson of Richard Strauss, and his wife. All that I found exciting about him was that he was RS's grandson. Otherwise he seemed to be a lugubrious old bore who is a great authority on his grandfather but appears to have little interest in any other music. Sadly his English is not good and my German is zilch, so I didn't get him to talk about him grandfather – which could have been such a privilege. He loathes Nikolaus Harnoncourt at present, because last week NH was on the radio saying that whatever Richard Strauss wrote after *Der Rosenkavelier* is crap. That was that as far as Christian Strauss was concerned. Off with Harnoncourt's head!

Cecily drove me to her family castle Rastenburg, which is one and a half hours out of Vienna. Beautiful countryside, a huge mediaeval castle high on a rocky outcrop which rises out of a beech forest. Pine forests in the distance. It was 30 degrees and as hot as hell, but inside the castle it was terribly cold because it snowed two weeks ago and it takes about a month for the stone to warm up. I shudder to think of the winter.

I walked alone for a couple of hours through the forests and got a bit lost. There was a trout stream at the bottom of the valley – and no rod!! Masses of birds in the forest. Lovely birdsong, and the loudest woodpecker I've ever heard pecking its brains out. I saw little shy violets, fields of daisies and forget-me-nots. I love discovering the occasional pink ones.

I slid on my bum some of the way through the pine forest ending up in a sea of nettles. I was in my khaki shorts and was stung badly on my legs and could find no path to get out of the nettles. Eventually I grew so accustomed to being stung that I gave up minding and it was a wonderful exercise of mind over matter.

Went from Vienna on to Prague by train to meet Thomas and Valerie and 30 other Irish – all part of an Opera Society. Prague stunningly beautiful. We all went to Smetana's *The Bartered Bride,* charmingly produced – mediocre voices.

The Irish lot and I stayed in an ugly modern hotel on the outskirts of Prague. I kept happening to be in the lift with the same man and eventually we chatted. He was the leading cellist in the St Petersburg Philharmonic Orchestra – Sergei Chernadiev. He invited me to their concert that evening. I was going to the *Battered Bride*, so he insisted that I come to his rehearsal with him. I went in the bus with him and the rest of the St Petersburg orchestra and had a wonderful afternoon.

From a postcard I sent to Jim from Prague:

"Picture this: Thomas and I are sitting in a huge piazza outside a church built in 1380, and two American women at the next table want to know how to

224

get tickets for the underground in Prague. Thomas tells them, and uses a knife and fork, crosses them then puts the sugar sachet where they cross, representing the Museum stop, talking all the while as if he knows every inch of Prague. He confuses them so much they are aghast and leave their table and walk fairly briskly away."

Back in London I was waiting for Thomas who was flying from Dublin and coming straight to my flat so that we could go together to hear the *Koln Musica Antica* at St James's Piccadilly. I waited and waited and gradually grew frantic because it was after 7 pm and we'd be late. The concert was beginning at 7.30 pm. The doorbell rang and in came Thomas – the plane had been delayed.

He started telling me about the giant lilies in flower at Tullynally, and supposing I had to give up on the concert, I offered him wine and my heart sank. Kevin Volans had told me how wonderful the Koln musicians were and I was very excited at the thought of hearing them live. Then Thomas said, "Weren't we supposed to be going to a concert tonight?" So I told him I was longing to go. He said, "Well why didn't you stop me talking, you silly goose? Come on, we'll get a taxi – quickly!"

We only missed five minutes of the concert. We had press tickets otherwise we wouldn't have been let in immediately. Other latecomers had to wait until interval. They were performing a work by Zelenka, 1679-1745, who was a psychopathic composer for the court of August the Strong in Dresden. Reinhard Goebbel led and played like a dream. At one moment there was a hooter outside the church and it was in perfect tune with what they were playing. I nodded to Goebbel and he grinned and nodded back. He is a wonderfully exciting musician.

Kevin told me of his first encounter with R__. Kevin arrived early in the morning in Cologne and was to stay with R__ and his partner, who was a friend of Kevin's. The partner was away at the time and R__ answered the door. He was stark naked. He ran off to the bedroom to fetch some boxer-shorts which he held clutched in front of him. He then led Kevin to the kitchen and insisted on making him coffee and giving him some breakfast. All the while covering himself with the scrunched-up shorts, he did everything with the other hand, walking on tiptoe. He wouldn't hear of Kevin helping in any way, and after a bit Kevin asked him why he was walking on tiptoe. R__ replied, "Because the floor is so cold."

I went to Sherborne to visit Simon Wilkinson whom I hadn't seen since Oxford and who has taught at Sherborne for decades. On the train going there were about 15 ex-railway employees on their way to a funeral in Cornwall. They were all dressed up to the nines and had a wonderfully happy journey. They were delighted to be in each other's company and have an excuse to chat and drink together for a couple of hours. Their chatter made the journey pass quickly and amusingly for me.

Sandy Baillie came and spent five hours with me in our London flat. He is super company and told me many tales about musicians. Stravinski as a child refused to shake hands with a man who had offered him one finger. He said, aged 10, that he would wait until he was worthy of shaking all five fingers.

Apparently when Galena Vishnevskaya, wife of Rostropovich heard that her husband had impregnated Ann-Sophie Mutter, she held his cello out of their 2nd storey window threatening to drop it. At a banquet she also tipped his hot soup over his lap. Fruity gossip.

3 AUGUST 1997 MONAGHAN
Kate O-T and I rode for over two hours chasing guinea-fowl into the guns. With success I might add. There were 10 guns, Jim shot expertly. How good it is for me to feel well enough to do this.

6 AUGUST 1997
Pixie-boy[33] turned 11 today. He said he didn't want to be 11 – serious sad expression on his face. I asked him how old he would like to be. He said seven. Poor Pix, he knows a thing or two.

10 AUGUST 1997
Edwin Cameron came for the day. I wish he were heterosexual because he should breed like a rabbit. We need little Edwins all over this country. He is such a deeply

---

33 Frederick

good man. We had a lovely walk on the game farm and saw an orange-breasted long-claw. This bird is a dust-coloured, nothing-to-look-at little bird, almost invisible in its being the same colour as the winter veld, and then it turns to face you and beneath its chin is a persimmon sunset. It is such a wildly unexpected surprise.

29 August 1997
I was lying on Helen Suzman's sofa after lunching with her, with her two kittens asleep on top of me and a lady popped in and said hello. I greeted her and asked her to forgive me for not getting up on account of the kittens being asleep, and said my name is Barbara Bailey. She said, "I'm Linda Chalker, and please don't move." We chatted a while and she went off to pack because she was flying back to England that evening. Later on Helen came in and told me that Linda Chalker wasn't too keen on the kittens because they had clawed her silk skirt – and typically, Helen said if she had to choose between the kittens and Linda, Linda could stay elsewhere.

Helen is besotted with her animals. I once found her walking like a hunchback because a cat was sitting on her shoulders. She has always been great fun and I do appreciate knowing this side of her. I admire her more than I can say, and in addition to all her honorary doctorates from universities all over the world and all the honours she has received everywhere, I feel she deserves even more recognition for standing alone in parliament for so long against such terrible odds, and with such honesty and guts.

September 1997
I am having a very frustrating and dreary time battling with the Department of Education over the appointment of a good headmaster for the farm school. It is truly ill-making. They do not answer the telephone or reply to faxes or letters – or acknowledge any form of correspondence.

The one big consolation is that Cassie Abodeelly has come to teach there. Cassie is Egyptian, lives in America, and is teaching voluntarily for a year as part of her training. She is hugely generous, good fun and is a great addition to the staff. She lives here in the garden cottage. I wish she were staying longer.

Gentle rain for weeks now. Mushrooms almost daily on the lawn. Nightstar has become a real love. I adore him, he is perfect for me, soft mouth, lively forward moving. And he and Mars Bar come into the bedroom whenever I forget to shut the door.

14 SEPTEMBER 1997

Pincus Zuckerman rehearsed the Beethoven violin concert with the orchestra at the SABC. I took Granny and she said it was the most wonderful moment of her life. He played a Guanerius like silken cream. For Beethoven I prefer him to anyone I have heard.

Pincus Zuckerman

Pinky and his accompanist Mark Neikrug came and spent Sunday on the farm. We were disappointed that he didn't bring his fiddle.

1 OCTOBER 1997

Stood on a bee. I gave myself the adrenalin injection, got the sting out, so that very little poison actually went in, BUT worst reaction ever. Vomiting, total and awful urticaria, kidney failure, arrythmia, freezing blue lips. Jim was wonderful. I fainted about four times, once while on the loo with my head practically on the floor, and Jim held me and carried me back to the bed. I really thought it was tickets. The worrying part is how little poison caused this. Oh dear. Dr Mark Holliday was on the other end of the phone guiding me thank God.

Prospero came back from California with his foot in plaster. He said he broke it in a climbing accident. He did. He was coming down a ladder out of an attic, forwards, and jumped onto a table that was wet. Oops.

20 December 1997
Our first baby giraffe was born.

JANUARY 1998 PLETTENBERG BAY

Plett. cold and rainy. Max Coleman speared a 10lb leervis, as well as stumpnose and blacktail. Max is almost as old as Jim and they meet with their spearguns at dawn on the beach. The old men of the sea.

We went to Cape Town on the way home and Simon Preston was there, run-

ning a Choir Festival. He and I finished a Spectator crossword!! – mostly Simon of course. It was lovely to see him, as always.

While I was in Cape Town I was tele-phoned by a young man in despair. He had his final cello exam at the University and had no accompanist. Neil Solomon suggested that he asked me! I played the whole Brahms E minor sonata with him at a day's notice. Frightening it was, to put it mildly, before an examining board. He passed, mercifully.

Simon Preston and B in Cape Town

9 FEBRUARY 1998

Kev arrived to stay. And then the Falloons and Dougie Boyd who is the first oboist for the Chamber Orchestra of Europe. He played the Richard Strauss concerto with our Chamber Orchestra – beautifully, and when he came to stay, I took an photograph of no less than four oboists lounging on my bed.

It has been a joy having Dougie practising here – even in the kitchen while I cook. He is a superb musician as well as a lovely oboist. During a long and rather alcoholic lunch with many Irish guests, Dougie and I escaped to my room and watched a video of the Mahler *2nd Symphony* played by the Chamber Orchestra of Europe. Dougie pointed out his cellist wife – he was 1st oboe – and then he went on to tell me who was in love with whom. It was great fun hearing all the gossip of the COE.

10 MARCH 1998 LONDON

Went to a rehearsal of *Cosi fan Tutti* with Colin Davis conducting. Jonathan Miller directed and it was very funny and very good. Ashutosh Kandekhar – editor of

Opera Now – took me to the opening night. It is quite alarming how poker-faced he has to be on the first night. All the critics are there and don't want to let on what each other thinks of the performance. Covent Garden opera is at Shaftesbury Avenue Theatre while the new Opera House is being redone. *Cosi* was wonderful.

Stayed with the Dick-Reads in Winchester and saw Tom Kiley in his house production of 'Guys and Dolls', which was excellent. The standard was as high as a school production could be. It would have done well in the West End.

How happy Jim would have been as a boy at Winchester now. When he was there in the 1930s it sounded more like Dotheboys Hall. I saw the House, du Boulay's or 'Cook's' where Jim was. It looks like a prison. I wanted to weep thinking of Jim being incarcerated there.

25 March 1998

Paddy Rossmore, first cousin to Jim, came to lunch. He is so like Jim to look at that it was eerie. A gentle soul and very unlike Jim in character. Same skin texture, same forehead, cheeks, and eye-shape. I remember Jim saying that Paddy was the most beautiful child anyone had seen. His smile is disarming. He told me his life was made miserable at Eton and he would never send his son there.

There are those I know that had a hideous time at their public schools and then still send their sons away to boarding schools at the age of eight. I suppose they fear to choose a different life for them. Thank heavens these institutions have changed considerably.

26 March 1998

My last day in London and I went to the Royal Festival Hall to hear Gidon Kremer rehearse the Sibelius concerto with John Eliot Gardiner conducting. For me Gidon Kremer is the most exciting violinist alive. His playing is quite different from anyone else's. His passion is terrific and singular in these days of technical perfection and so often there is nothing much more.

JEG was charming and friendly which was a surprise.

Then a lovely Thai lunch with Sandy Baillie. He joined me in the RFH and I didn't recognise him at first because Crystal had gone out of control with a new hair-cutting machine and he was almost shaved bald. Flew back to SA in the evening.

28 MARCH 1998 MONAGHAN
Jasper (aged two), Beezy and Nicci came to stay, and Jess and her two children came and we went to Keith Kirsten's Nursery where there is a children's play area. We all lay in the bed of plastic coloured balls. I loved it and must do it again. It is hugely relaxing. Other small children there thought it a bit odd finding adults lying in the plastic balls. Beezy and Jess enjoyed it as much as I did.

Hunt the B

Jasper has inherited Beezy's mind. He said "a Gleek is something that can't shut its mouth." He was singing "Ladybird ladybird fly away home" and he said the ladybirds can't understand it. So Beezy asked, "is it because they are too small?" "No," replied Jasper, "it is because some of them are German."

When Beezy was two, he cried for a star, to be able to hold it in his hands. He would only agree to go to sleep if Jim promised to climb the big ladder, buy a long feather-duster from Harrods-in-the-Sun (our name for the local farm store) and yank down a star. Eventually I made him one out of silver paper and tinsel. He was desperate hold it in his hands. And now Jasper asked his mother Nicci for the moon. She must climb the tree and get the moon for him.

231

Greyhornbill

26 April 1998
Heavenly day. A grey hornbill came whistling into the vegetable garden. I think it was the first time I'd seen one at Monaghan.

In America Friederich Gulda felt ill and cancelled a concert. He wanted to read his obituary so he telegraphed wherever he was engaged to play, and told them F Gulda had died. His obit appeared in the *New York Times*. When I heard him play in Vienna, he loped onto the stage with a little floral skullcap and gave a very original rendering of Mozart and Bach, and then started extemporising on the Mozart theme. He is a unique free spirit in the music world and has a great following. No wonder.

He was once billed to play at the Musiekverein in Vienna and when he heard that Kurt Waldheim was in the audience, he refused to appear. End of story.

1 May 1998
I went to Adam Seftel's memorial service. Dear good Adam died in a car. He fell asleep during a long drive somewhere. Poor poor Seftels. I saw Effie at the service. She was so stricken she kept hidden behind the building to avoid meeting people. When she saw me, she fell into my arms. What a sisterhood it is to be mothers of children that have died. We didn't have to speak. There are no words. There will never be words. Christ it is so sore.

Adam worked in the *Drum* Archives and did excellent editing of *Drum* books. It was lovely for me to have him working here on the farm. A gentle sweet soul.

One morning he came into my room with a nasty attack of asthma and asked if I had any medicine to help him. I have a good selection because of my bee allergy, so I offered him a choice of various pills and inhalers. He explained breathlessly that his mother and father never agree on the treatment (both are doctors) and therefore he didn't know what to choose. I helped him over his attack and we lay on my bed and giggled about it.

I will miss him very much.

Son-in-law John holding Saskia four months later

2 JUNE 1998
Saskia Honey Bailey born to Nicci and Beezy.

13 JUNE 1998 LONDON
Went to Hugh Whitemore's play, *A Letter of Resignation* at the Savoy. Edward Fox took the part of McMillan. I loved the play. Hugh is a genius. He is also wonderful company.

Ash and I went to Evensong in the Abbey and Tim Bavin gave the sermon. He is now a monk. I went to greet him afterwards and he fell into my arms. We hadn't seen each other since he was Bishop of Johannesburg.

Saw Alan Bennett's *Lady in the Van* with Maggie Smith for whom it seems as if it were written. Alan Bennett played the part of himself. I thought it was very very funny and brilliantly acted.

I went to Ireland. Lunched with the Stewart-Smiths and then Jane Falloon drove me to Laois, where she and Paddy live in the prettiest house imaginable. Jane has a great talent for making a home and she has extraordinary energy. Not only has she moved house from Kildare to Laois, but she has also set up a new home in Oxfordshire – at the same time. She and I went and sang in her church choir practice in Stradbally, a nearby village.

Jane introduced me to Robert Townley, Dean of Kildare. He is not of this era but straight out of an Anthony Trollope or Jane Austen novel. I don't think I have met anyone so anachronistic. He is enchanting and innocent beyond description.

I went to Tipperary to Judy and Christopher at Tullow, my favourite house in Britain.

Me: "What's the date?" Judy: "Yesterday was something so today's another day."

Much playing of scrabble and spite-and-malice, and plenty of laughter. Judy is the only member of the Protestant church choir in Fethard. There are no others in the choir. Christopher proudly claims that he goes to bed with an entire choir every night.

233

Went to Kevin, who lives in the Stableyard at Knockmaroon in Dublin. He has exquisite minimalist taste, rather like his music.

Took the train to Mullingar where Thomas Pakenham was meeting me to drive me to Tullynally. Opposite me on the train was a nun. A very swarthy masculine unlovely-looking person, who while reading her multi-beribboned missal, picked her nose constantly, ate it, licked her finger to turn the page, and then changed fingers to continue picking her nose.

My first reaction was to look away in disgust, and then as the journey went on, I became riveted. When the tea trolley arrived, we all had a cup and she was given no sugar. I offered her mine, which started her talking.

Staring at me intensely, without a smile, she said, "I would have done the same for you. Are you a stranger here?"

"Yes."

"Are you her on holiday or business?" I told her I was visiting friends.

"Are you married?"

"Yes," and I told her my husband was not with me because he was ill.

She gazed at me fixedly, silent for a while, and then leaning over, offered me a rather grubby tissue, and said, "You must be grieving."

She was *willing* me to cry. Her black eyes bored into me. I think she works with children, and makes certain the poor little things are utterly miserable. I kept wishing Jessica or Beezy were with me – we would have been in stitches.

Thomas feeding the ducks at Tullynally

Thomas met me at Mullingar wearing an Australian leather hat in battered condition, and an awful leather jacket. His opening words were, "How much do you think I paid for this jacket?" I had no idea. He said, "Absolutely nothing. It was left at Tullynally after a concert and no-one has claimed it." I am not surprised.

We stopped in Mullingar to do

the shopping. Thomas had a list of groceries to be bought. I wanted to go to the chemist so I told him I'd meet him in the supermarket when I had done. I spent at least 15 minutes queuing to pay the chemist. I found Thomas chatting to a lady telling her about a villain who had chopped down some trees and he led us both out to witness the stumps. He hadn't even started the shopping. So I did it.

22 JUNE 1998

From 10 am-1 pm and then again from 4-7 pm I was in King's College Chapel Cambridge listening to the choir practising for their recording of the Rachmaninov Vespers. Then the next day I took Rohan McCullough and Prospero and Lara Agnew to St Paul's Cathedral where the St Petersburg Choir were rehearsing the same Rachmaninov Vespers. Their pianissimo was such that Lara leant over and whispered to me, "I thought it was the wind."

What utter magic. It is senseless to compare King's and the Russian choir. They are both wonderful and I think Stephen Cleobury, organist and choirmaster of King's is doing an incredibly good job with King's. But the Russians are singing their own music and the power and earthiness of it is mind-blowing. I want the recordings of both.

16 JUNE 1998

Winged my way to Annie Campbell in Corfu, flying over snow-capped Alps, the intricate shoreline of Italy, spotted Venice, and when I saw we were landing on Corfu I was so excited I started to cry. It is thrilling beyond words to go somewhere new and beautiful.

I took a taxi to the north east of the island and was met by Annie and her enchanting daughter Elizabeth known as Weeny whose welcome was overwhelming.

It was dark when I arrived, so imagine my wonder in the morning when I opened my shutters onto a sparkling sea with the mountains of Albania only two and a half kilometres away. Wild rosemary was growing down to the gin-clear water – and it was all like a background to a Classical painting.

My mother brought us up on the Greek Myths and I was deeply in awe to see the beach where Odysseus was washed up to find Nausicaa and her friends. Corfu is heavy with myths and Annie is a great source of knowledge. I feel very much at home here.

235

The three-year-old son of Weeny saw a mother breast-feeding her baby. This was new to him and he asked her what she was doing. She told him she was giving her baby milk. He stood watching for a while and then said, "Can you do tea?"

A lot of men here are called Spiros, who is the patron saint of Corfu. Annie's house is right on the sea. They have their own little jetty where I can dive naked into the sea – or, if going to lunch at the local taverna, don my bikini and swim across the little cove to sit under the vine leaves, dripping wet and enjoy delicious food with the others who come by car.

Here is gentleness, time meaning absolutely nothing, good and loving company.

When I rise, the enormous decision I have to make is whether to walk through the olive grove to the village of Kassiopi and sit and sketch the boats in the little harbour; or swim off the jetty; or lie and read.

Corfu looks like a Cezanne - cypresses, vines, olive-groves, hills, and sea. The oleanders are so heavy in blossom they look like rhododendrons.

At night, from time to time, a flashing light can be seen on the Albanian coast. Smuggling is rife, and Albanians come over to Corfu in rowing boats during the night to escape into Greece. Some have actually swum across. We are near the narrowest crossing between the two countries, so the smuggling and escaping goes on right here.

Weeny was born and brought up a Corfiot so she knows all the locals in Kassiopi. She took me to a taverna where a good friend of hers, a wonderful Greek dancer was the central performer. Corfiots of all ages take part in the dance, three-year-old children up to aged crones. The island comes to life at about 11 pm and the music and drinking and eating is a total delight. Everyone has a siesta after lunch, so at night the villages throb.

As I wandered down the road in Kassiopi, the tavernas were alive with music and dancing, children running free under the stars. The sense of living with such simplicity and joy moved me to tears. I felt such a surge of elation watching the dancing, and then the whole village crowded in to see England beat Germany in the world cup on TV at half past midnight.

And so to bed in the small hours, and slept till 9 am. A very new kind of life – so relaxed and healthy.

The choir of St John's College Cambridge arrived from the airport and came straight to the farm in a huge coach. To prevent the coach driving into our drive where it would never be able to turn, I mounted my gallant white charger Nightstar and rode up the farm road to meet them. I guided the coach in to the barn above our house and the choir etc. followed me on my horse, on foot down through the garden.

Christopher Robinson, their choir-master, cannot sleep on a plane, so I ran him a hot bath and lent him pyjamas, which I later discovered were full of holes, and put him to bed to sleep for a few hours. It was about 10 am.

Although it is the end of winter and the water is at its coldest, all the choristers saw the pool, stripped naked and jumped straight in.

B with Christopher Robinson

The dean of St John's, Andrew McIntosh, and his wife Mary accompanied the choir on the their tour. Lovely lovely people. Mary fosters babies. She had fostered over 100 by the time she came here. After the 100th baby she has stopped counting. It is a rare gift she has. She is in her 70s.

Mary told me she once had a cat with a litter of kittens and she introduced an abandoned baby rabbit to the mother cat. After some time the mother cat was seen bringing grass for the baby rabbit. Only Mary could have caused such a miraculous happening.

Jim loved showing his library to Andrew who is a great Classics scholar. It is rare for Jim to have someone who can so readily appreciate his library.

Having them rehearse here and at the game farm was wonderful. We all had a picnic lunch under the trees in the sloot and there were choristers climbing in the branches wherever we looked.

I organised a concert at the Hertford in the evening. The thatched chapel is not acoustically enhancing, but the place was packed and the audience was very appreciative. From here they go off to tour the rest of the country.

After their game drive and before their concert, I had an hour or two to rest and I didn't want to go all the way back to Monaghan, so I went to the Piggery which is Prospero's home at the game farm. It really was a piggery and he converted it into his dwelling. He has been living alone there for over a year. I asked him if I might have a cup of tea. Of course, said he. There was no tea. And no milk. Then, having washed my hands and face I asked him if he would lend me a comb to smarten up a bit for the concert. No comb. May I have a brush? No brush. Where is a mirror so I can just tidy my hair with my hands? No mirror, but said he, if you sit on the floor of the kitchen you can see yourself reflected in the shiny metal of the fridge.

24 SEPTEMBER 1998 LONDON
Rohan McCullough married Hugh Whitemore in the church up the road from Peel Street where they live. I walked there and it was a lovely gathering. Edward Fox read a Shakespeare sonnet. He read it like Harold McMillan because he is at present HM in Hugh's play, *A Letter of Resignation*.

I greeted a lady who is obviously a neighbour and friend of Hugh and Ro – I couldn't remember who she was but she had a very familiar face. She turned out to be Polly from Fawlty Towers. It was a star-studded congregation on account of Hugh and Ro being playwright and actress.

Rohan, who is one of the most beautiful women I know, looked ravishing in a cream Indian outfit.

All the guests were taken in a bus to the Ritz where the celebration was held. Derek Jacobi gave the wedding speech which was hilarious and original. He and his partner Richard Clifford are delightful. Derek is twinkly and gentle and has an attractive humility and naturalness.

26 SEPTEMBER 1998
Lunched at Hugh and Ro. His stories about working with actors and producers are as amusing and riveting as Sandy Baillie's are about musicians. Hugh tells how impossible so-and-so is to work with etc. etc. and many quirky little tales about the various famous actors or actresses who one knows so well from the screen or stage. They suddenly take on a new light. Hugh is also deeply musical.

29 September 1998

Kevin and Hugh came for supper and Kevin played a video of a composition of his and Hugh really appreciated it. Wouldn't it be loverly if they worked together one day!

2 October 1998

Lara and I went to the film on Francis Bacon. We both cried a lot and were badly upset by it. Derek Jacobi played Bacon brilliantly. Out of the squalor and filth and drunkenness comes this genius.

16 October 1998 Cape Town

Jim and I flew to down for Beezy's Lee Ping Zing show at his factory. Lee Ping Zing is Beezy's mythical character based upon a Chinese ceremonial bank note. He and Brett Bailey (no relation) staged a street performance using street kids, closing the road in front of the factory. Beezy himself was Lee Ping Zing with an enormous papier mâché head, Vivienne Westwood red patent leather high heels, and a flowing golden Chinese cloak. It was a truly mind-blowing experience. Every window of the factory had some curious Beezy creation dancing or posing in it, as a backdrop to the show in the street. There were hundreds of people really enjoying themselves. Brett and Beezy work very well together.

Jim came to Cape Town specially to be there for Beezy – and didn't come to the show. He stayed at the house and read. Very Jim. Very puzzling.

23 November 1998 Durban

Spent time with Yanna and Denis Claude. They are Anna's parents and I do enjoy being with them. Denis teaches architecture at the University, and Yanna trains teachers. Anna is to become Prospero's wife. It is such a plus to be genuinely fond of in-laws.

6 DECEMBER 1998

Farm School prizegiving. The pre-school babies wore caps and gowns to graduate into Grade I next year. They looked enchanting.

13 DECEMBER 1998

Susie Cock conducted the Chanticleer Singers in the 'Christmas Cracker' instead of Richard Cock who had to conduct elsewhere. She did it beautifully. The singing was alive and moving.

19 DECEMBER 1998

Jonty Smulian arrived to stay. How I love him and what a treat it is that he is my cousin. The last time I saw him was when I was about 18. I feel close to him like no other relative. Sad that he lives in Houston. He is a great architect, designed the planning of the Aswan dam and goes all over the world doing major projects. He adores music and is very very funny. Oh how I wish he lived near me.

21 FEBRUARY 1999

Bundy died this day in 1985.

Two piano quartets of Mozart and Brahms were performed by Gerard [Korsten], Malcolm [Nay], Jessica and Jean-Louise [Moolman]. It was a ravishing and hugely passionate performance. I took Brigitte Zaczek who was out here from Vienna and she was really moved and impressed. I value her judgement enormously.

I am deeply grateful that Granny was there because the very next day she was gravely ill with a strangulated colon and had a huge operation removing a chunk of it. As she is 88, I didn't think she'd make it. I helped wheel her into theatre for the operation, reciting Walter de la Mare's *Martha* and she recited it with me with such joy, she loves it so. It was the first time I had ever seen her without her teeth, and she looked so tiny and old and helpless. I thought that was the last time I would see her alive. Happily she has proved me wrong.

25 FEBRUARY 1999

Jim has been incontinent for some time and I was advised to get help to look after him as it has become very stressful for me. He has lost his sense of smell so it doesn't worry him much. As he never has noticed what he wears, it has not been too awful for him to have to use napkins. It is very tiring for me to change him, particularly as he cannot see why it should be necessary. It is a sad state of affairs to say the least.

There was a tiny advertisement among the 'Positions Wanted' in *The Star* newspaper which read, "Wanted job as housekeeper, preferably on farm, ex-nurse." I phoned the advertiser, Thandrea Klem, and she came and has proved a success. Looking back I do not know how I would have managed without her. She has taken over all the part of the caring of Jim that I find so upsetting, and thus I can enjoy looking after him in every other way.

Ash and Michael on B's bed

26 FEBRUARY 1999

Ashutosh Khandekar and Michael Lee have come to stay which is a total delight. It is their first trip to South Africa. We went to hear Jess play quartets at Mount Grace in the Magaliesberg. Jim was not well enough to come but it isn't his cup of tea anyway. On the way home we stopped at Skeerpoort to shop for mangoes and litchis. While we were looking round the shop, Michael came to me and said, "There is an orang-outang coming into the shop."

Skeerpoort is a hillbilly rural area on the foothills of the Magaliesberg and some pretty rough-looking people live on smallholdings thereabouts. I peered across the dusty shelves of sweets and tinned-foods and saw a beer-bellied red-faced man, followed by his wife who was half-hidden by his huge frame.

Michael repeated, "There is an orang-outang!"

I shushed him and whispered to him not to make remarks like that. People could get very ugly and violent if they heard him.

241

He said, "But there really is an orang-outang." I was about to kick him hard on the shins when I saw the beer-belly's wife, and in her arms dressed in pink frilly knickers, was an orang-outang.

We all went up and had a good look at it and chatted to the woman who treated it like her adored baby. I thought it was odious – particularly its rather grubby pink knickers. Ash thought it was sweet.

4 MARCH 1999

Thomas Pakenham has been staying here on the farm and today flew to the Kalahari with Prospero in his little Kitfox to photograph baobabs for his book, *Meetings with Remarkable Trees of the World*.

They flew as far as Rustenburg and then Prospero phoned to say that he had forgotten his passport, so please would I send John Maswanganyi to fetch it from Prospero's house and deliver it to him while he waited there. John drove it all the way to Rustenburg. Thank heavens for him. How like Jim Prospero is!

Ash cooks superbly and has taught Thandrea some delicious recipes. I wish he and Michael could stay for a long long time.

When Thomas and Prospero came back they flew over the garden and we all waved. The trouble is I find myself waving to all sorts of little planes that might be Prospero. It gets so exhausting rushing outside every time I hear a little plane that I must make an effort to learn to identify the sound of the Kitfox.

11 MARCH 1999

Thomas left for London and I stuffed fresh sage and basil from the garden into his suitcase to take to Ash and Michael, who left a few days ago. Thomas didn't seem to notice, but they did get it so he is not as vague as he appears.

18 MARCH 1999

Took Squeeze to Plett. The sea is too strong for him so he swam in the lagoon. He finds his lack of strength difficult to accept. I find it heart-breaking. He is terribly anxious and has an expression of fear on his face which I have not seen before. When the day came to fly home, the plane was due to leave at 1 pm and he was packed and ready standing in the hall at 8.30 am. When I think of all the years I have known him when not only was he not ready on time, but I couldn't even find him. He missed planes and hardly communicated when he was delayed in another country. What a change! Since then I have been told this was the onset of Alzheimer's.

We did see about 30 dolphins dancing on their tails and leaping in formation. To share this with Jim was a precious gift.

31 MARCH 1999
There is a blue moon! I didn't know what a blue moon was. Now I do. It is a second full moon in the same month. There was one on the 1st of March. Fancy not being curious enough to know what it means until now!

22 APRIL 1999 LONDON
Ton Koopman and Yo-Yo Ma in the Royal Festival Hall. I was impressed but I wasn't moved, there was something too mechanical for me. Some years ago, Laurens van der Post arranged for Yo-Yo Ma to come and play his cello to a group of Bushmen in the Kalahari. They exchanged their very different music and Yo-Yo Ma remarked how strange it is that he has to dress up and play at a precisely given time to a silent audience in a huge building. He said that Bach is such a modern composer compared to those that must have first made the music of the Bushmen. Their music seems to happen naturally, like the wind or rain, at any time and anywhere. He was fascinated by their music and the instruments they used, and he comes over as a lovely, humble and natural person.

Gina Beukes is a violinist in the London Philharmonic who grew up in SA and played with Jess regularly over the years. They have been close friends since the age of seven. Gina often comes to play her violin with me at the flat in London and today asked Clint and me to come and perform Bach with her at South Africa House where there was a huge gathering of dignitaries, wonderful Zulu dancers and black choirs. We three white South Africans performed an aria from *St John's Passion* – Clint singing, Gina and myself on violin and piano. Having given it all of 10 minutes rehearsal it went surprisingly well.

5 MAY 1999

Melvyn Tan, one of my favourite pianists on earth, and Paull Boucher his partner violinist, both beloved friends of mine, invited me to a chamber concert at the Tabernacle Church off Portobello Road. There I was introduced to Anita Wallfisch whom I congratulated on her recently published book. In it Anita describes her life in a prison camp in Germany during the war, where her cello-playing saved her life. A very moving account. As Portobello is near where I live, I asked Anita where she lived, thinking maybe she was also a local. She hesitated and then replied, "Why?'"

Melvyn Tan, B and Paull Boucher

6 MAY 1999

Yonty Solomon. We met when we were both 18 in Cape Town. His playing of Bach's *Goldberg Variations* was unearthly in its beauty. He is one of the most sought-after piano teachers in Britain and has taught at the Royal College of Music for many many years where he has become a legend. His playing is also legendary.

Yonty Solomon

Deb Duncan remembers Yonty being auditioned by the Professor of Music at University of Cape Town when Yonty was 18. He played two bars. The Professor looked a bit puzzled and said, "Is that all?" Yonty said, "Isn't it enough?" After a few seconds silence, the Professor replied, "Yes. It is."

Now, 1999, at the Royal College of Music, Yonty asked me to come and listen to a pupil of his, Georg Lazaridis. Georg played Moussorski's *Pictures at an Exhibition*. I wept. This is something else – oh oh what energy and huge talent.

MAY 1999

Hugh Roberts, stepson of Michael Stern, has come to stay with us for five months.

Michael, who founded St Martin's School in Rosettenville and Waterford in Swaziland, was awarded the OBE for education.

My first job when I came back from England when I was 21, was teaching for Michael at St Martin's, which I enjoyed hugely. Michael was always game whether for hard physical labour or for sheer fun. Once when he was housemaster at Bedales in Hampshire, he was locked in his rooms by pupils on April Fools' Day. He made a rope out of sheets, lowered himself out of the first floor window, appeared at breakfast and got his revenge by saying nothing at all about it.

After running Waterford, he returned to England to live where he taught delinquents in London. At the age of 75 he climbed Kilimanjaro. He always longed to marry and only did so for the first time at the age of 65. His wife Sarah was a young widow in her 30s with a boy of seven, Hugh. Michael phoned me from England at dawn one morning with the joyous news that a little girl had been born to them. They named her Miranda and he gleefully suggested Miranda and Prospero must meet.

One morning Michael went to make tea for Sarah who was in bed with a headache. When he came back to the bedroom, she was dead with a brain haemorrhage. Miranda was three months old. Michael brought up the two children without help. He did everything for the baby, and was a wonderful father to Hugh. I remember going round to all my friends with babies who lived in London and collecting a big bag of clothes for Miranda. This all happened about 20 years ago.

Now, 1999, Hugh is going up to Cambridge in October to read English. A large part of his gap year is being spent here with us. He is a total delight and is using Jim's library with such enthusiasm. He's teaching at our farm school and loving it. The children are benefiting greatly from his input. He visits their homes, plays football with them, coaches the farm team, and is altogether hugely generous with his time and his deep and genuine concern for the kids.

In the evenings we share hours of Mozart and Shakespeare. I have not had a

245

houseguest that I have enjoyed so. He is an astonishingly fine young man. Not too surprising, being brought up by Michael Stern.

Sandy Baillie came to stay. He performed the Dvorak cello concerto in Johannesburg beautifully. He played his cello for the children here at Monaghan Farm School and he is obviously a born teacher and gives total loving energy when he is with the kids.

Sandy plays for the farm school

22 MAY 1999
Jessica and Albie van Schalkwyk played the Rachmaninov cello sonata and the Beethoven G minor, at Mount Grace. Albie is a terrific pianist. Sandy Baillie came with me and it was a great experience to hear Jess's playing with Sandy there.

26 MAY 1999
My children organised for me to go on a ride on Tweefontein as a birthday treat. We rode among eland, zebra, kudu, warthog, gemsbok and impala. The animals take little heed of us when we are on horseback, and one can ride right into the herds. It was heaven.

JULY 1999
Five of our stud bulls were stolen and cut up. Horrible. So sad that this is happening on our farm.

Jim's driving has become a danger to himself and to others. He cannot hold his alcohol and has made a daily habit of going to Ruby's or the Ocean Basket restaurant in Fourways and having a few glasses of wine while he writes. He comes home sloshed every evening.

He had a terrible accident some weeks ago. He was brought home by the police having been picked up about 20 kilometres away, completely off course. He had overtaken a car with a trailer and smashed into it so that his car was practically written off. He said it was entirely their fault, but paid for the damage to the other car immediately – so it was obvious that he knew he was to blame. His secretary told me about the payment later. He would never have admitted it to me.

How he gets home in his alcoholic state is a miracle. Our farm workers pulled his car out of the gutter outside the main gate today. Jim is always sweet and cheerful when he's drunk. Never nasty, thank God – just loud and silly.

After much heartache and careful consideration I organised for a friendly policeman to follow him home from Fourways one evening, and having told the policeman all about the driving problem, he agreed to take Jim's licence away. This seemed to be the only way we could stop him driving. When he reached the garage here, Jim actually fell onto the ground when he climbed out of his car, but was charming when we helped him up and together supported him into the house where he invited the policeman in to supper. The policeman was so pleased that he forgot to talk about the drunken driving. I had to call him out of the room and tell him to get on with it. I thank God I did this because it was becoming a nightmare.

Since then, John Maswanganyi, our reliable driver for over 20 years, has driven Jim to Fourways every afternoon. I find it so very very sad. According to the doctor, this too is part of Alzheimer's.

I went in to the Ocean Basket one evening after shopping, and there was Jim sitting at a table having his wine. When he caught sight of me he looked so desperately pleased and surprised. I went and kissed him and sat with him and my heart bled for him. He is so lonely. He has become comparatively silent, and repeats anecdotes verbatim over and over again. He always did, but he is now more monotone and if I tell him I have heard it before, he ploughs on regardless.

Hugh Roberts at St John's, Cambridge, with a view of Trinity Library and King's

12 JULY 1999 ENGLAND
St John's Cambridge were recording Britten all day. Heaven. Thanks to Christopher Robinson I am staying in St John's in the senior guest room overlooking Wren's Trinity library and King's Chapel. Hugh Roberts is up at Clare College Cambridge at present and came and had hot chocolate with me in these glorious rooms.

I went punting on the Cam with Hilary Jenkins who is a retired History don at King's, and I took over the punting for a bit. Not remembering how heavy it is, I dropped the pole on Hilary's head. He seemed all right, but I burst into tears with the shock of it. He was very brave and polite about it. Later we walked together to Grantchester along the river, past Darwin's house and the meadow where Francis Cornford wrote "Oh fat white woman who nobody loves". It was so hot we swam in the river in our undies. His wife Rosemary kindly fetched us in the car from Grantchester.

13 JULY 1999
I phoned Christopher Robinson and he invited me to come and sing in Mozart's *Coronation Mass* which he was conducting in the chapel with an orchestra to celebrate 40 years of recording. All the ex-choir members of St John's were invited to sing and it was so kind of him to include me. What a treat!

14 JULY 1999
Kevin's 50th birthday celebration was held in the Queen Elizabeth Hall, South Bank with various musicians playing a selection of his compositions. The hall was packed full, and it was a huge and glorious success. There was a party for him in the Festival Hall reception rooms afterwards and Kevin said apart from everything else, it was the most tuneful rendering of Happy Birthday he had ever heard. Kevin's music is thrilling and it was beautifully performed.

248

Healthy appetites have B and Kevin!

He wrote a percussion solo for Robyn Schulkowsky who performed it. She is partly American Indian, a wildly exiting exotic creature who made it an electrifying experience. Hugh Canning of *The Guardian* wrote: "...Volans' piece for solo drummer which, after the most astonishing feats of rhythmic battery subsides into a little tuneful epilogue on the marimba...this remarkable and exhilarating score... worked in abstract terms with a complete exposition of conventional drumming technique."

Kevin once brought Robyn to the farm to stay. I love having my back massaged. Robyn offered to do it for me. Can you imagine what it is like being an instrument played by one of the greatest percussion players on earth?

At the Festival Hall party, I met Simon Callow. Recently I saw him do a one-man show about Dickens, and his energy and power is enormous. After meeting him I read his book about Peggy Ramsay the legendary theatrical agent, *Love Is Where It Falls*. Callow was a 30 year-old gay man, Ramsay in her 70s and they loved each other passionately until she died. It was an unbridled intense and reckless love for 11 years. Curious and moving story.

16 July 1999

Yonty Solomon and I went to the Rembrandt self-portrait exhibition at the National Gallery together and had a lovely time choosing the one we'd want to own. We agreed on the same one. What an exhibition! How I love Yonty. It is always such a bonus when one has known a friend for so long. What a gifted and sensitive creature he is. He grows more beautiful with the years.

25 July 1999 Monaghan

Back at the farm we had one of the best shoots in memory. Jim, who turns 80 in October did only the first part of the shoot. 128 birds in total: two duck, 14 francolin, 112 guinea-fowl. Perfect weather.

Delicious roast pork for lunch. Thandrea a star in the kitchen. Both Neil Orford and Peter Moses said they had never seen the farm looking so good.

26 July 1999

Jim's sister Noreen died. Kevin turns 50.

30 July 1999

Bailey gathering for Noreen's funeral. All her children were there, and all ours. Paul Raben, her son and Beezy and Prospero met properly and liked each other very much. These sad happenings are good for kinship.

Jim was very affected by his younger sister's death. One tells this from his face. Little was said.

2 August 1999

With the help of generous sponsorship from BP, I purchased the Blair Atholl 'bus' for Monaghan Farm School. It is a revamped truck which carries 22 kids. It will be useful for trips and matches.

26 August 1999 Namaqualand

Phillida and I went to see the flowers in Namaqualand. We stopped at a garage in a dorp miles from anywhere which I decided was called Bokpoep. We were too early for the blooms and very few flowers were out but we had a great time together and laughed a lot, and on the way back to Cape Town we saw a whale almost standing on its tail, right up in the air. The sun was setting red and huge, and we stopped at Blaubergstrand and had fish and chips and watched the whale for about half an hour.

I skidded in the Toyota in Jan Smuts Avenue which was oily and smashed into the car in front of me. No-one hurt but I was shocked and drove on to Ian and Dawn Haggie's house, and they were so kind. What a noble pair.

Jim was invited to a concert at St Mary's school to celebrate his 80th birthday. Kerry Swift had organised the Johannesburg Youth Orchestra to play there for him. They made a great fuss of him and he loved it all. Sadly I was not well enough to be there with him. Boofer Rossouw, aged six, sat next to him and said, "I'm so proud of Jim. I didn't know he was famous. It's so nice when your friends become something."

29 October – 7 December 1999
Took Jim to Plett. He is badly incontinent and I am changing his napkins about five times a day. Here in Plett, without Thandrea's help I am finding it very gruelling and very upsetting. Luckily Jim doesn't seem too aware of the difficulties, but I am becoming ill.

Miles Crisp phoned to say that his company, Deloitte & Touche are donating 10 computers to Monaghan Farm School, bless him.

Kevin arrived to stay and he wasn't well. Bad timing while I am caring for my poor Jim. However the sea is almost too warm and the swimming gentle and calm and healing.

16 December 1999
Home with Jim who is so unwell. I went into the library and found him sitting in his usual chair, not reading. He said he finds it difficult to see. He added after a long silence, "Sweetheart, I think I want to go on to the next world."
I told him that if he could see to read he would be content. I took him to see Gavin Douglas who shoots with us regularly and is a good friend and brilliant eye surgeon. He diagnosed cataracts. I was thrilled because the operation is easy and

251

probably the most successful surgery of the century. Jim is booked for the first op on 6th January. He has never had an operation in his life and is frightened.

I spoke to Cecily who gave me valuable advice on Jim's condition: "Enjoy it. Don't fight it. It is here for you to learn and grow. Love it." How wise, and how strong I will have to be.

25 DECEMBER 1999

Lovely quiet Christmas Eve here on the farm with all us Baileys and Meg and her girls. I walked on Tweefontein in the evening and there was the best rainbow I have ever seen stretching hugely over a battleship grey sky on the eastern side, and golden flying saucers to the west.

31 DECEMBER 1999

John Amis arrived to stay. John and I went over to Prospero's New Century's Eve party at his Cradle restaurant. It is nearly finished being built. Jim was far too ill to come with us so we stayed for a very short time. Prospero gives wonderful parties. Dave Matthews was there and lots of lovely young friends.

2000 has arrived and rain rain rain. Pity for John Amis but good for the farms.

6 JANUARY 2000

I set off at dawn driving Jim to the Kenridge Nursing Home for his cataract op. He was so frightened. I stayed with him all the time and my heart bled for him. When he had gone in to theatre, I walked over to St George's Church in the next road and sat under a tree and wept. Gerald the priest there came and talked to me and I told him about Jim and he took me into the church to pray for him. He was comforting and kind. I drove Jim home in the evening and tomorrow we can take his dressing off. Thank God it is over. He is so weak and vulnerable, poor lamb.

7 JANUARY 2000

He can see!!! With his new lens he can see. It really is a miraculous procedure.

He seems to be in a lot of pain around the eye and the doctor cannot see anything amiss. It shouldn't be painful according to Gavin Douglas.

I feel desperate. Dr Boyce who diagnosed him with Alzheimer's, wants to do all sorts of tests on him. Jim refuses.

I cannot bear leaving him even for a short time.

27 January 2000

Mozart's and Julian's birthday. We had a cattle sale at Mooiplaats. It poured with rain throughout and we sold 170. Hopelessly bad weather conditions for a cattle sale. Mud, slush, heavy rainfall, very uncomfortable and a great pity.

Huge floods, the worst for centuries. I heard a tree-cricket. An autumn sound – what is happening?

30 January 2000

I drove Jim over to lunch with John and Jess in Pretoria. He was very silent but so pleased to see the grandchildren.

Robert Loder visited us and had a chat to Jim on the verandah. It did Jim good to be with such an old and valued friend. It would turn out to be his last chat with someone who has meant a great deal to both of us for over 40 years.

B with Robert and Jo

During these last few months I have walked him round the garden, our fingers entwined. He was so weak he needed my support. I told him that it had taken 50 bloody years for him to let me hold my hand! He giggled.

1 February 2000

Jeremy Isaacs and his wife Gillian came here for lunch with Prospero. Jeremy was wonderfully reverent towards Jim for his efforts in publishing *Drum* and in doing so, launching so many black journalists and photographers on their careers – some hugely successful. It was so warming for us both to hear.

I went to Betty Suzman's funeral. Saw all her children whom I have known all my life. We are all around 60 and agreed we are becoming orphans at a steady rate.

Jim's eye is red and sore. Saw the specialist again who has given him cortisone drops. He is terribly frail.

12 FEBRUARY 2000

Jim came through to my room and lay on my bed and said, "Sweetheart this is very difficult to say, but I'd like enough pills to pass on." I feel as if a grey rock is in my stomach. I told every medical friend I have and begged for help. It is impossible. Jim is in despair. I too.

14 FEBRUARY 2000

Jess came. She was wonderful and is such a support to me. She is gentle and perfectly sensitive to Jim's needs. When she left, he again asked for an overdose. Terrible to see such anguish. Why cannot he be allowed to choose to go now? Why has he to wait through this pain and indignity? Dr Boyce said his heart is against him. He has such a strong heart that it won't give up easily.

15 FEBRUARY 2000

Jim very very ill with a high temperature. Thank you God for Thandrea who nurses him so lovingly.

I went to pee at 1 am and found him lying on the floor next to his bed. I ran to him and he said he was sleeping on the floor so as not to worry me. He had fallen. He is so, so sweet and so, so ill. I needed superhuman strength to lift him back into bed.

16 FEBRUARY 2000

Dr Boyce came and says Jim has bowel cancer and has not long to live. This explains his incontinence for over the last two years. He also has cancer of the liver, the bones, the lymph, and it also explains the pain in his eye. It is cancer behind the eye which would not have been evident when he had the cataract op.

17 FEBRUARY 2000

Gran came and lunched with Jim. They had a wonderful time together – talking about old times and he was so touched. He loves her dearly. At lunch, partially-blind Gran tottered to the kitchen to help fetch her lunch. They were both to be brought trays in the bedroom. While she was in the kitchen, she looked round and there was Jim at the door. He hadn't been out of his room for days. He sat at the table with her. Then Thandrea and Mookie[34] helped him back to bed. Jim and Gran both realised how precious this meeting was. It was their last. I had gone out for lunch. Gran told me all about it when I came home.

18 FEBRUARY 2000

I went over to the Cradle and watched two rhino being unloaded. Prospero and I stood on the roof of the container when they were released and watched the female rhino and her male child hurtling out, Prospero with camera poised. When we told Jim about the rhinos he christened them Mrs Thatcher and Denis. I also saw a giraffe giving birth! I was away for one and a half hours. Jim said, "Thank God you're back."

19 FEBRUARY 2000

Paul Davis, a doctor and valued friend saw Jim and said I must get my children here soon. Prospero came to sleep here. It is a huge physical and emotional responsibility to go through this without one's family.

Why should he be in such pain? My darling darling. He goes through hell when we change his napkins. Thandrea and I change him together. While she takes on

---

34 Maria Masilela

the lower part of him, I hold him and stroke his head and quote poetry to him. He only once complained, saying very quietly and measuredly, "This is excruciating."

The pain-killing suppositories are not sufficient and it is hell for him when they are inserted. We didn't know at the time but all is cancer-ridden there.

21 FEBRUARY 2000

This is the day that Bundy died 15 years ago.

Susie Cock came and spent the day. She was loving and gentle with Jim. There are few people who could take the strain of being with someone terminally ill. She was terrific. She helped me feed him. He wants to eat chocolate mousse mostly, which we feed him off a teaspoon like a little bird.

24 FEBRUARY 2000

Thomas phoned from London, and I told him Jim was dying. He asked our fax number and immediately sent this:

FOR
Dr Squadron-Leader Jim Bailey, DFC, CBE, DPhil, OS

Dear Jim,
Or should I say Doctor Jim?
I'm writing this scribble on a beautiful sunny morning (crocuses yellow and blue everywhere) and send all my love and hugs to you and Barbara, Prospero, Beezy, Jessica –
I wish I could be with you all, holding your hand and telling you, Jim, what a wonderful friend you have always been to me for the last 30 years.
Yes, you are a SUPERMAN (that's your new honour, 'Order of the Superman') with all your amazing gifts as PILOT, POET, WIT, WRITER, PUBLISHER, FREEDOM-FIGHTER, PATRIOT –
And LOVING HUSBAND & FATHER.

Love from Thomas

I lay next to Jim, holding his hand and read him this precious fax. He lay very still. And then he whispered, "Read it again."

25 FEBRUARY 2000

Beezy back from India came straight here. The three children took over this day to look after Jim. Jess came over for the whole day, and Prospero took me out. They insisted I go. Much against my will.

Prospero took me to see a Cuban movie, then a Chinese lunch, then he bought me trainers. I kept wanting to go home to Jim. Prospero wouldn't take me home, and when I wanted to phone home, he spoke to Jess and wouldn't let me. Prospero spoilt me with treat after treat but I was desperate to get back to Jim. When I was driven home and hurried in to him, he whispered, "It has been terrible. Thank God you're back. Don't leave me again." I promised him I would never leave him again.

He has lost 60 lbs.

While lying next to Jim on his bed, Prospero told him that Bundy visited him in his dreams, and said to Jim, if it is at all possible to visit him in his dreams, please would he do so. Jim was silent for quite a while, and then said, "You can count on it."

26 FEBRUARY 2000

Jim is on morphine AT LAST. I asked Dr Boyce why he had to go through such hell before she would allow him morphia. She told me that she had asked him whether he wanted quality time with his family, or to be free of pain. Surely he wasn't in a condition to have rational judgement by this time.

After the initial dose of morphia he opened his eyes wide for the first time in years. I had forgotten how beautiful they were.

Jess and John came for a short while to help us bath him. It took four of us to do this. He disliked being washed on the bed and longed to be in the bath. He is so thin, and so grateful, and so weak. For the first time in years, yes years, his eyes are wide open. Free of pain.

27 February 2000

I was alone with him for the afternoon. The morphia makes him very restless. He kept trying to stand up, and muttered, "I've had enough of this." It took all my strength to prevent him from falling over. I had to run and ring for Thandrea, it became so hazardous.

Nicci came to say goodbye. Jim couldn't speak but he took her hand and gave it tiny tiny kisses. It was such a tender way of expressing his farewell. I will never get this out of my mind.

I was alone with him for about six hours today and it was hard work. He is very muddled and keeps thinking he can walk.

Beezy came for the night and brought some fresh salmon which he cooked for me. It was heaven to see him. Thank God for my children over and over again. They are trying to get me to eat more. I have lost 10 lbs.

28 February 2000

Jim's eyes stay wide open but do not see. It is alarming. He cannot close his jaw or his eyes and I find it very very hard to bear. Dr Boyce said he is not in a coma.

29 February 2000

If only his pain could be taken away. He was given more morphia today. John Spencer came and saw him with Prospero. Then this evening Hank Slack came and wanted to see him. I didn't want him to because I didn't want anyone to see him in this state. Hank insisted that it wouldn't upset him. When we entered the bedroom Jim recognised Hank's voice and tried to greet him, struggling to sit up and making a terrible effort to speak. He was trying so hard to be the polite host. It was intolerably sad. He cannot live on like this.

Jim died at about 10.50 pm.

Thandrea came and woke me out of a drugged sleep. She said, "It's Mr B."
I said, "Is he dead?"
She nodded.
I said, "What's the time?" She told me.

He had done it. He had died on the 29th, leap day of leap year. I had prayed he would die today.

I went straight to him. He had the sheet drawn over his face and I pulled it down immediately. I couldn't bear his face covered. Thandrea had bandaged his jaw shut, and had shut his eyes. I asked to be alone with him.

So it has happened. Jim is dead.

I kissed him, removed the bandage, crossed his arms over his chest, sat on the bed next to him and spoke to him. I was so relieved to see him rest sweetly. My beloved Jim has taught me that death is as natural and magical as birth.

It was the first time I had been with someone that is dead. It wasn't in the least frightening or even strange. It was such a privilege to be part of a normal death. He was 80. It was so different to Bundy's death which so early in his life and so unnatural.

I stayed with him for a while talking to him. He lay there not heeding, just as he did so often when he was alive. I said to him, "Thank you my darling Jim for preparing me for this all my life." Then I left him and went back to my bed and took another sleeping pill.

1 MARCH 2000

My first awakening to Jimlessness. At dawn I phoned Meggy and told her that Jim had died and said that the children were coming at about 8 am. She came straight over at 7.30 am to wait with me until they arrived.

Jess brought pink roses, and blue, white and purple flowers – masses of them from her garden and placed them either side of his head, and on his breast. He looked beautiful. His bone structure is so lovely and so nakedly visible now.

Prospero and Jess took over when the hearse came. I didn't want to see him taken away, so when the gate bell rang I went to the main house with John[35] and bawled my brains out, with my head on his lap. He was loving and supportive.

Prospero and Jess helped wrap Jim in a sheet and then when he had been driven away, we all lay on my bed in a heap. Jess asked me if I would like her to make a

---

35 Clarke

posy from the flowers on his breast. I said oh yes please. We went into Jim's room and the horses had been in and had eaten a whole lot of the flowers, others they had strewn over the carpet on their way out again. Jim would have roared with laughter.

Beez, Prospero, John and I chose a place to bury him on Mooiplaats, on the diabase reef separating the granite from the dolomite on one of the oldest geological sites on earth.

When Prospero came for lunch about a month before, he asked me where I would like to be buried, or would I be cremated? Jim was sitting with us. It was a very tactful move, to ask me. I told him at length what I wanted, and chose some of the music for my funeral, and then asked Jim what he would choose. He said he would like to be buried, not cremated. He said he wants to lie next to me. What welcome words! He will. He will lie next to me.

Susie Cock came and together we chose the music for Jim's memorial service. I told Judy that I regretted not being with Jim at the actual moment of his death, that I had gone to bed and wasn't with him. Judy said that Jim had to be alone to die. She said how could he do anything so profound as to die without being alone? He did everything alone, in his way. Fair enough. Her words comforted me.

Robert Loder sent me an email part of which read:

"... I heard the news this morning. My love and sorrow comes with this message.
    Thinking of you and the space left by the felling of a true giant of the forest I can't easily see South Africa without him ... "

2 MARCH 2000

Beezy and Prospero went into Jim's library to find the book of war poems that Jim had written. We wanted to have one of them read out at his Memorial Service. Beezy went across to the far side of the library to start searching for it. As Prospero went in, one of the light bulbs from the ceiling flew down near his feet and exploded. Beezy stared across at Prospero and raised his eyebrows. Beezy then walked across to the other end of the library where Prospero joined him, and another light bulb exploded at their feet. Beezy said, "I'm getting the fuck out of here!" and they scurried out. Jim wasn't ready to have anyone handling his books.

The following day they went back into the library, and without having the least idea where to begin looking, Prospero walked across to a shelf opposite the door and put his hand on the book straight away.

5 March 2000

Jim was buried today. A huge busload of people came from all the farms. It was a proper African burial.

Jess and Beezy bidding farewell

He lay in his coffin with his face visible, and vases of flowers were placed on and around the coffin. The people of the farm walked round it to bid their farewells.

Anthony Njango, a Shangaan from Mozambique and our gardener for decades, was the priest who took the service. We didn't understand a word he said but David, our cook Lizzie Mafatle's son, translated: ". . . We have not only lost our father, we have lost an important football player."

There was the wondrous sound of African singing under a blue sky with huge stretches of hills and bushveld. While everyone took their turn at filling the grave with spadesful of soil, Beezy in his usual passionate style grasped a huge earthenware vase of flowers and hurled it deep down on top of the coffin, which had by now been lowered into the grave. Jess, Prospero

B and Prospero at Jim's grave

261

and Nicci found this hilarious. I had brought several arrangements of flowers over from the house.

Jess had a basket of rose petals and we strew them into the grave while the stony soil was spaded in by the men. So rocky is that part of the farm that a machine was brought in to dig the grave. No human could have done it. Since then the whole area has been declared a World Heritage site so now Jim can be assured of being left in the peace he so wanted.

7 MARCH 2000
Jim's Memorial Service at St George's Church, Parktown.

I had asked Richard Cock if he would play the last double chorus of Bach's *St Matthew's Passion*. He not only played it, the whole of the SABC Chamber choir sang it in German with all the repeats, as it was written. Nothing could have been a better gift for me.

Susie brought her St Mary's Choir to sing *the Angel's Prayer* by Humperdinck. Many of the girls in the choir had been to one of Jim's '9th' birthdays at the farm. It was almost unbearably moving.

We sang Jim's favourite hymn, *Thou Whose Almighty Word*. Jim sang more out of tune than anyone I have heard, and often sang this hymn, putting great expression into it. Without any discussion the entire Bailey family sang it like Jim, completely tunelessly. My intensely musical mother who was with us and who didn't know the history of it, couldn't believe her ears. Luckily the family were seated at the front of the congregation so very few could hear us. Afterwards when my mother remarked on the awful singing she'd heard, Jessica said, "It would have been totally meaningless to sing it in tune! It's Jim's hymn."

Granny stood with Jessica and Frederick. Tiny little 89-year-old Granny who is not at all well. My two sons held my hands throughout the service. The church was full.

Kerry Swift spoke excellently. Aggrey Klaaste, one of the early *Drum* school and now editor of *The Sowetan*, spoke and partly used the pulpit as a political platform, making derogatory remarks about white millionaires no less than three times. The Oppenheimers etc. etc. were there. Oh well.

262

I flew to Plett. I so dreaded getting off the plane and going to the empty house that I asked the Bernings to meet me. Peter did and drove me to the house, bless him. I feel raw and peeled and lost. Too weak to swim.

Phillida came down and was very good to me. She is the only person I wanted with me. Spent ages replying to letters of sympathy, parts of which I shall quote.

From Deb Duncan Honore my friend for over 50 years:

"... what a timeless person he was, free of so many boundaries. We all know that this involved difficulties, but somehow those melt away in the wider perspective of his life. 'And think, this heart, all evil shed away, A pulse in the eternal mind, no less.'

And only you, of all the people I have ever come across, could have given him the freedom, lovingly, to be as fully himself as was possible this side of death.

In love and gratitude,

Me – Deb"

Deb's husband, Tony Honore added: "What a great man, with imagination, a challenging mind, courage and vision – and only you could worthily nourish all this talent in good and bad days."

From Ann Welsh in Oxford, who had known us for about 40 years:

"... But who oh who can really appreciate Jim's complexity and his incredible range of knowledge, his need to be loved, his severity, hilarity, cussedness and compliance except you.

What extraordinary perception drew you to him when you were 15 – or younger? And how it lasted, and how you managed and what heights you had to rise to keep your cool.

Your story is the hidden part of Jim's life. He could so easily have gone on making crashing mistakes. It is a sort of miracle that you were there, and he was there at a key time in both your lives.

I think you rose magnificently to the challenge of Jim, the farm, and all of

263

life. Now I would like to hear you saying some of it on the piano. As for me, I still wonder the way in which Jim enlivened life – treating it as a special gift after the war – he made of life something larger than life. Seeing you both so infrequently means nothing much – you were both planted deeply on whatever Ground I am."

from Val Pakenham:

"… The obituaries remind me of all the amazing things he did with his life and how rare he was, coming from his background, to have done them … He and Thomas had a lot in common (… obsessions with whatever they were investigating, not to mention, no doubt, hopeless impracticality …) What Jim would have done without you, heaven only knows …"

from James Fox:

"… I am proud of my association with him; to have been close to a really brave and wonderful man and one with a laugh like an Egyptian Goose. We must all get together and cackle like geese and praise a famous man. Much love, James."

Jim's niece, Starr wrote to me. I quote from her letter:

"… Jim's public record speaks for itself but to have Jim as my 'littlest uncle' was a huge bonus for me. Ever since my first memory of him, when he came into the garden – I must have been three or four – he was a golden man full of light and laughter. In the years since, whenever we have met unexpectedly, he has remained just that.

"He was the only one of the five [Bailey siblings] who managed to rise above the traumas of his childhood and achieve not only a full public life but also managed to give to his family a warmth and support that enabled them to develop unfettered in their different paths. All the cousins are full of insecurities and fears from parental put-downs. Jim was different – different by all standards, and after half a century of loving him you must find it very hard . . ."

Thank you Starr. Starr looks so much like Jim that I get a fresh frisson every time I see her. It delights me.

Jim knew so little of his parents when he was a child that he was practically brought up by the gamekeeper Alan Howe, at Bletchingdon in Oxfordshire. Alan was born in St Mary's Cottage, part of Bletchingdon Park and lived and worked there as gamekeeper all his 93 years. Jim spent every spare moment shooting with him. This is no exaggeration. I have all Jim's diaries from the age of 15, and almost every single entry is about shooting or fishing.

Thanks to Alan, Jim published his first book at the age of 15, *Jottings and Odd-ments*, which describes the wildlife of Oxfordshire. Alan was a true naturalist and taught Jim so much. Jim and I visited him together often and we made him god-father to Prospero. As I have already described, when Prospero was six, we took him over to meet Alan who was nearly 90 and was so thrilled about being his godfather. He always called us Master Jim and Mrs Jim and told us countless tales about Jim as a boy.

The BBC broadcast an hour's interview with Alan as one of the last of the great gamekeepers in Britain. In it Jim crops up with regularity even though Bletching-don Park had several owners over those long years – he keeps coming back to Mr Jim and his various antics. When we left to drive back to Oxford, Alan pressed a half-crown into Prospero's hand. His eyes brimmed. He knew it was unlikely that he would see us again.

He lost two sons in the war. His remaining son Bill, and daughter, Sophie have always lived at Bletchingdon. Bill is not much younger than Jim was.

I quote from Bill Howe's letter:

"Dear Mrs Bailey,
There is no need to say how sad we all are to hear of Master Jim's departure, from a first meeting of 1932, to 2000 is one long time to remain in touch . . . we gave him a thought and viewed the front steps of the Big House yesterday and paid a memory visit to the stable yard . . .

Perhaps we may all meet again in the GREAT ESTATE in the sky. Jim will be easy to recognise for IF THEY can get him to wear a halo it will be worn at such an angle he will stand out a mile.

But during the hunting season of 1937/38 (Bicester and Wardon Hill) JRA Bailey did (in those establishment days) the quite dreadful thing and popped over the fence before the MFH whose horse had refused. THIS WAS NOT DONE and to make matters worse, on a skewbald at that, at a time when coloured horses were considered only fit for circus rings. Even grooms in the tack rooms were shocked.

So indeed we at Bletchingdon can all agree life was richer for having known 'YOUNG JIM' as he was known to everyone.

May GOD BLESS YOU,
Yours,
Bill Howe."

I have been ill most of the time in Plett. I seem to have no energy at all. Phil went home on 19th and I am alone, and need the solitude.

1 APRIL 2000
Jess came with Frederick and Imogen to spend the night when I got back to the farm. So good of her to know how awful it would be for me to come home as a widow. Isn't widow a desolate word! I didn't realise how much I was dreading going back to be on the farm alone for the first time.

Every day there is a new hurdle and I suppose it will get easier.

21 APRIL 2000
Gentle autumn weather.

Gran is very ill and said to me she's had enough and means it. I wept myself empty. I have never heard her complain about anything in her life. She must be truly ready to die. I have promised her that I shall get the help of Hospice. The doctor wouldn't let me do this for Jim, and I didn't know at the time that this could be my decision and not the doctor's. Oh how I regretted this. Granny had seen how Jim suffered and has no intention of doing likewise.

I had a lovely person from Hospice come and meet Gran and finding how very ill she is, they have agreed to come whenever she calls. Hospice is wonderful.

Granny then made me promise to go to England and be there when she dies. She said I had had enough of dealing with the dying and I must bid her goodbye and go. She was adamant. Jessica, her favourite person on earth, will be with her throughout her last days. That is what she wishes.

I went and said goodbye to her on my way to the airport. It was not emotional because I always say goodbye to her when I go abroad. This farewell seemed no different to any other. I didn't allow myself to feel or think.

26 MAY 2000 LONDON

My birthday. I phoned Granny and Jess answered and said I won't be able to speak to Granny again. She is morphined and peaceful. I find it hard to swallow.

Ash came for breakfast on his way to work to be with me. Then I went to a service at St Clement Danes to hear what the choir was like – it would be singing for Jim. Ash then took me out for lunch so that I wouldn't be alone. Afternoon I went to Deb in Oxford where she made me a birthday supper.

Next day I stayed in bed. Feeling very battered by Gran. Deb is so good to me.

28 MAY 2000

My niece Sarah phoned me at Deb's to tell me that Granny had died. Jess was there but she was too upset to speak to me. Jess had lain with Gran on her bed during the days, having spent her last two nights on the floor next to the bed.

After her first shot of morphia, Gran smiled and whispered, "Oh wonderful." Then having a very peaceful silence of some days, she said, "I'm so grateful . . . mumble mumble . . . armsful of love." So Jess said, "What did you say Gran? Something about armfuls of love." Granny's voice strengthened enough to say quite firmly, "Armsful not armfuls." These were her last words.

I was in Oxford with Deb when I was told. I was sad, but I have no more petrol for feeling. It will sink in when it sinks in.

All the recent entries in this diary are about dying. One doesn't like to be caught mouthing platitudes but however well trodden this subject is, our own experiences concerning death are never banal. Our pain and grief are virginal.

Anthony Sampson and Anthony Smith were so helpful in advising where to hold the Memorial Service. We were trying to decide between Christ Church Oxford, and St Clement Danes London. The latter church was perfectly suited for our purpose – in the middle of the Strand where it joins Fleet Street where the *Drum* office was. In addition, it is the RAF church, so it couldn't be more apt.

13 JUNE 2000
Jim's Memorial Service at St Clement Danes. So many friends came from all the very different and separate parts of Jim's life. There was an extraordinary and interesting mixture.

Johnnie Johnson (Air Vice-Marshal JJ, CB, CBE, DSO DFC – Wow!) read the psalm. He is very old and frail and it was so good of him to make the trip to London to do so. He didn't hesitate for a moment when I phoned and asked him this favour.

Thomas Pakenham's tribute, which he read:

"To say that Jim was unlike others greatly understates things.

I remember once being accosted on the pavement in Notting Hill Gate by a tall, 60-year-old tramp, with a shock of fair hair; he was carrying what appeared to be all his worldly possessions in a battered cardboard box. I was talking with animation to someone else at the time. So I told the tramp, impatiently, that I had no change, and tried to wave him away. But the tramp stubbornly stood his ground. He was still there after five minutes and he repeated his question, which turned out not to be, 'Do you have any change?' but 'Will you come and have lunch as my guest?' For the tramp, of course, was Jim.

Then there was the Jim who took obvious pleasure in the things that money could buy; the beautiful farm besides the Jukskei River, the sleek cattle in the veld, and (more recently) the magnificent game reserve teeming with buck, zebra, and rhino. Of course, these were things he had bought for his family in whom he took such a passionate pride; for Barbara and the children. Without Barbara and the children he might have lived, like Diogenes, in a barrel.

And there was Jim the poet and artist with words – a world away from Jim the cattle tycoon and Jim the happy family man. And there was Jim the dare-devil pilot and hunter of Messerschmitts who had shot down nine of the enemy.

I remember wondering how Jim, who seemed vague enough in navigating a car, could ever have mastered the intricacies of piloting a Hurricane. But one day about 10 years ago I went to Soho Square where Group-Captain Peter Townsend and Jim were re-launching Jim's account of his war-time experiences in the RAF, *The Sky Suspended*. This book is one of the classics of war. At the book-launch Townsend could not conceal his admiration for Jim – and not merely for Jim's skill in flying. Townsend explained how the pain of war had left most of the young pilots silent, that is, the few who survived. Jim's eloquence had given them a voice, or, as he put it 'given wings to their thoughts'. And when you read it yourself the pain is at times almost more than you can bear, as Jim chronicles the death of his friends one by one.

How can one reconcile these Protean Jims: the hobo and loner, the loving and gregarious family man, the millionaire tycoon, the hunter and war hero, the sensitive poet?

I am tempted to say that Jim had to reconcile in his own nature two con-tradictory sets of genes: those of his father, buccaneering Sir Abe, born a fron-tiersman of the eastern Cape, the bosom friend of Cecil Rhodes, with the same huge gusto for life, money and power; and those of his mother, the shy, lonely, awkward Mary Westenra, the daughter of Lord Rossmore, for whom solo flying was a form of escape into a world of her own.

But perhaps it was more complicated than that. Certainly Jim inherited a sense of privileged alienation – you could call it the predicament of the in-sider/outsider – from both sides of his family. For his mother was Anglo-Irish, meaning she was trapped between two competing identities, Irish and Brit-ish, and his father oscillated between homes (and loyalties) in England and South Africa.

But what is so remarkable is that Jim's life did not follow that pattern of privileged alienation, the playboy's path. He became a doer on a huge scale.

And his wartime experiences did not leave him a burnt-out wreck (as he said, one felt one had lived one's whole life in a few years). Of course he was cruelly scarred. And the scars were deeper and more painful because they were to the soul, not to the face or hands. But he said he drew two lessons from the war. First, a faith in the essential goodness of the ordinary man. Second, a sense of indignation, a kind of holy rage, at the folly of politicians. These were the lessons, I think, that impelled him to launch his great idealistic venture, the founding of *Drum*.

And here one must observe how far he had travelled from the sad, lonely world of Mary Westenra – or the boisterous world of Sir Abe, Cecil Rhodes and white supremacy. *Drum* was a celebration for blacks, that orchestrated laughter and humour for tens of thousands of Africans spread right across the Sub-Saharan continent. *Drum* dealt with the dismal architects of apartheid as they deserved – with wit and mockery. It shouted to the heavens that apartheid was worse than a crime, worse even than a blunder. The thing was ridiculous! Jim was never a bleeding heart liberal. He despised political correctness. But few white people did more to help create the new South Africa.

Now let me finish with a short anecdote from the very last days of Jim's life. He was dying, and he could no longer read. Barbara brought him a fax from a friend and admirer in London – from myself, in fact. The fax was headed: 'To Commander Jim Bailey, DFC, CBE, OS'. And when Barbara read out the initials she said, I wonder what 'OS' means.

'Read on,' said Jim like a good editor.

Barbara read out the fax[36]. It ended . . . I should like to confer on you a new award – the OS, the Order of the Superman.

I should like to think that Jim gave one of his wonderful joyous, cacophonous laughs, as the trumpets sounded for him on the other side.

But his spirit remains with us – glowing in our lives, impelling us forward. You can repeat that last line. 'Read on'."

---

36 quoted on page 256

Anthony Sampson's tribute:

"Many of the most interesting people have sets of friends who never meet each other – until perhaps they come together at their memorial services and eye each other with surprise. Many people here saw very different Jim Baileys – a fighter pilot, a family man, a farmer – whom I know much less about.

I can only speak about Jim as a man with a unique gift – for turning people's lives upside down. And I know several of us here know that if we hadn't met Jim our lives would have been very much more boring. For us he was always the great disrupter, the un-rest cure. He was always shocked by watching people get duller and more complacent.

He thought we should be more adventurous. He asked us to do things we didn't think we could do, and then left us to do them. His motto might have been: go and see what Tommy is doing, and tell him to do the opposite.

I suppose I was an extreme case. When I first met Jim at Oxford I was an unconfident and unsatisfactory undergraduate, a would-be writer with nothing to write about. I got a dead-end job as a trainee in a printing works. Then I received a cable from Jim, asking me to join a new black magazine in South Africa. I'd never met a black man, knew nothing about journalism or Africa.

But Jim's challenge was impossible to refuse. 'It's rather like the Kon-Tiki', he wrote. 'It has a fair chance of reaching the Marquesas of an 80 000 circulation, but we are at the moment dicing with the waves.'

So of course I went out to the waves. Within a few months I was editing the magazine *Drum* while Jim kept flying off round Africa to find more readers. We were soon reaching the 80 000, and much more through Africa, with the help of others here. He never seemed to doubt we could do it, so we had to do it.

My four years on *Drum* gave me a new sense of commitment, something to write about and precious friendships, black and white, including Jim's friendship, which lasted my life. I could never forget how dull I would have been without that unrest cure.

But I was one of many. There's an odd club of people whose careers have been totally disrupted by Jim – some of whom are here today – who still love to exchange notes about his outrageous ideas, his exotic meeting-places and low dives, his disorganised parties with incompatible people, usually ending up with the game of Cardinal Puff.

They remember how maddening he could be, disappearing just when you wanted him, asking the impossible, giving bold but vague instructions ending up with 'that sort of thing.' But we also knew about his courage and independence of mind, and would never ever say, 'I wish I'd never met Jim' because we know how much more boring life would have been without that disruption. And what else would we have found to talk about?

And we'll never forget that long echoing laugh, with the head thrown back, with that great mane of hair. Some of us are perhaps hearing it now. We were never quite sure what it meant. Was it laughing at us, or at him? Or was it laughing at the human comedy, the absurdities of life, that no-one is quite who they think they are.

Certainly that is how I like to think of Jim, like Puck, encircling the world, laughing and saying, 'Lord what fools these mortals be.'

But there was a more serious side behind Jim's laughter. For he always had a long sense of history which gave him a detachment – which make him see through politicians, ideologies and tyrannies. In South Africa he knew some of the government ministers – including De Klerk – through his father who had befriended Afrikaners when they were the underdogs.

But he was never deceived by the racism and brutality of apartheid. And he was much more interested in befriending the blacks who had become the real underdogs. He could see the sweep of history. He knew that the whirligig of time brings in his revenges.

I was able to share with Jim the marvellous experience of watching apartheid come and go, autocracy become democracy, the underdogs becoming overdogs, the prisoner Mandela, whom we used to meet in a shebeen, becoming president.

I would never have had any of these experiences if I had never met Jim."

Anthony Smith, who ran *Drum* in West Africa in the 1950's, read his tribute but much of it was extempore, so I have chosen to quote part of the letter that he wrote to me when Jim died:

"Dearest Barbara,

Of course it was a shock when that fax arrived, a wretched shock, a tear-making shock, but I was glad to be informed.

Right now, on this Sunday, I believe you are burying him, apparently in a fine place with a great view over the surrounding land. A piece of me has therefore gone but a hugely bigger piece of you in particular, and all his family. I grieve distantly for every one of you.

... I have known him – and that laugh – since 1953, and have often wondered how he teased me out of a fine job with the Manchester Guardian to go to an uncertain future between the open drains of Accra, Lagos, and much of western Africa, but his mixture of charm, concern, and cunning made me resign from the MG and do his bidding.

It wasn't the money – certainly not. It wasn't the prospect of sweating it out in the Bight of Benin – even Manchester has a better climate. But I am delighted that he did, as my life and Africa have ever since been erratically entwined.

We tried to do our best for his memory over here, writing pieces, telling obit editors of the recent loss, and generally letting this portion of the world know that a sadness had occurred.

... To both of you I am deeply indebted – but also bloody miserable. So too, I know, are hundreds of this planet's citizens up and down the land, Africa in particular.

With love,
Anthony."

Beezy's address – very courageous of him it was to read it after such accomplished speakers – was from the heart, as is everything our Beezy does.

"... I recently dreamt that Jim turned up at his own memorial, and of how overwhelmed and touched he was by the flood of friends and their love. He said, 'Thank you for coming – well met!'

... Jim's father, Sir Abe Bailey, would have been well proud of his son. Sir Abe was a pioneer to whom this family owes a great deal. His source of

273

wealth, the metal of kings, was dug from the African earth. It was always Jim's lesson to us that we should try to put something back.

He lived by example by providing a home for many of Africa's finest writers. For over three decades Jim's Africa-wide publications gave voice to generations who had previously been silenced.

Jim was a warrior. One of the few to whom so many owe so much.

The war shattered a poet's heart. When a friend who had joined the RAF with him and fought in the Battle of Britain was killed on his 21st birthday, Jim wrote, 'That was the last occasion on which I wept. After that, the delicate mechanism had been destroyed.'

But the war also invigorated Jim's spirit. He said, 'God gave me fortune so that I may now speak for the dead.'

He arrived in South Africa shortly after the end of the war to sort out his late father's affairs. (His father died in 1940.)

The indifference he showed for his appearance throughout his life was not shared by the immigration officials who demanded a letter from a notary that he would not be a burden to the state before allowing him into a country. He went on to horrify, shock, and delight by holding the mirror of truth up to its face.

In Africa legends about Jim can still be heard in obscure drinking-holes, as well as African parliaments. Above all, he despised snobbery. His mission was to debunk the fake, and debag the pompous. Highly educated, he scorned universities for 'shining pebbles and roughening diamonds.' A war hero, he abhorred violence yet remained a freedom fighter. An independent anarchist, he was driven to do great things by his deep passion for beauty and truth, in the belief of the potential for greatness in us all – and by love."

Jim would have loved it all. There were so many people I haven't seen for ages. They came from far and wide.

We all walked over to the Cock Tavern in Fleet Street for the lunch. Jim had drunk with friends in the Cock Tavern regularly after being in *Drum* office a few minutes up Fleet Street. It was altogether a heartfelt celebration.

Many raved about the music for the service. I did love choosing the music, and having it performed by a good London choir was exciting. It was rewarding for me to able to do this for Jim. Jane Falloon and Robert Townley had helped me choose the prayers.

I had dreaded this occasion and it was truly wonderful.

11 JULY 2000 MONAGHAN

I gave a lunch at the Cradle for all Granny's friends. I asked her neighbour, Bea Katz if the Cradle was too far out of town for all the old people to travel. Bea said, "For Iris, they would go to the moon!"

It was very warming to see many of her old friends and to know how much they loved her. She was a great up-lifter of spirits and a deeply loyal friend to them all. I gave a short speech, because she wanted no funeral and there was no ritual of any kind to mark her death. They were grateful to be able to have this little gathering.

She could have won a medal for worrying about her family, but when it came to her own ill health and partial blindness she was devoid of self-pity. When I said to her how awful it must be not to be able to read, she said, "But I'm so lucky! I listen to music and tapes of books. And I saw perfectly for 80 years."

It is so unlike her to die.

4 APRIL 2001

Jessica played the *2nd Bach Cello Suite* at the Cradle. She is a born Bach player. At dinner afterwards, I sat next to Deborah Lavin and we spoke of losing our loved ones. She said I must understand that I am free now. I must keep Jim within my core, as it were, but go forward – free. As she spoke these words, the thick gold ring that my mother gave me and that I wore as a wedding ring, broke clean through!

I rushed to Jess and told her, and showed her the ring. She said, "Bar, isn't that enough of a sign that Jim is telling you to let go, for heaven's sake!" She didn't seem in the least surprised.

275

On this day our family gathered together at Jim's gravestone when it was laid.
Beezy wrote this verse and read it to us.

JIM

You sleep inside the warm
African earth, while above you
The silver grass whispers golden secrets
In our dreams.
Your soul flying, diving, soaring
Among the mother-of-pearl
Porcelain mountains in the sky.

Behind the moon at night
You ski the frozen slopes of Pluto;
At dawn you are inside the amber
Rays of sun dancing with the Angels
Celebrating; beating your *Drum*.

With the Kings you rest inside
The bosom of the African earth
Forever in peace.